The Roof of the World! A heart-stopping panorama looking due west from a rock shoulder at 12,800ft. (3,901m) above the Upper Arun valley in East Nepal. Makalu (centre) dominates the horizon, while Everest is hidden behind the peak on the right. All the territory to the left of these peaks lies in Nepal, that to the right lies in Tibet. Through this spectacular terrain in 1971 the University of North Wales Bangor Expedition passed on the adventure of a lifetime

ROY LANCASTER
A PLANTSMAN IN NEPAL

Antique Collectors' Club

First published 1981, and reprinted 1983, by Croom Helm Ltd.

This enlarged and revised edition published 1995
by the Antique Collectors' Club Ltd.

ISBN 1 85149 179 1

British Library Cataloguing in Publication Data: A catalogue record of this book
is available from the British Library

Title page: *Sambucus adnata*, an herbaceous elderberry commonly forming extensive suckering
patches in glades and pastures in the Himalaya. It is a red berried version of the European Dane's
elder *S. ebulus*. (September)

Printed in England on Consort Royal Satin from Donside Paper Mills, Aberdeen,
by the Antique Collectors' Club Ltd., Woodbridge, Suffolk IP12 1DS

Dedicated to the memory of my friend Len Beer who died in 1977.
Without his loyalty and companionship this book could never have been written

One of the most exciting plant features of the Nepal Himalaya are the primulas, many of which occur in large drifts. Spectacular enough when in flower in late spring and early summer, some such as *P. obliqua,* seen here in a bog at 13,000ft. (5,962m) in the Jaljale Himal, are equally colourful in autumn leaf. (October)

CONTENTS

One of the bonuses for the traveller in Nepal are the many spectacular mountains which dominate the sky. (October)

ACKNOWLEDGEMENTS

The writing of this book has been a story of help and encouragement and sometimes gentle bullying. Margaret Body gave me constant advice and support and Joan Parsons had the unenviable task of deciphering my notes for typing. Subsequent work on the manuscript was bravely undertaken by Hilary Bachmann and my wife Sue. Sue also kept my nose to the grindstone when deadline loomed. Hatton Gardner generously gave of his time and expertise in proof-reading and in the compilation of the indices whilst Paul Chester executed in record time the excellent sketches (not included in the 1995 edition).

As for the botanical aspects of this book I have to thank the staff of the Botany Department of the British Museum (Natural History) for their help and guidance and in particular Sue Sutton who bore with characteristic patience and phlegmatism my queries and demands. Such errors and imperfections as there may be are my own responsibility.

To my friends and to all those who at various times urged me to record my experiences on this expedition I extend my warmest thanks and gratitude.

ACKNOWLEDGEMENTS TO THE 1995 EDITION

Several friends have helped me in various ways with this new edition. Tony Schilling, besides writing the Foreword, has provided several excellent slides to boost the illustrations as well as getting out of bed frequently to answer late night queries, whilst Tom Spring-Smyth and his wife Jennifer helped me with a variety of information concerning Nepalese ways and customs. D. Woodland took Colour Plate 125, Jeanette Fryer updated the information on Cotoneasters, Hatton Gardner compiled the new indices, leaving my wife Sue to deal with the typing, still an unenviable task. Last but not least I thank my publisher Diana Steel for turning the idea of a new edition into a reality and my editor, the indefatigable Cherry Lewis, for her confidence and encouragement.

FOREWORD

When this book was first published in 1981 the ecological frailty of Nepal was already apparent. This Hindu kingdom may hold some of the highest mountains on earth but in spite of this immensity it is a land with an ecologically fragile landscape subjected to an exploding population and overburdened by the ever-increasing demands on its natural resources. In the next twenty-five years Nepal's nineteen million population will almost certainly double, putting what is already the most densely populated mountain community in the world on course for ecological tragedy with all the human misery which inevitably goes with it.

Deafforestation far outstrips reafforestation programmes and mankind is clearly asking too much from too little; this situation is not sustainable and in due course, if the problem is not addressed, the price must be paid.

When I first walked the long trails to Everest and elsewhere in 1965 I seldom met another foreigner. Nowadays on the same routes one sees hundreds if not thousands of tourists trekking through the beauty of Nepal and, whether they intend it or not, eroding a small amount of that beauty by their very presence. Ideally one should 'take only photographs and leave only footprints' but this philosophy falls down unless one is totally self sufficient.

Tourism has undoubtedly brought wealth to a percentage of the Nepalese, but generally it has only served to make the entrepeneur richer whilst the poor get poorer. The only Nepalese who can actually afford to buy eggs in the Everest National Park these days are the wayside hoteliers who sell them to the tourists at mealtimes.

Long term political decisions urgently need to be made if Nepal is not to become a degraded alpine desert. Maybe the country's best chance of blunting the adverse pressures of tourism is to adopt the wise tactics of its near-neighbour Bhutan where tourist numbers are strictly controlled by fixing low numbers and high prices. The new wave of ecotourism may alleviate the pressure to some degree but it may not be sustainable in the long term. The earth is amazingly resilient and, given the right chances, it has the ability to heal and recover, but will it be given those chances?

In spite of the many problems which face present day Nepal it remains a country which fires the imagination of all who love the beauty of the mountain world, especially those who also enjoy the plants which grow there. A large number of people assume that plant exploration in the wilds of the Himalaya is a rather genteel and romantic activity carried out amidst idyllic surroundings with the sun ever shining and the mountain air laden with the sweet scent of flowers and full of the songs of birds. Whilst it undoubtedly has its rewarding moments, more usually the physically demanding rigours of travel, the danger of swollen mountain torrents, of landslides and the frequent discomforts caused by leeches or occasional illness frequently make the rewards hardwon. Much of lasting pleasure is in fact retrospective when time has helped to blur the unpleasant moments and hardships in the field are tempered by the warm feelings of fulfilment and friendship.

Roy Lancaster and I have been close friends for more than thirty years, but apart from the odd day or two in the Brecon Beacons or the New Forest we have never

A fine colony of the Himalayan fern *Dryopteris wallichiana* on a wooded slope. Such plants may well disappear if deafforestation and devastation in Nepal are not brought under control. (April)

managed an expedition together. Being where he is today, professionally respected and widely acclaimed, it is hard to believe he was once 'wide-eyed and innocent', eager to realise his first expedition and envious of my personal experiences in Arctic Norway and elsewhere. In 1971 his dreams were eventually realised when he was invited to join the University College of North Wales' expedition to East Nepal – his chance to search for plants in the wilds of the Himalayas had come.

This expedition was instrumental in opening the door for the author to extend his horizons over the years to other botanically rich corners of Asia, especially China, and to enable him to follow more fully his chosen career as a freelance horticulturalist, plantsman, lecturer, writer and broadcaster.

Several of the plants which came into cultivation from the 1971 Nepal expedition have successfully established themselves in horticulture and may be found accompanied by their B.L.&M. collecting numbers, in gardens around the world. One can see them in the Asian collection at the University of British Columbia Botanic Garden in Vancouver as well as in numerous botanical collections in Britain including Kew, Edinburgh, Windsor, Wisley and the Sir Harold Hillier Gardens and Arboretum in Hampshire where the author's story begins.

Many of the 415 seed collections have for various reasons faded away, or the all-important field collecting numbers have been lost from the records – such are the frustrations and disappointments of plant collecting. It is a well known fact that the best custodians of plant introductions are often the collectors themselves, for they are naturally charged up with a potent cocktail made up of sentimental nostalgia, practical knowledge and, most important of all, personal

The Deorali Pass at about 10,500ft. (3,200m) in the Annapurna mountains of central Nepal. The trees in the background are Himalayan Silver Fir *Abies spectabilis* with a *Rhododendron arboreum* understorey. The dwarf shrub covering the near slope is *Berberis concinna*. The prayer flags were erected by Tony Schilling in memory of Len Beer a few weeks after the latter's death in 1977

enthusiasm. Some of the collections have proved to be too tender, others too difficult to cultivate, whilst some have succumbed to disease or other natural disasters, but thankfully the cream survives.

What also survives is the invaluable personal experience, satisfaction and knowledge which Roy Lancaster has gained from the adventure itself. Couple this to the friendship and camaraderie which evolved between the members and one begins to realise that the positive sides to such an expedition are many. The gardening world should be grateful to the author for turning his memories and adventures into the reality of this book, thereby giving others the opportunity to share the experiences even if only from the comfort of their armchairs.

The expedition leader Len Beer tragically died of cancer in 1977 long before his allotted time. He was a total enthusiast fired by the thought of what plants may lie beyond the next ridge or round the next bend in the trail. A few weeks after Len's death, at the request of Roy Lancaster, I set up prayer flags high on a forest-clad ridge in the Annapurna mountains of central Nepal. I left them there as an expression of respect for someone we had both, as fellow plantsmen, had the pleasure of knowing. May this book, which tells the story of the expedition he brought about and subsequently led, be another 'prayer flag' to his memory.

A.D. Schilling, V.M.H., M.ARB., F.I. HORT., F.L.S., F.R.G.S.
U.K. Colombo Plan Adviser to the Royal Nepal Government (1965/6) and
Deputy Curator of the Royal Botanic Gardens Kew (Wakehurst Place) 1967-91

PREFACE TO NEW EDITION

It is fourteen years since this book was first published and twenty-four since the events it describes. During this time a great deal has happened in Nepal, particularly as regards the natural environment, and Tony Schilling, a long-time visitor and friend of Nepal and an authority on its flora, has kindly provided a foreword to this new edition in which he discusses among other subjects the problems caused by deafforestation and the pressures of tourism.

It is mainly because of the increasing number of visitors travelling the mountain trails that this new edition was considered in the first place. There is no greater fuel for destruction than ignorance and to walk through one of the world's most beautiful and botanically exciting landscapes without knowing, let alone appreciating, what one is looking at, is an intolerable situation and of no help to Nepal.

I do not claim this book to be anything other than a personal account of a journey through a small area of the country. It is not a flora, neither is it a guide to Nepalese plants, but enough favourable comment has been received over the years from those having taken the original book with them into Nepal that I am encouraged to believe this new edition will prove useful to future visitors as well as to armchair travellers and those botanists and gardeners with an interest in Nepalese plants.

Given that this is a new edition, I have taken the opportunity of updating the nomenclature, correcting errors and adding new information wherever this was felt to be necessary or helpful, though I have not deemed it necessary to take on board every change of name that has occurred. The opportunity has also been taken to add a new chapter, 'Return to the Milke Danda', based on a botanical trek I led to East Nepal in 1973. The greatest change however is in the illustrations. The first edition contained only twenty photographs, albeit in colour, and numerous line drawings. In the present edition the number of photographs, thanks to the generosity of the publisher, has been increased to nearly 350, of which some 270 are in full colour. This means that many of the plants, people and places, not to mention the magnificent landscapes, described in the text can now be seen as well as imagined.

This preface would not be complete without a reference to the leader of our expedition, the late Len Beer, and his activities following the expedition. After our return in December 1971 Len played an active role in distributing our seeds to as wide a clientele as possible and continued the task with plants propagated from the first seedlings. Over the next few years Len continued to travel in Europe and Turkey as a leader of bird and plant treks for a specialist interest travel firm, but in July 1975 he was back in Nepal again leading another expedition, this time with his wife Sheila.

The expedition lasted five months and resulted in good collections of seed, spores and herbarium material covering a wide range of plants from ferns and flowering plants to agricultural crops, mainly barley and wheat. It had been Len's intention to visit the Walunchung region near the border with Sikkim but, owing to the activities of Khamba (Tibetan) guerillas in the area, permission was refused. In the event he obtained permission to visit the Upper Arun valley region and in August of that year headed for Sedua which he had visited four years before. High above Sedua is the valley of the Iswa Khola which Len had briefly explored in 1971. It was hardly known botanically and he believed that a more prolonged visit might prove fruitful. His small party spent a month in this area collecting seed and specimens of many fine alpines including primulas, androsaces and meconopsis at altitudes varying from 9,000 to 16,000ft. (2,743-4,877m). In early October they transferred their attentions to the Arun river between Lambagar Gola and Num and thence up the Wabak Khola valley and over the Lumbasumba Himal to Thudam near the Tibetan border. From here they retraced the route of our 1971 expedition to Topke Gola, returning to Dharan via the Tamur river valley.

Shortly after his return to Bangor, Len applied successfully for the post of Horticultural Officer to the University of Durham which he held from June 1976 until his untimely death from cancer in March 1977 at the age of thirty-four leaving his wife and a daughter, Abigail, of six months. Some years later Sheila remarried and is now Sheila Hargreaves whilst Abigail is now a young woman. I remain in contact with them, and a couple of years ago Sheila kindly sent me roots of an *Inula hookeri* collected as seed in Nepal in 1971. Len's mother Alice and sister Doreen still live in his home town of Ivybridge in Devon. Recently, they presented to the town's Gardening Association a Len Beer Trophy for Alpines which will help keep his memory alive among local gardeners.

On a national if not international front, Len Beer's name will be remembered by all who profess a keen interest in the Nepalese flora and its introduction to cultivation. Two seedlings grown from seed he collected have been named after him, and although neither is currently widely available *Rhododendron glauco-phyllum* 'Len Beer' and *Bergenia purpurascens* 'Len Beer' are well worthy of the plantsman's attention.

Len's death was a great shock not only to his family and friends but to those who had come to know him in the horticultural and botanical world, including the many members of gardening and other societies and clubs who had heard him lecture. Cut off in his prime there is no doubt in my mind that had he lived, he would most certainly have continued his plant exploration and become a leading figure in the recent resurgence of botanical activity in China. Like the Scottish plant hunters David Douglas and George Forrest, Len Beer was able to endure long periods alone in wild terrain and weather and was indomitable in his search for new and interesting plants. He was also a helpful and good humoured companion and my memories of him are rich in incidents like that which occurred during one of our wettest days in Nepal's Jaljale Himal in 1971.

We had squelched our way through mist and rain for most of the morning, eventually seeking shelter beneath a large rock overhang. It was time for lunch but none was forthcoming as our cook had gone missing in the gloom. As any traveller in wild mountain terrain will testify, it could have been a tricky situation but Len characteristically began singing and I immediately joined in, the two of us serenading the barely visible hills for a good hour until our cook arrived guided by our warblings. Len's physical strength also proved useful in the field enabling him to surmount what for others might have been impassable barriers. In dangerous terrain he naturally led the way and on several occasions carried the packs of porters in precarious situations.

A brief but accurate account of Len Beer, especially relating to his activities in Nepal, appeared in the July 1992 Newsletter of the Sino-Himalayan Plant Association, an organisation of whose work and ideals Len would have approved.

Those visiting east Nepal today intent on trekking in the Arun valley area will

Primula listeri, seen here on a shady bank in woodland at around 10,500ft. (3,200m) on the Milke Danda, is but one of an estimated 6,500 flowering plants native to Nepal. (April)

find one major change since the events described in this book. This concerns access to the Milke Danda. It is now possible to travel by bus in a day from Dharan to Hile along what is by Himalayan standards a modern road. In 1971 it was a three-day hike on foot.

More easily accessible, the Milke Danda and the mountains beyond are now more vulnerable. If this book helps the visitor to identify plants seen without the need to pick them I shall be well pleased. As for collecting plants I would advise visitors, especially tourists, to take only photographs and to resist the temptation to remove plants just for the sake of it or because they are there.

It should be remembered that most of the Himalayan, including Nepalese, plants of garden merit they are likely to see have long been available from established and reliable stock in western nurseries, gardens open to the public and via the regular plant sales and auctions organised by the many specialist societies and groups.

Measurements

Wherever possible, the approximate height of a plant seen in the wild state has been given. Measurements are given in Imperial with the approximate metric equivalent in parentheses.

Measurements of leaves, flowers and others parts of a plant have mostly been taken with a rule, while figures for the height overall of trees and shrubs including the length of climbers are estimated. Where both height and girth or width are given, the height appears first. Measurements given for Nepalese trees in British cultivation have mainly been taken from Bean's *Trees and Shrubs Hardy in the British Isles* (8th edition revised) and are largely from the work of Alan Mitchell – dendrologist and tree measurer extraordinaire. Further examples are quoted from *Champion Trees in the British Isles* by Mitchell, Vicky Schilling and John White.

A typical hillside in the mountains of East Nepal supporting a wealth of trees, shrubs and climbers
beneath which flower in season a host of perennial plants. Of such things dreams are made. (October)

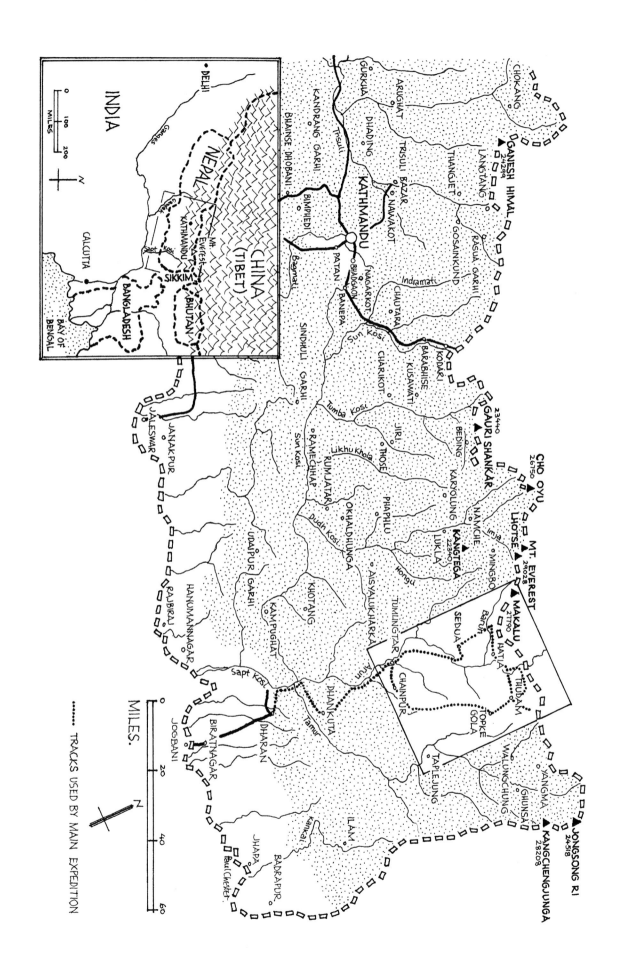

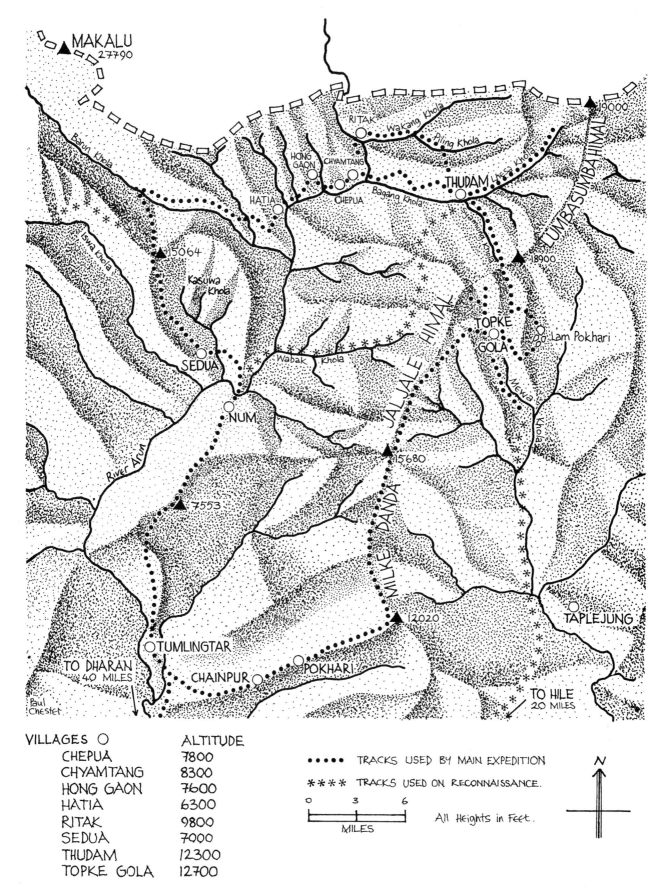

VILLAGES ○

VILLAGES ○	ALTITUDE
CHEPUA	7800
CHYAMTANG	8300
HONG GAON	7600
HATIA	6300
RITAK	9800
SEDUA	7000
THUDAM	12300
TOPKE GOLA	12700

•••• TRACKS USED BY MAIN EXPEDITION

**** TRACKS USED ON RECONNAISSANCE.

0   3   6
MILES

All Heights in Feet.

N

Colour Plate 1. To plant enthusiasts the Nepal Himalaya is a land of snow peaks, vast screes and mist-shrouded valleys, home to a wealth of weird and wonderful plants and flowers. *Saussurea obvallata* on the screes above Topke Gola. (October)

Colour Plate 2. I had long dreamed of Himalayan valleys like this one high in the mountains of Nepal, filled like an Aladdin's cave with exotic and exciting trees, plants and flowers. Valley at 12,500ft. (3,810m) above Topke Gola. (October)

1. PREPARATIONS

It was a chill March day with an overcast sky; an unkempt rose scraped the panes of my office window. I stared at the list of names on the sheets before me on the desk, and for the umpteenth time read carefully through the 159 entries under the genus *Salix,* beginning with *S. acutifolia* from Europe and ending with *S. yezoalpina* from Japan.

I was checking the page proofs of *Hilliers' Manual of Trees and Shrubs,* and a task which over the last five years had seemed unending was now nearing completion. The phone rang and, my eyes not leaving the list of names, I answered automatically, 'The Hillier Gardens and Arboretum, Roy Lancaster here.' The voice on the other end asked a simple question. 'I am leading a plant collecting expedition to East Nepal, can you come?' My gaze shifted from the proofs to the blank sky outside. 'Could you repeat that,' I asked incredulously. The voice obliged and it was then I recognised it as that of Len Beer, with whom I had spent a happy year at Hilliers back in 1962. Beer was now horticulturist at the University College of North Wales, Bangor and this was his second attempt to organise an expedition to the Himalaya.

Beer explained how a member of his five-man team had suddenly withdrawn to join another expedition and that I had next option on the vacancy. 'We intend leaving in September and will probably be away for three months, can you get time off?' Beer asked.

'Time off?' My mind was in a whirl – 'Time off? – of course I can get the time off, even if it means losing my job I shall get the time off.' Beer seemed satisfied and outlined the plans and objectives of the expedition. He then mentioned a problem. 'Before I can say for sure that you can join us you will have to meet the others, John, Dave and Martin. Can you come up for an interview one weekend?' I replied that I could, and a date was fixed.

Ever since my schooldays at the Castle Hill County Secondary in Bolton I had dreamed of plant hunting abroad. In those happy far-off days my plant exploring revolved round the moors, spinneys and roadsides of South Lancashire. Even slag heaps, rubbish dumps and flooded subsidence (known locally as flashes) yielded their treasures. My initiation into the plant world had begun with my discovery of a Mexican tobacco plant (*Nicotiana rustica*) growing on an allotment close to my school, and my subsequent interest in foreign plants led me to all manner of sites from a hen-pen at Knob End, Farnworth, to the fabulous Crown Wallpaper tip at Darwen. On the latter, rejected scum from the vats of the nearby factory gave birth to the most exotic plants, of which the ice plant *Cryophytum crystalinum,* now known as *Mesembryanthemum crystalinum,* and the date palm *Phoenix dactylifera* ruled supreme.

An unforgettable eighteen months as a national serviceman in Malaya introduced me to a completely new world of plants and gave me the desire for travel in foreign lands. Meanwhile I was earning my living as a gardener and slowly becoming familiar with plants of the temperate zones and, just as importantly, with their names.

I forget when I first read about the famous plant hunters, but I had long known some of the plants they had introduced. I do remember reading accounts by E.H. Wilson of his travels in China, and then there was the memorable story told by George Forrest of how he was hunted by Tibetan monks for twenty-three days before escaping to the safety of Tali (now Dali) in China's Yunan province.

However, in March 1971 I had reached the stage where it was no longer enough for me to read of others' adventures. Not enough to read how Forrest or Kingdon Ward had felt on first surveying the vast colourful rhododendron tapestries covering the Tibetan plateaux, or standing beneath tall fir and spruce in some staggering river gorge. I wanted to know how I would feel in those shadowed forests, listening to the rain on a high canopy, or wading through Himalayan scrub full of plants familiar from English gardens. Maybe now that dream was about to come true.

Next morning, I walked through the arboretum with a new sense of purpose, my eyes searching for those plants with a claim to Himalayan ancestry. I noted *Euonymus hamiltonianus*, a big deciduous spindleberry, and nearby the drooping funereal foliage of the coffin juniper *Juniperus recurva* variety *coxii, Spiraea bella, Ephedra gerardiana* and *Cotoneaster microphyllus.* I was heading for Jermyns House (Colour Plates 3 and 4), home of Harold Hillier, head of the firm and family, to find out whether I would be leaving for Nepal with or without official blessing. He had agreed to meet me in his study, a small room with four exits, one leading through French windows on to a paved area. This exit was flanked by a tall cinnamon barked tree from Santa Catalina called *Lyonothamnus floribundus* variety *asplenifolius*, and by a large bushy specimen of *Magnolia delavayi,* a magnificent Chinese evergreen with leathery paddlelike leaves.

Mr. Hillier sat at his bureau sifting through a sheaf of papers. The interview was brief and to the point. All he would say after hearing my inarticulate reasons for wanting to go was, 'I shall consult my partners and let you know our decision.'

It was a few days before I was asked again to Mr. Hillier's study. The meeting was shorter than before but the answer had been 'Yes'! Later that day I made a phone call to Beer to tell him the news and we discussed my trip to Bangor in order to meet the other expedition members. On the appointed weekend I drove to Bangor and thence to Menai Bridge on the Isle of Anglesey where Beer had a flat above a hairdresser's shop. Later the same day we drove into Bangor and made our way to a Chinese restaurant. John Witcombe, bare browed, bearded and slight in build was a lecturer in plant genetics and a Vice-President of the University Mountaineering Club. He was in charge of the Agricultural Project and intended making seed collections of cultivated crops and those of potential economic importance. Martin Mortimer, an agricultural botanist, was to assist Witcombe. He had long dark hair and sported a drooping moustache. The fourth member of the group, Dave Morris, was the tallest and looked down at me from a height of six feet. A research botanist, he was the expedition's organiser and would assist Beer in the work of the Horticultural Project.

I attempted to justify my inclusion in the team, Beer supporting my case with vigour and conviction. Questions were fired at me. Why did I want to go to Nepal? What did I know of the plants we might find? What was my knowledge of Himalayan plants in cultivation? I then found myself relating my life history, emphasising my early interest in plants and subsequent experience with plants in cultivation. The questioning continued until, our meal finished, we left the restaurant and retired to the nearest pub where the grilling was continued over pints of beer. We then made our way to a hall of residence on the University Campus where Morris had a room and here the debate continued. I was asked if I had any medical knowledge. I replied that I had not. Did I think it wise or essential to have a medical man as a member of the expedition? I said I would feel happier if there were, to which they replied that a medical man had applied to join the expedition and it was either him or me. Twice I was asked to leave the room whilst they debated in private and I drank cups of coffee in the kitchen. On the second occasion I was called back to find the members silent and serious – they had come to a decision. I forget now who told me but it was probably Beer. 'We would like you to join the expedition,' he said rather formally. The others looked expectant and then their faces creased and all hell let loose as congratulations were shouted, my hand was pumped and back slapped. I believe that tears actually came to my eyes but we all seemed to be laughing after the tension of the evening and a drink was called for to toast the occasion.

This was to be the first of several weekends in Bangor, and at an early stage it was agreed that I should be responsible for organising the food for the expedition. This entailed writing letters to manufacturers in the hope of donations or discounts. During the next few months, as a result of my efforts, a large assortment of dehydrated soups, meats and vegetables found their way to our Bangor headquarters, demonstrating the generosity of manufacturers in supporting worthwhile and well-organised projects. We had high hopes of supplementing this basic fare with fresh locally grown products. Meanwhile

Colour Plate 3. The Hillier Arboretum and the valley below Jermyns House looking across to the area known as Three Acre Paddock. Part of the *Cotoneaster* collection occupies the foreground whilst the white stems of an Australian Snow Gum *Eucalyptus pauciflora* subspecies *niphophila* can be seen far right foreground. On the top of the slope right is the white ramrod-straight stem of *Eucalyptus dalrympleana.* (November)

Colour Plate 4. Jermyns House and the Hillier Arboretum, near Romsey in Hampshire, with cherries and magnolias in bloom. It is here that the author became familiar with many Himalayan trees and shrubs. (April)

Colour Plate 5. Tony Schilling, one of the most experienced plant explorers in Nepal and an authority on its flora, seen here in the Everest National Park, Ama Dablam 22,494ft. (6,856m) in background. Schilling gave the author his first taste of the Himalaya at Wakehurst Place in Sussex

Morris was busy with the thousand and one things which are an expedition organiser's lot, principal among which was the business of raising money. We were offering shares in the seed we hoped to collect, Ordinary shares at £25 and Special shares at £50. Several correspondents with special interests in *Primula* (Colour Plate 7), *Rhododendron* and other specific genera bought the more expensive shares to secure first choice or larger quantities in their chosen groups. Of course we all rose to the challenge of selling shares and eventually something in the region of £1,500 was raised this way. Initially the expedition budget was set at £6,000 but later was increased to £7,000. Many trusts, scientific institutions and private concerns made generous donations and each expedition member made a personal contribution of £100.

Witcombe, in the meantime, was selecting equipment, including tents, sleeping bags, boots, warm clothing, compasses, seed bags and envelopes. A certain amount of climbing gear was purchased which reminded me that Witcombe, Morris and Mortimer were experienced climbers. I compared their manoeuvres in the mountains of North Wales with my strolls up and down the 300 feet of St. Catherine's Hill near Winchester, and I had unhappy dreams of being left behind on the first day of our march into the hills of Nepal.

Organisation of the expedition had begun the previous August and much of the groundwork had been completed by the time I joined the team. We had secured the blessing of Sir George Taylor, F.R.S., Director, Royal Botanic Gardens, Kew, and Sir Charles Evans, Principal, University College of North Wales, as patrons, while Professor P. Greig-Smith, also of the University College of North Wales, had agreed to be our home agent.

Beer's contact with the Botany Department of the British Museum (Natural History) had resulted in the loan of plant-collecting material such as presses, drying paper and several packing cases. John Williams of that department was particularly helpful. He had visited Nepal on four occasions as a member of plant collecting expeditions and knew some of the problems we might face. Another person whose help proved invaluable was Frank Ludlow. As the remaining member of that famous plant hunting partnership Ludlow and Sherriff, his advice was supremely sound. Both Beer and I met him on visits to the British Museum, and before leaving England he spoke to me of the things to be careful about in the Himalaya. 'The most important thing is to look after your stomach,' he said. 'Treat it gently and sensibly and you won't go far wrong. Equally important are your feet', he continued. 'Wear sensible boots and break them in before you go.' After all the discussion about the plants we would see this was a wise after-thought. Without a qualified doctor in the team our physical well-being would be in the hands of Morris. Taking professional advice, he assembled pills, ointments, tinctures and drugs, together with bandages, plasters, splints and enough bits and pieces to satisfy an army of hypochondriacs.

During this time I was briefing myself on the Himalayan flora, especially that relating to Nepal. Beer knew the alpine plants to search out and Witcombe was similarly well informed on the broad range of cereal crops he would find. Although I had already promised myself to look at everything that grew, walked, crawled or flew, I was looked upon by the others as the woody plant expert, and it was this diverse group which claimed much of my attention. I was acquainting myself with those trees and shrubs in gardens which had originated in Nepal or thereabouts. Much as I am familiar with a plant in cultivation though, when I see that plant in its native state I am deeply moved. It is like meeting an old friend far from home.

Visits to the gardens at Kew, Wisley and Exbury brought me into contact with Nepalese plants, but one of my most significant experiences occurred at Wakehurst Place in Sussex. I was being taken round by the man in charge, Tony Schilling, who had lived and worked in Nepal for two years and was well attuned to the country and its people (Colour Plate 5). He took me to a place in the garden which was the closest thing in Sussex to a Himalayan glade. We made our way along a path which led into a steep-sided valley filled with rhododendrons and large trees. After a few minutes we stopped beneath a giant beech. 'Close your eyes and don't open them until I tell you,' Schilling said. I did as he instructed, and holding on to his jacket we continued along the path before plunging to our right, down a sharp incline. Hard leaves cracked underfoot. We stopped and Schilling told me to open my eyes. I found myself supported by a tall stem, one of several forming a colony on the slope above the stream. My eyes followed the nearest stem upwards to a dense canopy some 20ft. (6m) above. We were standing in a plantation of the noble tree rhododendron, *R. arboreum*, which I had been told covered the lower regions of the Nepal Himalaya (Colour Plate 6). Schilling also pointed out a Himalayan bamboo, and across the valley a giant *Magnolia campbellii,* another native of Nepal. Many other Himalayan plants were shown to me that day, and months later when I finally made it to the Himalaya, I remembered that Wakehurst Place had been a convincing, albeit miniature, version of the real thing.

It had been agreed that Beer should leave alone for Nepal in June on a three-month reconnaissance, during which time he would locate and mark worthwhile plants in flower for seed collection later. He would also check on suitable routes and promising collecting locations and campsites. Beer's departure caused a great flurry of activity as stores and equipment were assembled and packed to accompany him.

Expeditions rely on many things, not least good fortune – and ours was no exception. Arrangements had been made with the Royal Air Force to fly expedition members and baggage from England to Singapore on one of their regular weekly flights, space permitting. We should have to use civil airlines in order to get us from there to Kathmandu.

Beer reached Kathmandu on 9 June. Our main contact there was Mike Cheney of Mountain Travel, a well-known and experienced trekking firm which had been established by an Englishman and old Indian Army hand Col. Jimmy Roberts in 1965. Mike Cheney was to arrange for Sherpas, as interpreters and camp staff, and cooking equipment and would help us obtain trekking permits for the area to be visited. An approximate route had been decided earlier but had been modified as time went by and new information became available. We intended our operational area to be in the north-east corner of the country, mainly between the Tamur and Arun rivers (87°10'E and 87°40'E). On 3 August, a little over two months after Beer's departure, Witcombe flew out to begin a similar but shorter reconnaissance investigating crops grown at lower altitudes. With him went the main bulk of food and equipment which, together with Beer's allowance and that of the remaining members of the team, amounted to more than one ton overall.

Colour Plate 6. 'Little Nepal' at Wakehurst Place in Sussex, dominated by *Rhododendron falconeri* (yellow) and *R. arboreum* (pink) in background right. Other rhododendrons native to Nepal are represented, as is *Daphne bholua*. It was here that Tony Schilling brought the author for a taste of the Himalaya. (April)

During this period we received several letters from Beer, deep in the hills and by all accounts having a hard time of it. Summer in the Himalaya brings the monsoon, and this year's rains were the worst for more than a decade. He wrote of swollen rivers, dangerous bridges, landslips and leeches, and suggested an altogether unwelcome environment.

On the evening of 14 September I was driven to Oxford by my future wife Sue Lloyd and met Morris and Mortimer at a small hotel. We worked into the night writing last-minute letters, compiling lists, packing, unpacking, then packing again, in a room which resembled a quartermaster's store after an earthquake. In the early hours of the morning we staggered to bed and thanks to Ken Burras, Superintendent of the University Botanic Garden, who lent us a small truck and driver, we arrived at RAF Brize Norton in time to take off at 2.30 p.m. on 15 September.

We made two stops on our flight to Singapore. First, briefly, Bahrain in the early hours and then the tiny island of Gan in the Maldives, south-west of Sri Lanka. The runway began and ended by the sea and there were coconut palms, flame-flowered poincianas – *Delonix regia* – and the equally brilliant flowers of the African tulip tree – *Spathodea campanulata*.

By mid-afternoon we were 35,000 ft. above Sumatra, a vast green forested land intersected by winding ochre-coloured rivers. An hour later we touched down at Changi Airport, Singapore, to be met by the fragile figure of Yong Fan Chin. I had known Yong some years previously when he was a student first at Hilliers Nursery and then at Kew and I had written to tell him of our expedition

Colour Plate 7. *Primula denticulata:* a particularly fine form of the Drumstick primula, one of the most popular and easily recognised Himalayan plants. It is found over a wide area from Afghanistan through Kashmir and Nepal to Bhutan, Burma, south-east Tibet and south-west China. (April)

and our passage via Singapore. We had the rest of the day and all the next to enjoy the island and Yong insisted on being our guide and provider; it was a brief respite from the organisation and headaches that we had left in England and which most assuredly awaited us in Nepal. We spent our time in Singapore enjoying its food and its rich variety of plants.

Frangipani (*Plumeria* species) was particularly plentiful with flowers of white, pink, yellow and red. So too the ubiquitous bougainvilleas clambering over walls and houses and into the branches of trees, their flowers varying from orange, crimson and purple to a rather dirty white; *Cassia fistula* with yellow flowers and long truncheon-like pods; scarlet-trumpeted *Hibiscus rosa-sinensis;* flame poincianas and yellow-flowered *Thevetia peruviana.* I was particularly struck by a line of clove trees *(Syzygium aromaticum)* whose flower buds are the cloves of commerce; even the crushed leaves were clove scented.

After further stops at Bangkok and Calcutta we were on our way to Kathmandu. We approached the Nepalese border through dense cloud which gradually thinned as we flew high above a vast white mantle whose horizons seemed boundless and whose surface was incredibly even, save for a series of eruptions to the north. It was some minutes before we realised that these 'eruptions' were of a solid nature – it was our first view of the Himalaya. The plane then banked suddenly and descended at an alarming rate into the cloud layer. We were flying over the Mahabharat Lekh, the range of mountains stretching in an east-west direction through southern Nepal, for many centuries the main barrier between this once remote kingdom and the outside world to the south. Green terraced hillsides gave way to equally green fields as the plane sank lower into the widening valley of Kathmandu. We could see strange buildings and trees, many of unfamiliar hues, and the brown band of the Bagmati river. A crowd was gathered around the airport terminal. From the seething throng a figure emerged dressed in an orange T-shirt and baggy khaki shorts; it was Beer.

2. CITY OF THE GODS

'And about time, too,' was Beer's first greeting, accompanied by a grin and followed by much back-slapping. He was obviously pleased and relieved to see us, the last contingent, and whilst he and Morris sorted out the baggage for Customs' inspection, Mortimer and I drove into the city in a car that was long past retiring age. The road was pot-holed and strewn with reclining cattle which our driver negotiated at speed as though taking part in some giant obstacle race. Other cars raced ahead, their lurching shapes obscured by great clouds of dust which entered our vehicle to leave a grey deposit on its occupants.

In a short while we were moving through narrow streets between wooden canopied buildings and all around us a sea of people and a din of car hooters and clanging gongs and bells as a religious parade passed by. Then we turned through a narrow opening and pulled up at the entrance to the Panorama Hotel. It was a tall building with whitewashed walls, a dark entrance and a constant coming and going of tricycles and taxis. Perhaps the best amenity was the view from the hotel roof which attracted most guests at some time or another but most of all in the early morning and evening when the sun rinsed the landscape in gold.

Eventually Beer and Mortimer arrived with the baggage and for the next hour we listened to Beer recounting his adventures in the hills, occasionally throwing in questions which he answered with authority and obvious enjoyment. There had been many problems, most of which he had overcome and it seemed the greatest disappointment to him had been the non-arrival of many of our letters

Plate 1. A street in Kathmandu: the bazaar area late one afternoon. The whole place held an air of mystery and excitement, the shadowed shop fronts buzzing with people and the sound of haggling

Colour Plate 8. *Photinia nussia,* a handsome evergreen, shown in fruit in the Hanbury gardens at La Mortola near Ventimiglia on the Italian Mediterranean coast. It is too tender for all but the mildest gardens in Britain. (January)

Colour Plate 9. Garlands made from the colourful flowerheads of marigolds *(Tagetes)*, poinsettias, zinnias and chrysanthemums on sale in Kathmandu. These garlands are popular in Nepal and are worn on special occasions, such as religious festivals, celebrations, welcomings and farewells. (December)

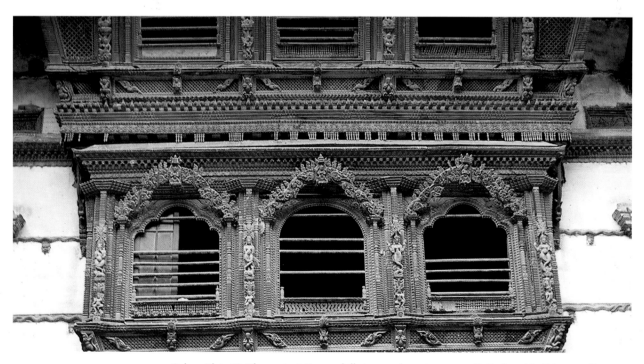

Colour Plate 10. The ancient Newar skills in wood carving are well displayed in this magnificent window surround in Kathmandu

30

Colour Plate 11. The Royal Botanic Gardens at Godavari are easily reached by a sealed road from Kathmandu. Here the members of the expedition picnic in the shade of a magnificent *Photinia nussia*, a native tree which pre-dates the garden. (September)

and news of the expedition's organisation in the UK. Difficulties of travel and certain unexplained delays had been the main culprits and the next hour therefore was spent in bringing Beer up to date with the situation.

When we finally ventured into Kathmandu it was mid-afternoon and hot. The next few hours brought a bewildering series of pictures and impressions as we walked through narrow streets, dust underfoot, flanked by shops whose open fronts exhibited an incredible array of goods (Plate 1). Strange sights and smells assailed us on all sides and there was a constant babble of unfamiliar tongues. Fruit-sellers abounded, their pumpkins, papayas, durians, mangoes and bananas tumbling into the street in piles. The colours of these tropical fruits were more than matched by the heaps of dyed cottons and wool and garlands hanging in rows and bunches from rails and hooks. These garlands, made from the fresh flowerheads of marigolds, poinsettias, zinnias and chrysanthemums are popular in Nepal for wearing on special occasions such as festivals, family celebrations, welcomings and farewells (Colour Plate 9). The bazaar areas were seething with people of many distinct races – Newars, Thamangs, Rais and several others. It was the Newars, or rather their ancestors, who were responsible for the plethora of carvings and decorative work on the exteriors of many buildings especially the wooden window frames, door surrounds, panels and awnings, some of which were incredibly elaborate and ornate (Colour Plate 10).

Temples rose like islands from a sea of wooden and whitewashed hovels. This contrast between the exotic and the ordinary amazed us. One minute we would be walking down a thoroughfare of temples and carved exteriors, the next we would turn into an alleyway of filth and stench where mangy dogs scrabbled and scavenged like rats, eating whatever man had discarded or deposited. The splendour, magic, mystery and the squalor of the city roused alternating feelings of wonder and disgust, and our heads swam with the whole colourful experience as we wound our way back to the hotel.

We found Ed Hammond sitting in the hotel lobby. He was the leader of a small climbing expedition, the other members of which were travelling from Britain in a jeep. We had met during the previous spring and he had given us a great deal of useful information and advice based on his previous visits to Nepal. It was growing dark when Hammond suggested a place to eat, whereupon we hailed a taxi and piled in. The small candlelit restaurant was apparently full when we arrived but a table and chairs were extracted from a particularly dense concentration in the darkest corner and we were soon seated. The room was full of foreigners like ourselves, many of them members of climbing teams, whilst others were on long overland hikes. Others had come to Nepal to make special studies, and then there were those here as volunteers helping in various social or agricultural projects. American, Australian, New Zealand, Japanese, German, French, Danish and British accents combined in a multiple conversation with loud exclamations, table banging and hand waving, indicating the various national temperaments. It was exciting to be part of such a gathering and the sense of adventure and the unknown lay thick in the air.

The heat and excitement made sleep impossible for me that night. We had returned to our hotel during the early hours after a marathon session of story telling and jokes accompanied by glasses of rakshi which, like most initially nasty drinks, improved as the night wore on. It is a spirit distilled from mash of any one of a number of sources including fruit, though grain (barley, millet,

Colour Plate 12. *Roscoea purpurea* in the author's garden. It was collected by Tony Schilling under his number 1185 at an altitude of 7,000ft. (2,133m) at Nagakot on the eastern rim of the Kathmandu valley. (August)

rice) is the most popular. A simple test for pure rakshi, according to my old friend Major Tom Spring-Smyth, is to dip your fingers in it before drinking and then flick them at a fire. If this produces blue sparks or a small flame, then it is safe to drink.

During the previous day we had made brief telephone contact with Spring-Smyth and his wife Jenny who were then living in Kathmandu and had arranged to take us to see the Kathmandu Royal Botanic Gardens at nearby Godavari. After breakfast next morning the Spring-Smyths arrived at the hotel in a jeep complete with picnic basket. I had met Tom Spring-Smyth on two occasions in England, both in the Hillier Arboretum. He had lived and worked in Nepal in various capacities on several occasions since his first trek in western Nepal in 1955 and knew the country well. More to the point, he had also, in 1961-2, accompanied an expedition organised by the British Museum (Natural History) to east Nepal. When we had last met, this irrepressible raconteur had with his stories fired my imagination, though I never in my wildest dreams thought our next meeting would be in Kathmandu. Joining us for the trip to Godavari was Dawa, a Sherpa guide, who had been sirdar (chief Sherpa) with Beer's party and who had been engaged in the same role for the main expedition. The route to Godavari led us through Patan, a place of temples and wooden structures both domestic and religious. The dusty road looked as if a squadron of planes had bombed it and Morris's head beat a regular tattoo on the roof of the jeep as we lurched first this way then that. All round lay paddy fields splashed white with cattle egrets, and when we passed through small villages we saw scenes of domesticity.

Eventually we arrived at the Royal Botanic Gardens, situated at the foot of a densely forested 9,050ft. (2,758m) hill known as Phulchoki. The garden had been cut from the forest and contained a number of native plants which occurred in far greater numbers in the thickets outside. A particularly large specimen, some 60ft. (18m) high, of *Photinia nussia (Stranvaesia nussia)* caught our attention, so much that we decided to have our picnic beneath it. This is a handsome evergreen, with rather leathery leaves varying from lanceolate to obovate, and with flattened heads of white flowers during summer (Colour Plates 8 and 11). It is occasionally met with in gardens and collections in the milder regions of southern and western Britain, but is generally too tender for our climate. It grows much better in the Mediterranean regions of the world and I have since seen fine specimens in the Strybing Arboretum, San Francisco, and in the famous Hanbury gardens at La Mortola on the Italian coast near Ventimiglia. Scattered throughout this area was a wild pear – *Pyrus pashia* – a small thorny tree with ovate, sometimes taper-pointed leaves, which on strong or sucker or juvenile shoots were often deeply three lobed, not unlike those of our native hawthorn *Crataegus monogyna*. A few flower clusters still showed, quite attractive with their white petals and red anthers, but the branches were mainly hung with small fruit up to 1in. (2.5cm) across, rounded, hard and acid to the taste. Later we came across a man going through the fruits searching for and eating those which had ripened and sweetened, turning brown and soft (bletted).

A small stream ran through the garden and the banks were peppered with the rich blue single pea flowers of *Parochetus communis* which grew here as freely as the white clover – *Trifolium repens* – in Britain. I had often seen this little gem cultivated in cool greenhouses in England, and in particular I remember it being sown annually on the sandstone rock garden at the University Botanic Garden, Cambridge. It was a thrill to see it in the wild.

In the scrub around the garden's boundary, three shrubs caught our attention – *Berberis asiatica* reached 10ft. (3m) in height and its evergreen leaves, 1½-3in. (4-7.5cm) long, were elliptic to rounded and few spined. They were hard and leathery in texture and made conspicuous by the striking whiteness of their undersurface. This handsome shrub has been tried in the Hillier Arboretum but without success because it is liable to frost damage, although it is suitable for warmer areas and there is a large specimen in the gardens of Dunloe Castle in County Kerry, south-west Ireland. *Sarcococca coriacea* was an evergreen with strong growths up to 7ft. (2m) tall. The leathery leaves were 4-6in. (10-15cm) long and rather narrow, ending in a slender point. The flower buds were apparent in the leaf axils, but their greenish-yellowish floweres are no match for those of *S. hookeriana* which also grows wild in the area on Phulchoki. As far as I am aware, *S. coriacea* is very rare if at all in British cultivation, being less winter hardy than most other species. The wood of this shrub is hard, like boxwood, and further east is used for walking sticks. *Pyracantha crenulata*, the Himalayan firethorn, grew here in some quantity. Its narrow, minutely-toothed leaves and small orange-red fruits are no competition for the popular firethorns in cultivation, and its tender nature also prevents it from becoming better known in British gardens.

We left the gardens and drove along a track which wound its way through the forest and up the side of Phulchoki. Many plants caught our attention and I was pleased to see *Coriaria napalensis* throwing its long arching stems 6ft. (2m) in the air. Unfortunately this handsome shrub is only suitable for the warmer areas of the British Isles although it has succeeded for several years in the Hillier Arboretum.

On the lower slopes *Alnus nepalensis* formed groves with dark green stems 60-70ft. (18-21m) high and handsome slender-pointed leaves 4-6in. (10-15cm) long, the petioles with conspicuous stipules. It is a pity that this alder is so tender because in the British Isles its attractive foliage, bark and autumn catkins would be in great demand among tree planters and landscape architects.

Although long past flowering, the Himalayan musk rose – *Rosa brunonii* – impressed by its powerful scrambling growths reaching into trees and swamping less sturdy plants. Hips were swelling but still retained the green of youth. *Stachyurus himalaicus* put in an appearance between the 5,000 and 6,000ft. (1,524 and 1,829m) contours. Its flower spikes were already formed, lining the undersides of the branches ready for the winter ahead. Unlike the Japanese *S. praecox* of our gardens, this species has dusky red flowers and is quite startling as a result. It is vigorous in growth, reaching 8-10ft. (2.5-3m), but unfortunately is too tender for all but the mildest areas of the British Isles. I remember a large specimen growing in a border on the north side of Jermyns House in the Hillier Arboretum during the mid-1960s. It flowered but timidly two years running before succumbing to a persistent frost.

We left the jeep parked by the track and scrambled up the steep slope beneath trees of a handsome evergreen oak – *Quercus semecarpifolia*. Many were gnarled specimens 30-40ft. (9-12m) high or more and the fallen leaves of summer lay in thick carpets crackling under our feet. The current leaves were obovate to oblong in shape, 3-4½in. (7.5-11.5cm) long, dark glossy-green above and covered with a dense pale buff to rust-coloured felt beneath; even the young growths were similarly covered. The leaves varied in amount of toothing, those on old trees entire or few toothed, whilst on vigorous, especially sucker growths, they were spine toothed and larger. Occasionally we came across stumps where trees had been felled and these had produced dense growths bearing prickly leaves as hostile almost as those of an English holly. This diversification of armature is not unusual with evergreen oaks and is commonly seen in the holm oak – *Q. ilex* – in Europe. *Q. semecarpifolia* has an immense range in the wild from Afghanistan to western China, reaching an altitude of 12,000ft. (3,657m) in the western Himalaya. It is strange, therefore, that it should be so rare in cultivation, the only tree I had previously seen being one from the north-west Himalaya introduced by acorns sent to R.S. Gamble of East Liss, Hampshire, in 1900 and still going strong.

Sharing the same zone as the oak were two other handsome evergreen trees, one of which, *Rhododendron arboreum,* formed characteristic dense, gently tapered columns up to 40ft. (12m) or more. The other tree was another species of oak – *Q. lamellosa,* an attractive tree 50-60ft. (15-18m) high with striking leaves shaped like those of a Sweet chestnut (*Castanea sativa*) 6-10in. (15-25.5cm) long. These were boldly toothed and parallel veined, and the glossy dark green of the upper surface contrasted effectively with the glaucous undersurface. It is little wonder that Sir Joseph Hooker, who saw this tree in Sikkim, regarded it as the noblest of all oaks. A specimen of this oak flourishes in the woodland at Caerhays, Cornwall, although along with many other fine trees it was badly damaged in a devastating storm in January 1990.

Colour Plate 13. The grounds of the Singha Durbar, the former palace of the Rana Maharajas of Nepal, and now Kathmandu's administrative centre

Colour Plate 14. Pancakes of dung being dried on a sunny wall in Kathmandu. Once completely dried they will be used as fuel

Colour Plate 15. A young Lhasa Apso outside one of the many monasteries at Bodhnath

Colour Plate 16. A typical wall painting on the plastered wall of a monastery at Bodhnath

As the tree cover thinned out a little towards the summit of the hill, several small perennial plants became more frequent, including two species of pearly everlasting *Anaphalis triplinervis* and *A. busua*. Both had grey woolly stems and foliage, those of the latter narrow and lacking the distinctive triple-venation of the other. In full flower was *Roscoea purpurea*, a member of the ginger family, with erect leafy stems to 1½ft. (46cm) and lovely orchid-like pale purple flowers (Colour Plate 12). This species, the first of the genus to be named, is rare in British cultivation, the closely related *R. auriculata* often doing service for it. I grow the true plant in my garden from a Tony Schilling collection made in Nepal at Nagakot in 1972. In cultivation this is the last roscoea to flower, usually in August-September. The name *Roscoea* commemorates William Roscoe (1753-1832), the son of a publican and market gardener who became a leading figure in Liverpool, as well as a banker, politician, historian, lawyer, painter and patron of the arts. He was instrumental in founding the Liverpool Botanic Garden in 1802 and became a specialist in the family *Zingiberaceae* to which *Roscoea* belongs.

Two white-flowered perennials appeared in the shape of *Thalictrum javanicum* and *Anemone vitifolia*. The former preferred shady places, throwing up erect stems 1-2ft. (30.5-61cm) high, whilst the *anemone* sought the sun. A curious saprophytic plant was the diminutive *Monotropastrum humile* which poked its creamy-white flower spikes above the leaf mould of the rhododendron and oak forest floor. This plant is closely related to our native Yellow Bird's Nest – *Monotropa hypopitys,* an uncommon little plant of leaf litter in woods, especially pine and beech as well as on sand dunes.

On our return to the jeep we encountered several shrubs well known in gardens, of which *Hypericum uralum* was the most frequent. Its graceful habit with arching frond-like stems, small leaves and yellow flowers like nodding buttercups was a constant pleasure.

Hydrangea aspera is a variable species which is not surprising considering its distribution, which stretches from Nepal eastwards through China to Formosa, and then leaps a couple of thousand miles south to appear in Java and Sumatra. Many of these forms are too tender for British gardens and the plants we found growing on Phulchoki would doubtless fall into this category. There were several specimens from 6-10ft. (1.75-3m) high with large velvety hairy leaves, pale beneath, and flattened heads of blue-tinted fertile flowers surrounded by conspicuous white ray florets. Interestingly, this species was first described from Nepal in 1825, though the hardy forms in cultivation today are of Chinese origin, several having been collected by the great plant hunters E.H. Wilson and George Forrest. Both *Viburnum cylindricum* and *V. erubescens* were present in some quantity, the former with its unusual evergreen leaves which are covered above with a thin coating of wax. When scratched or folded the wax ruptures and turns grey, and Beer chose a large leaf on which to draw a face with a sharp-ended twig. Both species are of borderline hardiness in Britain, but I had seen several specimens of *V. cylindricum* in collections such as Exbury Gardens, Wakehurst Place and the Hillier Arboretum.

A Himalayan privet – *Ligustrum indicum (nepaulense),* tender in British cultivation, occurred frequently in open scrubby areas and an evergreen form of *Daphne bholua* appeared as scattered individuals over a wide area of forest and clearing. Climbing in the main stems of several trees was an ivy – *Hedera nepalensis* – with ovate entire or three-lobed leaves. It looked very similar to our native species *H. helix*, but the fruits, when they ripen in spring, are amber-yellow rather than black, otherwise it is just as effective, and almost if not as hardy. As if called to complete the partnership, we found a Himalayan holly – *Ilex dipyrena* – forming a small tree up to 20ft. (6m). The oblong, slender pointed, dull-green leaves measured 4-5in. (10-13cm) in length with entire or spine-toothed margins, borne on short purple-tinged petioles. The fruits were green and immature. Several trees had been cut down recently and the resultant sucker growths carried leaves which were fiercely armed with large spine-tipped teeth. Phulchoki opened our eyes to the rich variety of the Nepalese flora and yet it was merely the beginning, the first glimpse, an initial taste of things to come.

Returning to Kathmandu we were surprised at the number of hill people we passed on the road, their backs bent beneath huge loads of faggots bound for the city. Given the scarcity of forest in the Kathmandu valley, wood cut from the ever decreasing hill forests was in great and constant demand whilst alternative fuels were no less important. Never having encountered such a thing before, we were amused to see pancakes of cow dung smeared on walls to dry in the sun (Plate 14). Productive of more smoke than flame, these animal wastes are nevertheless relied upon as fuel by a large number of people.

There still being several hours of daylight remaining, we decided to pay a visit to Swayambhunath. Situated on a hill to the west of the city this famous Buddhist temple is dominated by a huge concrete stupa (religious structure) topped by a large gold-coloured block on each face of which the watchful eyes of Buddha gaze out across the valley covering the four cardinal directions.

Plate 2. Kathmandu, the stupa at Swayambhunath. This Buddhist temple is situated on a hill west of the city. From each face of the gold-coloured block the watchful eyes of the Buddha gaze out across the valley covering the four cardinal directions

Below the eyes where the nose should be is a symbol like an elaborate question mark. This is simply the Nepali number ek (one), a symbol of unity. Between and above the eyes a smaller third eye symbolises the Buddha's clairvoyant powers (Plate 2).

The stupa's white painted base represents the four elements, earth, fire, air and water, whilst the lines which lead from the spire are hung with small prayer flags bearing mantras (prayer formulas) which Buddhists believe are carried away on the slightest breeze. The sacred mantra 'Om mani padme hum' (Hail to the jewel in the lotus) is printed on the scrolls in the prayer wheels below, each spin of the wheel sending its message far and wide.

According to legends, the hill on which Swayambhunath stands was once an island in a vast lake covering the entire valley. During its long history the site has received many important visitors including, it is said, the Indian Emperor Ashoka over two thousand years ago. One of the blackest days occurred in 1346 when Muslim invaders from Bengal broke into the stupa in search of gold.

Locally, the temple is known as Monkey Temple because of the rhesus or macaque monkeys which frequent the hill and the temple complex. We saw them soon after we arrived and were amused by their tricks and escapades, although our laughs turned to indignation when one of them snatched a camera lens brush from my hand, speeding off with its prize chased by others of its troop.

The views of the valley from Swayambhunath are breathtaking and with a fast setting sun painting the stupa a rich orange we took one last look before departing for the city now twinkling with myriad lights.

The next morning we awoke early. This was to be a day of visiting and organisation, beginning with Mike Cheney, a friendly, capable man of immense

Colour Plate 17. A dhamye (or damai) – professional musician – at Bodhnath. His stringed instrument is known as a sarungi

Colour Plate 18. A temple guard with an ancient muzzle-loaded rifle in Durbar Square, Kathmandu

Colour Plate 19. A dead Bunya-Bunya (*Araucaria bidwillii*) opposite the Annapurna Hotel, Kathmandu. The bare branches are strung with sleeping fruit bats looking for all the world like withered plums. (December)

Colour Plate 20. Kathmandu, the Buddhist stupa at Bodhnath on the eastern side of the city. This is the largest stupa in Nepal and one of the largest in the world. The religious centre for Nepal's Tibetan population, it is surrounded by thriving monasteries. The thirteen steps of the golden spire represent the thirteen degrees of knowledge and the thirteen stages on the journey to Nirvana, represented by the umbrella. Note the many strings of prayer flags draping the spire

Colour Plate 21. *Eucalyptus globulus*, the Blue Gum of Tasmania, demonstrating its powerful stem and pale flaking bark. Such trees have been planted in Kathmandu since the nineteenth century and bring welcome shade to squares and parks. (September)

41

activity. He introduced us to our Sherpas – Da Norbu, Namgyal, Pema our cook, Namcha, Perma, Jangbu and, of course, Dawa our sirdar whom we had already met. The latter accompanied us on a shopping spree for last-minute stores and equipment which included five black umbrellas made in the Republic of China. These would serve the dual purpose of protecting us from the hot sun and the worst of the rain – a comforting thought even to adventurers.

Another foray took us to the Singha Durbar, a former palace and now Nepal's administrative centre, whose lawns were parched and fountains choked with debris (Colour Plate 13). Behind the gull-white façade lay a quiet dark world, a rabbit-warren of corridors and offices, each with its attendant cluster of people outside the doors. Here we successfully applied for our visa extensions and our trekking permits for the north-east. In 1973 the Singha Durbar was devastated by a fire, since when several courtyards have been rebuilt and the façade restored.

There was still time after all this to grab a taxi and pay a visit to the great Buddhist stupa at Bodhnath on the eastern side of the city. The stupa, which is the largest in Nepal and one of the largest in the world, is the religious centre for Nepal's Tibetan population and is surrounded by thriving monasteries and workshops. It was certainly a scene of intense activity, life and colour when we arrived (Colour Plates 15 and 16) and I was immediately struck by the stupa's magnificent spire, its thirteen golden steps representing the thirteen degrees of knowledge and the thirteen stages on the journey to Nirvana (man's final escape from the cycles of existence) which is represented by the elaborate umbrella at the spire's summit (Colour Plate 20). The spire was well draped with strings of prayer flags, and sitting in the streets below we saw sewing women surrounded by piles of colourful material used both for flags and other religious purposes (Plate 3). We watched for a while an elderly professional musician or dhamye (damai) playing a native stringed instrument known as a sarungi (Colour Plate 17) until a loud chanting voice announced the arrival of a visiting lama of the Kaphupa sect. In his right hand he held a prayer wheel which he kept spinning with a deft flick of the wrist (Plate 4).

Whilst still in England I had received a request from Spring-Smyth to bring two small plants of the Dawn redwood – *Metasequoia glyptostroboides*. He had a hunch that this tree, then unknown in Nepal, might prove suitable as a rapid source of timber. The two specimens we carried, however, were destined as gifts to the British and American Embassies in Kathmandu, and on our last day before heading east, we joined the Spring-Smyths for a luncheon engagement at the British Embassy. The Ambassador and his wife, Terence and Rita O'Brien, were charming hosts and showed great interest in the aims of the expedition as explained by Beer and Morris. We sat for a while on the terrace drinking beer, the Ambassador pointing out to us a pair of Spotted owlets, small, dumpy, sleepy-eyed birds, in the branches of a tree above. We then selected a place in the garden where the Dawn redwood might flourish and related to the O'Briens the story of this remarkable tree, of how it was known only as a fossil until 1941 when living trees were discovered in a remote corner of central China and six years later introduced to the world as a result of an expedition financed by the Arnold Arboretum, Massachusetts.

The afternoon we spent on a final tour of the city beginning with the Annapurna Hotel. However, it was not the hotel so much as the surroundings

Plate 3. Colourful prayer flags being sewn beside the famous stupa at Bodhnath

that interested us. In a garden opposite the hotel entrance stood a group of tall conifers from Australia – *Araucaria bidwillii,* the Bunya-Bunya. One of these was dead and from a distance its naked branches appeared strung with fruits like withered plums. Closer inspection revealed these 'fruits' to be Indian fruit bats or flying foxes *(Pteropus giganteus).* They hung by the claws of their feet with their wings folded around them like a cloak (Colour Plate 19). The only movement came from an occasional outstretched wing, but they kept up a continuous chatter reminding me of a British rookery. Their main activity takes place at dusk when they fly to the fruiting trees where they eat and then rest and digest their meal for several hours before flying back to their roosting trees before dawn.

One of the most fascinating areas we found in central Kathmandu was Durbar Square with its collection of temples, a royal palace and the Kumari Chowk or Kumari Bahal (Colour Plate 18). The last-named, its door guarded by two stone lions is the home of the Living Goddess, a young girl specially selected to fill this role until she reaches puberty when she reverts to being an ordinary mortal. We stood for a while outside this building admiring the magnificent richly ornamented façade and staring at a window in which it was said the Living Goddess sometimes sat, but we could detect no sign of movement and after a while we moved on to examine the exotic and often erotic carvings beneath the temple roofs. All around us the square seethed with people, a continuous, colourful ebb and flow of humanity which had us trying to look in every direction at once. Chattering women haggled over piles of vegetables of every description, ironmongers hovered above heaps of steel wire, brass and copper pots and teetering pyramids of tin mugs, whilst on mats in the dust rose mini Everests of salt and sugar buzzed by an assortment of flies. From walls and canopies hung wood and papier mâché masks, garishly painted to ward off demons and evil spirits (Colour Plate 26). In places loads of wood lay in the sun, dumped there by the hill people who now squatted in close groups, their long drawing on cheap cigarettes interspersed with noisy bouts of spitting.

We eventually arrived at the Old Royal Palace or Hanuman Dhoka, named for the Monkey God whose statue, built in 1672, stands outside the palace entrance. It was cloaked in red and sheltered by an umbrella but was difficult to recognise as its face had long since been covered by a coating of red paste applied by the faithful.

Kathmandu is truly the city of the gods for Hanuman is but one of a great

Colour Plate 22. Bougainvilleas creating a spectacular display in the Kathmandu valley where, as in other warm temperate and tropical climates, they are commonly planted and thrive. Two species, *B. glabra* and *B. spectabilis*, as well as a hybrid, *B. × buttiana*, provide a wide range of named selections differing most obviously in flower colour. (December)

Colour Plate 23. *Eriobotrya japonica,* a bold-leaved evergreen shrub or small tree is native to China but commonly planted in Kathmandu and other warm temperate and Mediterranean climates, where its small orange-yellow fruits – loquats – are commonly sold in markets and bazaars. Here photographed in Spain. (August)

Colour Plate 24. *Plumeria rubra* forma *acutifolia*. A native of Mexico to Panama, the frangipani is a familiar sight in tropical and warm temperate climates, including the Kathmandu valley where it has long been planted for its fragrant flowers. The species is variable in flower colour from rose-pink to white, yellow, bronze or a combination of all. (September)

Colour Plate 25. The long 'tongued' flowers of *Hibiscus rosa-sinensis*. In Kathmandu it is commonly grown as a specimen in a lawn, sometimes even as an informal hedge. The flowers vary enormously in colour and size and in the tropics many selections have been named, especially in Hawaii. (September)

45

many Hindu and Buddhist deities to be found there: Shiva, Brahma, Vishnu and the elephant-headed Ganesh – all have their popular images depicted in statues, carvings and murals, and if we had had more time we could have spent an enjoyable few days seeking out and identifying their numerous manisfestations.

The trees of Kathmandu are a mixed bag including several introduced from Australia during the nineteenth century. Pride of place must go to the occasional giant gums – *Eucalyptus* species – which dominate the squares and grounds in which they are planted. *E. globulus,* the Tasmanian Blue Gum, seems the most common (Colour Plate 21). Another magnificent tree is the Australian Silky oak – *Grevillea robusta* – which is not an oak at all but is related to the waratah (*Telopea*) and the *Protea*. This is a popular pot plant in Europe where its large finely divided fern-like leaves and reddish-purple young growths are much appreciated for decorating conservatories and as a 'dot plant' in subtropical bedding. It is too tender for growing permanently out of doors, however, which is why the sight of such large trees as those in Kathmandu interested me. In spring their dense elongated clusters of golden-yellow flowers bring an added pleasure.

Those of us familiar with the bottle-brushes (*Callistemon*) were amazed to see large tree specimens of *C. citrinus,* their drooping wand-like branches moving in the slightest breeze. *Jacaranda mimosifolia* from Brazil was commonly planted along main roads and in recreation areas, but its panicles of incredible lilac-blue flowers would not be appearing until the spring.

Many colourful shrubs crowded gardens and parks alike and included the ubiquitous frangipani (Colour Plate 24); *Hibiscus rosa-sinensis* (Colour Plate 25); *Lagerstroemia indica;* Chinese persimmon – *Diospyros kaki;* and the loquat – *Eriobotrya japonica* (Colour Plate 23), all commonly found in warm and temperate climates. Bougainvilleas scrambled everywhere over walls, fences, roofs and into lofty trees, bringing a dazzle of colour which, intensified by the sun, was almost blinding. The 'flowers' of this scrambler consist of three small tubular white-mouthed corollas enclosed in three large brightly-coloured bracts. Natives of Brazil, they are represented in cultivation by many forms and hybrids with flowers ranging in colour from purple to red, rose, orange and white and untold variations thereof (Colour Plate 22).

The following morning our plane was due to leave Kathmandu at 11a.m. and we were up and about in plenty of time to have our baggage transported to and checked in at the airport. We were flying south-east to Biratnagar, just north of the Indian frontier, where we would meet up with Witcombe, the fifth member of our party who had come out in August to do the crop reconnaissance. An aircraft was trundling along the runway to the airport terminal as we fought our way through the crowded arrival and

Plate 4. A lama of the Kaphupa sect (the same sect as the Dalai Lhama) visiting Bodhnath. In his right hand he holds a prayer wheel, whilst larger versions can be seen in the niches in the monastery wall behind. As the wheel is turned the mantra or prayer it contains is believed to issue forth to the world at large

departure hall. But it appeared that something was wrong with the engine and mechanics swarmed over and under the fuselage, while the waiting passengers walked over to watch the action. The efforts of the mechanics were mystifying to me so I left the others and watched the circling Griffon vultures high above.

At last the trouble was located and dealt with and soon we were all aboard and the plane was racing down the runway. Minutes later, at a height of 15,000ft. (4,572m), we peered below us to the north where peculiar rib-like hills rose from the valleys, whose water courses appeared dry and filled with silt. Further north the hills grew progressively larger until on the horizon, stretching east-west like some gigantic white wall, we saw the Himalayan massive, regularly punctuated by peaks in excess of 20,000ft. (6,096m). The plants we had come to collect would be found mainly below the snow line, between the 10,000ft. and 15,000ft. (3,048m and 4,572m) contours. In order to reach this area we would need to walk along the ridges, travelling north, maintaining as far as possible a steady progress and altitude in order to keep within our schedule. Soon beneath us we could see the comparatively flat and fertile strip of Nepal known as the Terai which stretches from the foothills of the Himalaya south to the Indian border.

There was neither steward nor stewardess on our flight, no boiled sweets, nor friendly reassuring noises from the captain, and our descent to Biratnagar airport was signalled by a sudden loss of height accompanied by a rapid movement of the adrenalin. My first glimpse of the airfield, while still aloft, revealed a short runway in a parched field with what appeared to be cattle wandering about. On landing I was able to confirm that cattle had indeed been occupying the runway and had been pushed away by a cowherd just prior to our landing. Now safely down, the plane was immediately surrounded and inspected by interested villagers and their assorted dogs, whilst the cattle returned to bask on the hot surface of the runway. Beer, who had flown in the previous day, was waiting to meet us.

For the next few days we were to be guests of the Officers' Mess at the British Gurkha Headquarters in Dharan, and their hospitality had extended even to the provision of a jeep to carry us and our luggage to the camp some miles north of Biratnagar. We found Witcombe discussing the money situation with a rather benign bank manager who immediately offered us cigarettes and cups of tea and threw in what he explained was a Muslim Christmas card for luck. Witcombe looked tired and thinner than when we last saw him and later we heard that he had been ill whilst in the hills and had returned in a weak and unhappy state on horseback. Our arrival, however, seemed to cheer him and during the subsequent journey to Dharan he rarely stopped talking. The only interruptions came when we saw things of interest in the surrounding villages and fields. In some areas by the road jute (*Corchorus capsularis)* was being grown. The fibre comes from the stem of this tall herbaceous plant, a member of the lime or basswood family (*Tiliaceae*), so fields are thickly planted to encourage long slender stems. After cutting and de-leafing, the stems are laid in rivers or pools to decompose, a process known as retting (Plate 5). The fibres that remain are hooked from the water and laid out in the sun to dry. Eventually these are bundled up and taken away in trucks or bullock carts (Plate 6). In a group of dead trees in the middle of a cultivated area we saw some strange-looking birds with scrawny necks and hunched shoulders. One or two rose on heavy wings at our approach and we recognised them as Adjutant

Colour Plate 26. Brightly coloured masks are hung on walls in Kathmandu to ward off demons and evil spirits

storks, ugly birds with a huge wing span and a grotesque ruddy pouch hanging from their chests. The roadside telegraph wires were a favourite perch for a host of interesting smaller birds including the Black drongo with its characteristic deeply forked tail and the small Green bee-eater, a delightful species with slenderly pointed bill and tail. Once we saw a Blue jay or roller, a brilliant flash of blue, like a giant kingfisher. Two common inhabitants of the rice fields were the white Cattle egret and a biscuit-coloured relative of the bittern, appropriately known as the Paddy bird.

Plate 5. Bundles of cut jute stems, *Corchorus capsularis*, being soaked in a pool, Biratnagar. The fibres are later separated and dried. (September)

Plate 6. Carrying bundles of dried jute fibres. The jute is chiefly used for sacking and matting. (September)

The road eventually passed through a stretch of the Terai forest, a mere fragment of a once vast green tropical and subtropical jungle, much of which has been destroyed to make way for agriculture. The dominant tree here was the sal *(Shorea robusta),* one of the most important timber trees in Nepal, long used by builders and woodcarvers who value its strength and durability. It can reach 100ft. (30.5m) or more with a straight clean stem, and in spring when its white flower sprays appear with the pale green young foliage it provides quite a spectacle, especially when viewed from the air in a plane.

For several miles we drove through the forest, dense undergrowth crowding the road and wherever trees had been cleared. We saw several birds including the all black Jungle crow contrasting with the slightly smaller black-and-grey House crow – a bird similar in appearance to the European hooded crow – which frequented villages and towns.

Towards the end of the afternoon we arrived at Dharan Bazaar where we headed for the Gurkha Headquarters. Here we were given a large clean and airy room with four beds and plenty of room for stacking our belongings.

We spent the next few days sorting and repacking our food and equipment and Dawa, our sirdar, arrived with twenty-four porters, Sherpas from the village of Sedua, who had just returned from a Japanese climbing expedition to Makalu. We agreed to employ them at ten rupees (30 pence) per day and sent them off to Tumlingtar to establish our first camp while we waited for the weather to clear in the hills. We then went for a walk around the camp ending up by a pond where we spent some time watching small frogs jumping from the bank and moving across the water in a series of leaps rather like a flat stone skimming the surface, a most amazing sight. Because of the crop research being tackled by Witcombe and Mortimer, the Food and Agriculture Organisation of the United Nations had offered to fly us and our baggage into Tumlingtar, thus saving us an initial four or five days of hard slogging on foot. Eventually our plane, a Pilatus Porter arrived piloted by a chain-smoking nervous-looking Swiss and the first two of us, Beer and myself, were being shuttled north towards a seemingly impenetrable barrier of hills and ravines.

3. UP THE MILKE DANDA

It was a curious sensation flying above foothills, any one of which would have ranked as a mountain in Britain. The slopes were steeply terraced and intensely cultivated with what appeared from our height to be pocket handkerchief-size rice fields. We saw the river Tamur where it joined the Sun Kosi and then we headed up the valley of the Arun. Suddenly the valley widened on all sides and before us on a raised plateau stood the village of Tumlingtar some 1,500ft. (457m) above sea level. We could see no runway, just a level area of rough grass on to which our pilot lowered his plane with the expertise born of long experience.

A plane landing in the valley was not such a common event that it passed unnoticed and it was not long before a good-sized crowd had assembled to watch us unload our gear. One man, a Thamang clad only in a pair of shorts, was covered from head to foot in a white powdery substance and looked as if he had fallen into a vat of flour. We were told that he came from a village on the hillside above and that he had been engaged in white-washing the walls of a

Plate 7. A Thamang man who had been white-washing the wall of a house, and came just as he was when he heard our plane landing at Tumlingtar

Plate 8. A villager who turned up at the Tumlingtar airstrip to watch us making camp was in need of help with his spectacles

house when the sound of the approaching plane had caused him to drop everything and come running to see what it was all about (Plate 7). Another man with bow legs and an engaging smile wore a pair of spectacles in which one lens was missing and the bridge stuck together with plaster (Plate 8). He was introduced as panchayat leader, the head man of the village, and when we made to shake hands he placed his own together and greeted us with a welcoming 'Namaste'. We smiled and repeated the greeting which then spread through the crowd. The pilot meanwhile had turned his plane round and taken off, and two trips later the expedition's five members and Sherpas were standing on the plateau surrounded by an assortment of bags, boxes and baskets (Plate 9).

Pema, the cook, got busy with preparing a meal as we began the task of re-sorting the baggage into 60lb. (27kg) porter loads. After lunch we made our way through fields planted with maize, soya beans and, surprisingly, cotton. Fifty years ago cotton was commonly grown in the hills of Nepal. It was a shifting cultivation with a rapid turnover and resulted in the destruction of huge areas of virgin forest. The industry declined, however, mainly due to the importation of cheap yarns from India. We found ourselves at the edge of a deep ravine through which the Sabhaya Khola flowed to join the river Arun at the foot of the plateau. We reached the river after a long, hot, dusty descent and plunged naked into the cold water. The surrounding soil was a red laterite which baked in the sun and dazzled the eyes. It was therefore pleasant lying in the fast-running water wedged between large rocks staring at the hillsides above. Two hours later we climbed out of the ravine and returned to camp to find the tents erected and fuel brought from the village.

Tumlingtar was something of a modern miracle. Ten years earlier it did not exist because of the malarial mosquitoes which swarmed from its waters. Then DDT had been introduced and the mosquito was said to be no more. The plateau was certainly fertile and it was claimed that the best chillies in Nepal were grown here. We assumed that by best they meant the hottest, as was confirmed when we were served a curry at dinner that night.

At breakfast next morning we discussed the non-appearance of our porters hired in Dharan; but half an hour later nineteen men, women and children padded into camp carrying home-made bamboo baskets and an assortment of bamboo sheets and ropes. We needed more porters so Dawa, Namgyal and Da

Norbu were sent to recruit some in the village. In the early evening Dawa returned with extra porters, a strange looking bare-footed bunch of various ages (Plate 10). One of them gave me a cigar which he had made by rolling together the dried leaves of *Lyonia ovalifolia*, a large native deciduous shrub or small tree of the *Ericaceae*. It had a strong flavour and though crude, compared with western versions it was nevertheless an acceptable substitute and cost nothing.

That night we were besieged by all manner of biting insects, most of which homed in on the light cast by a Tilley lamp which we sat around writing our letters and diaries. The shrill sounds of crickets and other creatures of the dark filled the air but failed to prevent us from sleeping until a call from Pema announced the day of departure. It was 5.30a.m. and it was just beginning to get light. Through the steam of our porridge we could see the porters arriving in dribs and drabs to stand in small groups awaiting instructions. Then Dawa and his assistants began issuing orders and the groups broke up and milled around the piles of baggage, sorting and weighing each item, discarding it if it proved too bulky or heavy. With the pale light of dawn bathing the valley our camp looked like a scene from an ancient history book of the east. The porters scurried about testing each other's load, talking, shouting and arguing like a pack of hounds in a mêlée. They were a mixed group, Sherpas from Sedua, Chetris from the valley, Thamangs and Limbus. Some of the women wore rings in their ears and ornamental nose pins. They would be carrying loads as heavy as those of the men and were being paid the same rate, ten rupees per day. The bamboo baskets were home-made and narrowed to the base so that the bulk of the load occurred at the top. A band passes around the basket and round the carrier's forehead so that the weight is borne mainly by the head. The porters, as a result, develop strong neck and shoulder muscles, contrasting with their often thin though muscular legs (Plate 11). All possess broad, flattened feet with wide gaps between the first and second toes from long use as an anchor in the making of bamboo ropes and straps.

Half an hour after leaving camp with the heat of the sun already making itself felt we decided to stop and change into something looser and lighter, Mortimer opting for his pyjamas which he reasoned would keep him cool whilst protecting him from the burning sun (Plate 12). Shortly afterwards, we left the plateau and followed a steep track down into the valley to the edge of the Sabhaya Khola. At this point the water was waist deep and running fast, too fast for the porters to chance fording. A discussion took place and a man was sent down river to summon the ferryman and his boat. Meanwhile we settled ourselves in the rocks and had a lunch of chapattis and eggs, the porters doing likewise, some of them using as bowls the large leaves of the sal tree – *Shorea robusta* – pinned together with slivers of bamboo (Colour Plate 29). My hat had just fallen into the river and been carried away, when the ferryman appeared paddling towards us in a dunga (dugout boat). It was with some difficulty that he steered to where we waited, the current continuously threatening to push his boat back in the direction he had come. At last he moored and we were better able to examine the boat, which was simply a tree trunk (probably that of the simal tree, *Bombax malabarica,* a tree of the tropical deciduous forest in the Terai whose wood is light and buoyant) hollowed out with hatchet and fire (Colour Plate 32). He told us it had taken him four days to make at a cost of 800

Plate 10. One of the villagers who offered his services as a porter at Tumlingtar flashed us a smile revealing an unusual example of native dentistry

Plate 11. In the Arun valley. A young porter carrying one of our boxes for dried specimens supplied by the Natural History Museum in London. Behind him the river Arun below Tumlingtar. (September)

rupees. Stepping into the boat I could not help but notice the handsome outcrop of bracket fungus which had established itself for 2-3ft. (61-91cm) along the water level down one side.

It took less than an hour and several trips to get us all across, some of the porters being understandably apprehensive of the boat's safety Having made it we lost no time in regaining the track.

There was no let up in the steepness nor the direction of the track which climbed straight up and out of the valley heading for the distant ridge above. We were moving in an easterly direction towards the village of Chainpur, which we hoped we would reach in time for tea. It certainly had not looked too great a distance on our map, but then the map was an unknown quantity as we were to discover many times in the days to come. Any excuse to stop for a rest on that long haul was quickly seized upon and we began to take photographs on all sides and at regular intervals (Plate 13). Once, it was a colourful pair of grasshoppers *(Aularches miliaris)* (Colour Plate 28) copulating in the grass, another time a group of three hoopoes in nearby scrub, their black-and-white barred wings and crest attracting our attention and that of one of our young porters who shouted to us and laughed pointing a finger in their direction.

Pines were frequent on these hills sporting large handsome bunches of 9-15in. (23-38cm) long grey-green, drooping needles. These were the Chir pine – *Pinus roxburghii (P. longifolia)*, a three-needled species occurring in the warmer

Plate 12. Expedition members taking time out to change into cooler clothing before facing a hot climb to Chainpur. Mortimer chose to wear his pyjamas to help protect him from the sun's rays. (September)

valleys of the Himalaya from Afghanistan in the west to Bhutan in the east. Here above the Arun it grew at 3,000ft. (914m), and individual trees reached 50-60ft. (15-18m) in height (Colour Plate 27), though there was evidence that many larger specimens had long since been felled. The Chir pine is too tender for general cultivation in the British Isles, although I understand it has been grown with limited success in Cornwall and similarly favoured areas. It should be mentioned here that William Roxburgh (1751-1815), after whom this pine is named, was a Scottish medical man and botanist who for twenty years (1793-1813) was Superintendent of the Calcutta Botanic Garden and Chief Botanist for the East India Company. He wrote many books including the two-volume *Flora Indica,* published posthumously between 1820 and 1824 (Plate 15).

After what seemed like a month we found the track gradually levelling out and looking ahead we saw that a number of porters had stopped to rest in the shade of two huge trees with vast spreading canopies. Crawling the last few feet we sank thankfully to the ground to lie on our backs staring up at the high mosaic of green leaves and needled sunlight. The trees were the banyan – *Ficus benghalensis,* and the Bo tree or Pipal tree – *F. religiosa,* both popular as village trees and both commonly planted on stone-walled platforms called chautaras above steep tracks in the foothills to give welcome shade to weary travellers. Here in Nepal they were often referred to as 'marriage trees' because their branches interlocked. The leaves of the banyan were elliptic and short pointed, rather like those of the evergreen magnolia – *Magnolia grandiflora* – with a rounded or heart-shaped base strongly contrasting with those of the Bo tree which were remarkably like those of a Black poplar – *Populus nigra* – but with a characteristic and conspicuous 'drip-tip'. These leaves are commonly pressed and dried, painted with religious themes and sold as souvenirs in Kathmandu.

It was dark before the dancing lights on the ridge ahead announced our arrival at Chainpur and the rough and rivened course of the track gave way to a paved main street. We tramped along the street to where a brick and wooden building stood before an open grassy space. This was the British-Nepal Medical Centre, one of several operating in Nepal for the treatment of various ailments, but especially tuberculosis. At the time of our visit there were four British nurses in residence. They welcomed us and made a large kettle of tea which soon helped us forget the long march (Plate 14). After that we paid a visit to the

Centre's lavatory, reputedly the best in town, which was a deep pit covered by a bamboo platform with a hole in the middle.

It was with difficulty that we hauled ourselves up the ladder into the Centre's attic, where our torches revealed piles of boxes, bottles and stores of one kind or another. We needed no rocking that night, and apart from the occasional involuntary kick when rats ran over our legs, we slept soundly until morning when Pema awoke us with mugs of hot tea. The porters were already assembled outside, having spent the night in various hostelries around the village. Now we could see Chainpur sitting astride a 4,500ft. (1,371m) ridge, its houses strung out along the paved street (Colour Plate 31) eventually climbing the hill in a series of broad steps. The village was celebrating a festival – Dashira, and many of the shop fronts had been freshly painted for the occasion. Chainpur was an isolated Newar stronghold as evidenced by the comparative cleanliness and intricate carvings on stone and wood exteriors. Around the wall of the Medical Centre was a narrow stone band in which numerous faces of animals and humans had been carved, and which might well have been taken from an old English cathedral or church (Plate 17). There were many merchants and craftsmen living here, especially those dealing in metalwork, and their tapping and banging could be heard all through the day and into the night. Outside on the village square a roteping, a type of ferris wheel, had been erected on wooden uprights (Plate 18). It supported four seats and was pushed round by two youths. Not far away children were queuing for a turn on a gigantic swing formed by two tall stout bamboo stems tied at the top with a rope suspended between. Once in the seat they shouted to be pushed higher and higher, their screams of delight and fear ringing through the valley below. As we stood watching this entertainment we saw gliding high above us on the warm thermals a group of six Himalayan Griffon vultures, as magnificent on the wing as they are repulsive on the ground.

The sun had so burned my legs in Tumlingtar that I could not bear to wear trousers and yet I needed somehow to protect them, so I decided to make a cotton skirt or lunghi similar to those being worn so gracefully by the women and purchased for 8 rupees two yards of a suitable material, which I proceeded to wrap around my lower half, tucking the end piece securely into my waist band. The merchant and his cronies, not realising the material was meant for me, were startled by my antics and broke into loud guffaws when I tried my first steps in the new creation, for I had wrapped it round too tightly and could walk only with difficulty. In view of the gathering audience, and to save further embarrassment, I decided to keep moving until safely out of the village before attempting a readjustment. I managed a further two or three yards before tripping up at the feet of the local policeman. Beer and Morris were no help and actually asked me for an encore. That was it, and without further ado I abandoned the lunghi, revealing my bright pink legs protruding from corduroy shorts. Once we had left the village well behind I again donned my lunghi, this time taking care to wrap it loosely. It survived only until the next day when the rains came.

Shortly, we entered a scrub area where we were surprised to encounter a familiar fern from home (bracken) – *Pteridium aquilinum,* which is said to be one of the most cosmopolitan of all plants. It was certainly common in these parts, whilst two evergreen trees – *Lithocarpus elegans,* with large leathery leaves, and *Schima wallichii –* occurred as isolated specimens (Colour Plate 33). The last named commemorates Nathaniel Wallich (1786-1854) (Plate 16). Of Danish birth, Wallich studied medicine before joining the Danish settlement at Serampur near Calcutta. He was later employed by the East India Company and became one of the most famous Superintendents of the Calcutta Botanic Garden from whence over a period of twenty-six years he sent home to England a vast amount of living plants and herbarium specimens including many from Nepal. He was a man of tremendous energy and played host, friend and adviser to numerous botanists and gardeners arriving from England wide eyed and full of wonder and apprehension.

Wallich developed his own technique of establishing collected seedlings and cuttings in the Calcutta Botanic Garden prior to shipping them to England, and such was his authority on the preparation, packing and transportation of living plants by sea that a paper which he submitted on the subject was read to the Horticultural Society of London (now the Royal Horticultural Society).

Both lithocarpus and schima were heavily pruned, whilst the latter, with a fairly hard close-grained, reddish wood, was used for ploughshares and in house building. Neither would be hardy in the British Isles, although the schima with its attractive white fragrant camellia-like flowers in April to June makes a magnificent tree of 60ft. (18m) or more in the eastern Himalaya. Its bark is said to be a skin irritant as well as being fire resistant. In the branches of one of these trees two small, brilliantly coloured birds were active. Their fiery-red and glossy black plumage identified them immediately as male Scarlet minivets.

Our path ran freely along the ridge now and afforded views of hillsides devoted to rice cultivation, creating pale green wavy bands following round the contours. The village of Side Pokhara appeared ahead of us and we noticed its pond on the outskirts choked full of Water hyacinth, *Eichhornia crassipes,* those on the marginal mud much larger and greener than those in the water. They were in full flower and quite beautiful (Colour Plate 30) and I should not have been at all surprised to see them decorating houses and shops in the village, but their value here was far more prosaic – they were used as pig fodder. The water hyacinth seemed a very long way from its native Amazon, and nearby in a garden grew another introduction – *Brugmansia suaveolens (Datura suaveolens)* from tropical America, its large white trumpet flowers

Colour Plate 27. *Pinus roxburghii*, the Chir pine on a hillside above the Arun valley below Chainpur. This fine specimen may have been planted or it could be the sole remnant of a natural grove or woodland. (September)

Colour Plate 28. *Aularches miliaris*, a strikingly coloured grasshopper mating on the hillside below Chainpur. (September)

Colour Plate 29. The leaves of the Sal tree – *Shorea robusta* – pinned together to make a simple expendable food bowl. (September)

Plate 14. The British-Nepal Medical Trust Centre, Chainpur, where we spent a night in the attic. Porters' loads litter the foreground whilst Mortimer catches up on his diary

hanging from the axils of the upper leaves. The smaller species of *Datura,* such as *D. metal,* have been cultivated in Nepal and India certainly for a very long time, and J.D. Hooker, for instance, in his *Himalayan Journals* published in 1854, described the use of this plant's seeds as a drug employed by thieves who frequented travellers' resting places.

By nightfall the porters had collected bundles of faggots, and soon fires were crackling and sparkling in many directions attracting people from a wide area who came to watch us eat They were dressed in their best clothes because of the holiday and some of the men had their foreheads dyed deep pink or studded with pink or orange rice; more people, returning from a religious ceremony, arrived and they all milled about among the many camp fires, talking and shouting, whilst a boy blew continuous blasts on a horn, the light from the fires flickering on their faces and the smoke curling in a dozen trails through the street. Added to this the smell of our meal – chicken supreme, vegetables and noodles, followed by fresh picked bananas and chocolate sauce. After this, and not surprisingly, we began to sing, which immediately attracted the crowd's attention especially when we sang Old McDonald's Farm and they joined in the chorus, 'eei-eei-o' echoing through the hills. Our every laugh, our every grimace drew a response from the crowd. Every action and reaction was noted by a hundred pairs of eyes that drank in every detail. We felt like a travelling circus here to entertain and we were eager to please. It seemed a natural progression to start dancing, and the sight of five foreigners making fools of themselves almost caused a riot. Thus singing and dancing we burned the midnight oil before our energies deserted us. The night being warm and the sky filled with stars, we opted to bed down on the veranda of a nearby house and were soon asleep.

The next morning we climbed the steep hillside through terraced fields of rice and small vegetable patches where buckwheat – *Fagopyrum esculentum* – presented masses of white flowers to lighten the green around. There were houses scattered over a wide area and the track we followed snaked its way past many of these, most of which were stone based with wooden and bamboo superstructures. Sometimes we were invited to stop and examine some inmate with a troublesome sore or sprain or maybe worse. It was in such a house that we were invited to have our lunch, and as soon as Pema and the kitchen porters arrived they got busy preparing our meal on the family fire. Meanwhile

Plate 15. William Roxburgh (1751-1815). Born at Craigie in Ayrshire, Roxburgh studied medicine at the University of Edinburgh, becoming a surgeon for the East India Company. In 1793 he was appointed Superintendent of the Calcutta Botanic Garden and Chief Botanist for the East India Company, but due to ill health brought about by the many hardships he suffered in botanical exploration, he eventually resigned and returned to Scotland. He was the author of many classic botanical studies including the two-volume *Flora Indica,* published posthumously. Several Nepalese plants bear his name including *Pinus roxburghii* (Colour Plate 27)

Plate 16. Nathaniel Wallich (1786-1854) was the Danish-born surgeon employed by the East India Company at Serampore and later as Superintendent of the Calcutta Botanic Garden. He travelled extensively in India, including Nepal, collecting plants and employing others to do likewise. He gave constant help and advice to other botanists visiting India and successfully introduced many plants to British cultivation, some of which bear his name, including *Pinus wallichiana* and *Dryopteris wallichiana*

our hosts busied themselves making us feel comfortable, mats were placed on the floor for us to sit on and we were offered roasted corn to eat. It was a typical Nepalese house of two storeys, each of a single room. A notched log led from the living area in which we sat through a gap in the ceiling to the sleeping quarters above. The fire lay in a hole or depression in the floor and the smoke made its exit via the open windows and door. The living area was becoming quite crowded, and as the porters arrived they too squeezed inside to escape the rain. Small fires were lit and pots of water and rice were set to boil. The room became so warm and full of smoke that Morris decided to sit on the porch outside, where he soon busied himself flicking leeches off his legs. Although we were at the end of the monsoon period, which lasts from June to September, the hillsides were quite wet. The leeches favoured the bushes and low vegetation bordering tracks, dropping on to any passing animal, be it pig, cow or man (Plate 19). I remembered being advised by someone before leaving Britain, to sprinkle a pinch of salt on their tails. Considering the number of

Plate 17. Newar gargoyles on the front of the British-Nepal Medical Trust Centre, Chainpur. Evidently the craftsman had a sense of humour

Colour Plate 30. The Water hyancinth, *Eichhornia crassipes,* a native of the Amazon region in South America, is commonly grown in Nepal as pig fodder. (September)

Colour Plate 31. The paved main street of Chainpur, a Newar village perched on a ridge above the Arun valley at 4,500ft. (1,371m)

Colour Plate 33 (right). *Schima wallichii* flowering on the sun-baked slopes of the Arun valley below Chainpur. This attractive evergreen is a member of the *Camellia* family, *Theaceae,* as can be seen by the flowers. (April)

Colour Plate 32. Porters and their loads crossing the Sabhaya Khola, a tributary of the Arun river, in a dunga or dugout boat. (September)

Plate 18. Rotepings or ferris wheels such as this one on the trail below Chainpur are very popular, along with other amusements, during Dashira, an autumn festival. The structures are dismantled at the end of the festival leaving the uprights in position

leeches we did encounter we would have needed a large barrel of salt to have dealt with them all. An old ex-Indian Army officer had even described to me in gory detail the effects of a leech attack: 'A Tiger leech will drain your arm of blood in an hour, your leg in two hours and your whole body in a day.' As if that were not bad enough, he then proceeded to tell me about the dreaded Bull leech which was on record as growing up to 4in. (10cm) or three times the size of the Tiger leech, although he had once 'shot' a giant specimen fully 6in. (15cm) long. The next time we met, a few weeks before my departure, the colonel unwittingly repeated the story but this time his Bull leech had gained three inches whilst the appetite of his Tiger leech had increased to the point where it had drained the body of his gun bearer as he slept in the night. I had not the heart to tell him that I had been on very close terms with leeches in Malaya many years previously when serving in Her Majesty's Forces. I knew well their capacities, and knew also that the simplest method of persuading them to disengage was to touch them with the lighted end of a cigarette. Unlike the weevil, the bug, the spider and other maligned creatures of this world, the leech has to my knowledge never been celebrated in poetry or song and is likely ever to remain one of nature's contemptibles although its importance in medicine as a blood letter should not be underestimated.

Cherry trees grew in some quantity around this and other houses in the neighbourhood. When we enquired of their origin, we were told that they were wild and that they had pink flowers in December. They were heavily lopped for firewood and as a consequence had the appearance of giant hat stands. We were later to identify them as *Prunus cerasoides*.

Many familiar shrubs had appeared during the last thousand feet of the climb, chief amongst which were *Pyracantha crenulata* and *Viburnum cylindricum* (Colour Plate 35). *Lyonia ovalifolia* formed a large shrub or occasionally a small tree up to 30ft. (9m) in height. This is a most attractive almost spectacular sight in late May and June when the racemes of small white pitcher-shaped flowers crowd the branches creating a singular effect, especially when seen from afar. Its leaves are used in the manufacture of native cigars or cigarettes and it was common for our porters to stop and stuff their pockets with the leaves for later use. It is a pity that this species is rarely seen in cultivation where, for some strange reason, it rarely thrives. In the Hillier Arboretum it is represented by variety *elliptica*, of China and Japan.

An evergreen – *Symplocos theifolia (lucida)* – occurred as a dense shrub with clusters of blue fruits, and the retaining walls around each house were clothed with moss and *Selaginella* species in which were embedded pink polygonums of several kinds, ferns, begonias and other small flowering plants. The most frequent *Polygonum* by the wayside was *P. runcinatum* whose red-tinted fleshy stems carpeted the ground. Its rounded-terminal heads of pink flowers contrasted well with the deeply lobed leaves marked with a dark V-shaped blotch.

By mid-afternoon we had left cultivation behind and now walked through pastures with scattered islands of trees and scrub. We had reached the Milke Danda, a euphonious name for the ridge which would be our companion for the next few days. We were, at this point, approximately 7,000ft. (2,134m) above sea level and life was becoming exciting as more and more plants appeared to indicate the approach of the cool temperate zone. The scrub included *Sarcococca hookeriana* and *Mahonia napaulensis* (Colour Plate 34), the latter a handsome large shrub, or small tree even, with numerous stout ascending rough-barked stems and bold ruffs of evergreen, spine-toothed pinnate leaves. The yellow flowers are borne in crowded cylindrical racemes up to 10in. (25.5cm) long in clusters from the ends of the branches and can be quite spectacular against the dark green foliage. All the mahonias we saw in east Nepal were autumn flowering which, together with their large leaves composed of seventeen to twenty-seven leaflets, place them in what some authorities believe to be a distinct species – *M. acanthifolia*. The last named also occurs at higher altitudes. Typical *M. napaulensis*, say the experts, grows lower down the mountains and is therefore less hardy than *M. acanthifolia* in British cultivation. It also has smaller leaves with fewer leaflets (up to fifteen) and produces its flowers later – in early spring (in cultivation certainly). Other authorities, on the other hand, regard the two above as merely variations of the one species, i.e. *M. napaulensis*. Certainly, what I have seen of plants labelled *M. acanthifolia* in cultivation suggest that it is the better garden plant, especially when given sheltered or woodland conditions. In some areas the hard bright yellow wood of the mahonia is used to make handles for the kukris carried by most village men. The wood of *Rhododendron arboreum* is also used for this purpose.

The pastures were studded with the slender pink flower spikes of *Spiranthes sinensis*, a pretty little orchid, a relative of our native Autumn Ladies' Tresses *(S. spiralis)* which, according to the latest authority, belongs to the variety *amoena*.

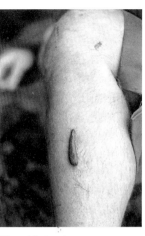

Plate 19. Leeches were common on the Milke Danda ridge despite the end of the monsoon. This one attached itself to Beer's leg at 8,900ft. (2,713m)

Colour Plate 34. *Mahonia napaulensis,* a bold-leaved evergreen shrub or small tree as seen on the Milke Danda, its yellow flowers borne in cylindrical racemes above the leaf ruffs in autumn. Some authorities believe this form to be a distinct species – *M. acanthifolia.* (November)

S. sinensis has an incredible distribution, being found from Afghanistan in the west right through the Himalaya to China, Siberia, Japan, south to Malaysia and Australia.

After a while our track left the open spaces and entered an evergreen forest in which the two main trees, *Rhododendron arboreum* and *Castanopsis tribuloides,* formed a dense dark canopy. The former was variable in leaf indumentum, ranging in colour from silver through buff to brown. Those with thin silver-backed leaves generally have crimson flowers and are more tender in cultivation, coming as they do from lower altitudes. The castanopsis surpassed in size the 30-40ft. (9-12m) columns of the *Rhododendron* and several specimens must have been in excess of 60-70ft. (18-21m). The dark green, toothed, chestnut-like leaves were pale or subglaucous beneath. The prickly-fruit clusters were borne in dense spikes, each capsule, when opened, containing two to three Sweet chestnut-like nuts. Both trees were full of epiphytic plants, especially lichens, ferns and orchids, and included *Agapetes serpens,* an unusual member of the *Ericaceae,* with slender trailing stems each lined with a double rank of narrow box-like evergreen leaves from the axils of which hung a profusion of tubular, inch-long, red-veined flowers. At its point of attachment with the tree the stem of the agapetes becomes conspicuously

Colour Plate 35. *Viburnum cylindricum* is a common evergreen shrub at lower altitudes in the mountains of east Nepal. The leaves are coated above with a thin layer of wax which cracks and turns white or grey when scratched. (September)

swollen into a hard turnip-like structure. One specimen we found still attached to a fallen branch had a swelling the size of a football. I have always wanted to see this plant tried in some of the moist, mild, woodland gardens of south-west Britain and Ireland, but frost of only a few degrees would, I suspect, dispatch it and it will, I suppose, remain forever a cool house or conservatory subject here.

The forest floor supported a wide variety of shrubs and herbs especially *Impatiens* species with yellow, pink or purple flowers. Two were later identified as *I. puberula* and I. *hobsonii. Eupatorium adenophorum,* a bushy sub-shrub up to 3ft. (91.5cm) crowded the paths and formed drifts beloved of leeches in glades and open spaces. A native of Mexico introduced to the Himalaya in the late nineteenth century, it occurs over a wide altitudinal range and had accompanied us from the plateau at Tumlingtar. In the darkest places there were large clumps of *Sarcococca coriacea (pruniformis)* with stems several feet high and axillary clusters of greenish-yellow flowers with long exerted stamens. Growing in moss on the forest floor we found a small creeping shrublet with small shiny leaves and prickly stems. It looked very similar to a plant Spring-Smyth had once brought to the Hillier Arboretum which has since been identified as *Zizyphus nummularia.*

Mahonia napaulensis (or *acanthifolia*) was now frequent and included many old gnarled specimens covered with epiphytes. We also collected seed of two large thorny *Zanthoxylum* species. One had pinnate leaves with a winged rachis and axillary clusters of small, wrinkled, orange-red, peppercorn-sized fruits. Both male and female plants occurred, and it reminded me of the American species *Z. americanum,* the Toothache tree, whose sharp-tasting shoots and fruits were once chewed by the Indians to relieve toothache. Our plant proved to be *Z. acanthopodium,* whilst its companion, whose red fruits occurred in terminal clusters, was *Z. oxyphyllum. Symplocos dryophila* here formed a handsome evergreen tree up to 30ft. (9m) with clusters of immature greenish fruits (Colour Plate 36). In spring the crowded stiff racemes of yellowish-white flowers are quite conspicuous. The only place I have ever seen this species in cultivation is a George Forrest collection in the woodland at Caerhays Castle in Cornwall.

Eventually we chose a glade in which to make camp for the night and helped our Sherpas to erect the tents. The glade was full of *Sambucus adnata,* forming extensive patches in the manner of *S. ebulus,* the Dane's elder. It differed from that species however in the large flattened corymbs of orange, ripening to red, fruits (see title page). These fruits are sometimes taken by the hill people as a laxative, a power which is lost however on being cooked.

Many climbing shrubs and vines thrust their way into the canopy and we quickly recognised the grey downy leaves of the Himalayan musk rose – *Rosa brunonii* – even without the masses of fragrant white flowers which cream the stems in May and June. Equally powerful were the stems of a giant bramble – *Rubus paniculatus* – which scrambled and clawed its way into several neighbouring trees to send its branches tumbling down from heights of 40-50ft. (12-15m), terminating in crowded inflorescences of white flowers followed by small blackberries. Its ovate-lanceolate leaves were cream or grey felted beneath. A single plant grown from this seed was planted out in the Hillier Arboretum and flourishes there still in a tree. We were pleased to find a climbing honeysuckle – *Lonicera glabrata,* despite its name a softly hairy twiner carrying axillary pairs of black shiny fruits. One of the most exciting finds however was *Clematis buchananiana*, a strong-growing climber with trifoliolate leaves and drooping panicles of tubular-bell-shaped, greenish-yellow flowers 1in. (2.5cm) long. The entire plant (including flowers) was clothed with a dense pale tomentum. Sadly, this species is not winter hardy and is rarely seen in British cultivation.

On a much smaller scale were two very choice plants with slender twining stems. The first of these – *Dicentra scandens* – had the typical locket-shaped flowers of the tribe, ¾in. (2cm) long, white with a greenish puckered mouth. They hung in loose clusters to be replaced by 1in. (2.5cm) long, bullet-shaped, pale purple fruits. The leaves were much divided and fragile in appearance. *Tripterospermum volubile* meanwhile belongs to the gentian family and was at one time assigned to *Gentiana*. It twined its way into large bushes or small slender-stemmed trees, bearing its long pointed ovate to ovate-lanceolate leaves in pairs. The nodding tubular deep-blue flowers, up to 1½in. (4cm) long, were borne singly from the leaf axils and gave way to fruits which reminded me of small purple radishes 1-1¼in. (2.5-3cm) long. An occasional plant with white flowers was seen.

All these climbers are represented in British cultivation mainly in the collections of specialists although the *Dicentra* is becoming increasingly available. *Rosa brunonii* is generally represented in gardens by a selection known as 'La Mortola' after the Italian garden in which it was raised.

Our campsite was at approximately 7,800ft. (2,377m) (Colour Plate 37), and for up to an hour after our arrival the porters were turning up thoroughly soaked and anxious to get a fire started. Dawa told us he had paid two porters off because they had changed their minds about going any further, whilst he had dismissed another two after finding them lying in a house drunk on rakshi. He had, however, managed to hire an extra five porters.

It was dark by 6p.m. and we busied ourselves by the Tilley lamp writing plant notes and pressing material. In the house where we had taken our lunch we had been given soya beans *(Glycine max)* but we then did not connect these hairy pods with the soya bean milk which Morris, Mortimer and I had sampled in Singapore. Soya beans were being grown by the villagers along the edges of their fields. The main crop in this area appeared to be maize *(Zea mays)* which was later underplanted with Finger millet *(Eleusine coracana)* to ripen after the maize was harvested.

Witcombe and Mortimer were sharing a tent as were Morris and I, whilst Beer had his own. At some obscure hour in the night we heard a commotion from Witcombe's and Mortimer's tent and at breakfast next day we were told that Witcombe had suddenly awoken to find his hair wet and sticky, which when Mortimer shone his torch on it proved to be blood from a leech bite. Pema too had been bitten on the ankle but did nothing about it until much later when it had turned septic.

The rain had not stopped and we climbed into a change of clothes and donned our boots before doing a quick exploration of the campsite and its environs. Two polygonums I recognised at once like old friends – *Polygonum campanulatum* was very common on the edge of the clearing and alongside the several streams nearby. Its leaves were beautifully parallel veined beneath and clothed with a silky fawn tomentum, whilst the clusters of flowers were

Colour Plate 36. *Symplocos dryophila* is a handsome evergreen tree or shrub, especially when sporting its crowded inflorescences among the glossy leaves in spring. (April)

Colour Plate 37. Camp 4 on the Milke Danda ridge at 7,800ft. (2,378m). Here we found many plants familiar from cultivation in Britain, and here also we encountered more leeches

Colour Plate 38 (right). The *Rhododendron arboreum* forest on the Milke Danda. It reminded me of the description of Mirkwood in J.R. Tolkien's book *The Hobbit.* (September)

typically white with a pink tinge. The other species was almost certainly *P. molle*, forming handsome bushy clumps to 3ft. (91.5cm) covered with panicles of snow-white flowers. Scattered across the grass of the glades and clearings were at least three species of *Anaphalis* including the narrow leaved *A. busua* previously seen on Phulchoki (Colour Plate 40). Another species which somewhat resembled *A. triplinervis* was later identified as *A. contorta,* which has since been introduced into cultivation by Tony Schilling who speaks highly of its autumn colour.

The main party moved off leaving Beer, Morris and me to collect seed. Pema had stayed behind to cook us a light lunch, after which we all set off up the track. After a short while we entered a *Rhododendron arboreum* forest and everything darkened. It was eerie as we picked our way through the tall crooked stems dripping with mosses and lichens, now and then obscured by drifting patches of mist. It put me in mind of J.R. Tolkien's description of Mirkwood in *The Hobbit* (Colour Plate 38). We passed through several small clearings containing rock outcrops on which grew large colonies of *Cautleya cathcartii,* evidently quite at home in the thick pelt of leaf mould in which its rootstock spread. It grew equally happily on mossy tree trunks. This species is closely related to *C. gracilis* and is similar to it in flower. It was named after J.F. Cathcart (1802-1851), a Calcutta judge and amateur naturalist who employed natives to collect and paint plant specimens. The fruits we collected have subsequently produced established plants in the Hillier Arboretum, Wakehurst Place and several other gardens in England.

Climbing all the while the track led us through the evergreen forest on to an open ridge. Here *Piptanthus nepalensis (laburnifolius)* formed great thickets together with an equally robust *Elsholtzia fruticosa (polystachya)* whose 5-6ft. (1.5-1.85m) shoots produced, from their tips, branched spike-like racemes of small creamy-white flowers. This has made a robust foliage plant in British cultivation although it is by no means common there. For many years a large clump from our collection flourished at the Royal Botanic Gardens, Kew, in a border by the old wood museum. *Edgeworthia gardneri* (Colour Plate 39) and *Daphne bholua* became frequent, suckering to form clumps up to 6ft. (1.85m) tall, whilst I was surprised to see *Hydrangea heteromalla* growing as an epiphyte. There were several specimens of the hydrangea 8-10ft. (2.5-3m) tall perched in the crotches of trees an equal distance from the ground, and then we found one growing normally, a tree-like specimen of 25ft. (7.5m) with a distinct trunk. The flowers occurred in broad flattened corymbs, both fertile and ray florets white, the latter 1-2in. (2.5-5cm) across. This species is variable, more so than *H. aspera,* and many forms from China especially have at some time been treated as separate species.

Mixed with the piptanthus in the more sheltered sites we recognised *Leycesteria formosa,* the so-called Himalayan honeysuckle, with its characteristic jade-green hollow stems and white flowers protruding from clusters of purple-tinted bracts. The dark purple juicy berries are a favourite food of several birds, especially the many pheasants which skulked about in the undergrowth. The genus commemorates William Leycester (1775-1831), a judge in the Bengal Civil Service and one-time President of the Agricultural and Horticultural Society of India. He was a friend of Nathaniel Wallich who named it.

Beer pointed out to me *Pieris formosa* growing just below the ridge path on the south-east slope. It formed large bushes up to 15ft. (4.5m), but much higher amongst the trees. Most of the upper reaches of this slope were covered with scrub and one of the commonest components was *Spiraea micrantha*, its erect 5-6ft. (1.5-1.85m) stems terminating in broad flattened corymbs of white flowers. Where it pushed its way through the branches of the pieris it reached 10ft. (3m). On the edge of the forest we found 15ft. (4.5m) specimens of an evergreen with dark green, narrow, serrated leaves arranged in pairs along the slender twigs. We decided that it was probably *Osmanthus suavis* which one sees occasionally in cultivation in the warmer regions of the British Isles and elsewhere. I have a 10ft. (3m) bush of this species in my garden, grown from a Tony Schilling seed collection, whilst there are much larger specimens elsewhere in the south and west. It produces in spring the sweetly scented white flowers which are a trade mark of the genus.

By now we had attained somewhere in the region of 8,800ft. (2,682m) and the track ran a comparatively level course, snaking in and out of the forest heading north-east. At this altitude other trees made an appearance and Beer and I were overjoyed to see our first wild Magnolia – *M. campbellii* – even though we had missed its white flowers by several months. A large-leaved sycamore-like maple proved to be *Acer sterculiaceum (villosum)* (Colour Plate 41) and accompanying it in some quantity was *A. campbellii* commemorating Dr. A. Campbell (1805-1874), Superintendent of Darjeeling and Political Agent to Sikkim. He was a friend of J.D. Hooker, accompanying him on his famous journey through Sikkim in 1849, during which time they were seized and made prisoners by Sikkim Bhotias (Tibetans).

I was surprised to see a yew tree growing in the forest and then others appeared resembling our native *Taxus baccata* in appearance but referred to by some authorities as a separate species – *T. wallichiana*. According to Hooker, the red bark of this tree was used to make a dye for staining the foreheads of Brahmins in Nepal, and perhaps this is the source of the dye we saw being used for this purpose in Side Pokhara. Beneath the forest canopy a bamboo ran riot pushing between stems and rocks, out into the open and into the scrub. Its slender bluish-green canes reached 10-15ft. (3-4.5m) with characteristic scabrous internodes. The narrow leaves, 4-7in. (10-18cm) long, we were later told are commonly given to cattle and ponies as fodder. It proved to be *Yushania maling (Arundinaria maling)* which is uncommon in cultivation, although I remember once examining a whole drift of it growing in Hilliers Chandler's Ford Nursery in the 1960s.

The flora here was tremendous and neither Beer nor I could contain our excitement as each new plant appeared. Morris, whose horticultural experience was understandably limited, was infected by our enthusiasm and searched as diligently as we for seed and specimens of each new find. A single shrub of what appeared to be a *Corylopsis* species, possibly *C. himalayana,* grew by the track, and whilst I was examining this Morris emerged from the thicket triumphantly holding a section of creeper from which hung a large sausage-shaped purple pod. The leaves were compound, composed of five pointed leaflets 3-6in. (7.5-15cm) long and there was no doubt that it was *Holboellia latifolia,* a forest climber with twining stems up to 15ft. (4.5m) or more. The pods are filled with a pale pulp in which the black seeds are embedded. *Vaccinium retusum* grew as an epiphyte on several trees, its wiry stems 1-3ft.

Colour Plate 39. *Edgeworthia gardneri:* an autumn-flowering shrub of the *Daphne* family found in warmer areas of the Himalaya. (October)

Colour Plate 40. *Anaphalis busua,* a common perennial on the Milke Danda ridge, distinct in its erect stems crowded with narrow leaves. (September)

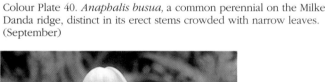

Colour Plate 41. *Acer sterculiaceum,* a strong-growing maple, here seen in Bhutan. Resembling *A. pseudo-platanus,* the sycamore, in some aspects but belonging to a different section. This tree was common in the woods of the Milke Danda. (May)

Colour Plate 42. *Lilium nepalense.* A most distinct and striking lily in flower. Photographed at 9,500ft. (2,895m) in Jumbesi-Solu region *en route* to Everest National Park. (July)

(30.5-91.5cm) long, densely clothed with obovate, notched, evergreen leaves ¾in. (2cm) long and carrying short terminal racemes of small blue-black berries.

Hypericum uralum appeared again and with it the handsome *Berberis insignis* with smooth virtually thornless stems 4-5ft. (1.2-1.5m) high, sporting clusters of large dark evergreen leaves up to 5-7in. (13-18cm) long, boldly edged with spine-tipped teeth. This distinctive shrub is occasionally found in collections in Britain but is not the hardiest of species, nor is it particularly striking in flower.

We found the track narrowing beneath a tall bush of *Enkianthus deflexus,* and then skirting a rock face exposed to the south-east. The rain was blowing into our faces all the while but this was forgotten when we saw several 1-2ft. (30.5-61cm) stems of a lily above our heads. Each was clothed with linear leaves and supported a single terminal nodding capsule. All around it were small seedlings, especially plentiful at the base of shrubs. It was *Lilium nepalense* whose strange green flowers in June are stained deep crimson at the base within (Colour Plate 42). It was quite at home in the mossy chinks and pockets and some seedlings were growing on the moss-carpeted rock itself. Sharing the same situation but preferring the fully exposed rock was a *Pleione* species, possibly *P. humilis,* unfortunately not in flower. The small flattened pseudobulbs clung to the rock surface like limpets and were loosely covered by a ½in. (1.25cm) layer of moss. The whole rock face was running with water, a situation which must dramatically change after the monsoon when the sunny weather of autumn would shrivel the moss and dry out the face until the snow of winter arrived. We were so pleased with the lilies and fussed about the pleiones looking for a sign of seed capsules but with no success. Instead we found the delicate golden-backed fronds of a pretty fern – *Cheilanthes farinosa* – which thrived here despite the seemingly unhelpful conditions. This is a most variable fern in which possibly several species are involved and I cannot understand why it is rarely seen in cultivation. It would surely enjoy the damp shady walls beloved of our native spleenworts. On reflection, however, it is probably of borderline hardiness, though collections from the highest altitudes might prove more successful. It is a pity that hardy ferns figure so infrequently in the introductions of plant collectors unless, of course, the collector is a pteridologist. We saw many excellent ornamental ferns in Nepal and made numerous spore collections. As the light faded we hurried along the track ignoring many tempting pieces of forest and hillside, finally succumbing to another *Clematis* species – *C. tongluensis* – which scrambled over neighbouring vegetation its general aspect suggesting a relationship with the well known *C. montana.* A single flower with four narrowly elliptic, creamy-white tepals confirmed our diagnosis.

4. LOST IN THE MIST

Gales in the night had played havoc with the camp and the large jouster tent had been blown down and its metal frame broken. The gales had spent themselves but the rain remained to remind us of the heavy cloud which hid the sky. Dawa and several porters left soon after breakfast and headed up the hill on their way to the village of Topke Gola several days' journey away, whilst the rest of us spent the day collecting in what seemed a botanically rich area.

Our presence on the Milke Danda ridge was based solely on a story Beer had heard on his reconnaissance. He had travelled to Topke Gola on foot from Dharan via Dhankuta, Hile and Taplejung, following first the Tamur valley and then the Mewa Khola to establish his base camp. On his return journey he had stayed one night in a hill village and huddled round a fire with the Sherpas and porters. The porters chatted with a group of villagers talking of the journey and the strange foreigner who collected flowers and seeds, not to eat but to press between paper or to store in bags. One of the villagers spoke of a sacred lake high on the mountains of the Jaljale Himal above the Milke Danda. According to the storyteller, on a special occasion each year, shepherds and others would go on a pilgrimage to the lake which was set in a place where many wonderful flowers grew. Dawa had translated the story to Beer and on repeating the story to us on our arrival at Dharan we had agreed, after some discussion, that the lake might be worth a visit even if it did mean a new and higher route unknown to our Sherpas and porters who preferred lower, well-known routes in the valleys. This route up the Milke Danda ridge through the Jaljale Himal to Topke Gola was full of promise and a sense of the unknown – anything might happen; we had instructed Dawa to leave indications of any change of route so that we might follow in his footsteps.

Beer, Morris and I meanwhile returned along the ridge to the rock face where we made a detailed search for more seed of the lily. We found a large individual carrying three plump capsules and again many seedlings growing mostly at the base of *Spiraea micrantha* clumps. It was whilst we were so engaged that the rain ceased and on turning round we could see a long streak of blue on the south-east horizon. From then on the weather improved and with it our attitude, which until then had been one of resignation in face of rain and leeches. *Rosa sericea* was plentiful with its small nodding, pear-shaped, red and yellow hips, but out of flower this is a poor relation compared with its blood-winged Chinese form *pteracantha.*

We returned to camp for lunch and then plunged into the forest on the north-west slope to spend a happy afternoon in what was to us a paradise. There were several *Magnolia campbellii* 60-70ft. (18-21m) high, their branches green with algae and moss and the fuzzy grey beards of a lichen. We grubbed in the litter beneath these trees but most of the fruits were worm-ridden. A large poplar – *Populus jacquemontiana* variety *glauca* – had sticky buds and ovate-cordate, grey-green leaves, glaucous beneath, borne on angular shoots. As far as I could remember I had neither seen nor heard of it in cultivation. However,

Plate 20. Victor Jacquemont, a French botanist who travelled and collected briefly in Kashmir in 1831. He did, however, discover a number of new species which have found their way into British and European gardens, most notably *Betula utilis* variety *jacquemontii*, a beautiful, white-stemmed birch. Some of his discoveries also extend in the wild to Nepal, for example *Arisaema jacquemontii*

Plate 21. *Sorbus insignis* growing from a fissure in a large boulder at 9,000ft. (2,743m) on the Milke Danda ridge. A bold foliaged mountain ash, the large clusters of tiny fruits which Beer is attempting to collect proved immature. (October)

it has since been successfully introduced by Tony Schilling and is represented by strong young trees at Wakehurst Place and the Hillier Arboretum, perhaps elsewhere. The species commemorates a young French botanist and plant geographer Victor Jacquemont (1801-1832) who travelled mainly in Kashmir although many of his plant discoveries there are also found in Nepal (Plate 20). Both maples of the previous day – *Acer sterculiaceum* and *A. campbellii* – were plentiful with individuals 50-60ft. (15-18m) in height. A third maple – *A. pectinatum* – was also present growing to a similar size and with three-lobed leaves on red petioles, the veins beneath clothed with fulvous hairs. Even the fruits, in pendulous clusters, had attractive red wings. The name refers to the fringe of fine hair-like teeth on the leaf margin, a characteristic which easily distinguishes this tree in gardens from the similarly three-lobed Chinese species *A. forrestii* which some authorities now regard as a subspecies of *A. pectinatum*. A small tangled currant occurred as an epiphyte on several trees and proved to be *Ribes laciniatum,* but of no ornamental merit. We were struck by the various members of the ivy family *Araliaceae* present, in particular *Pentapanax leschenaultii* with its large long-stalked palmate leaves. The ground where this small tree flourished was swampy and crowded with ferns of the *Dryopteris* clan. The sinister mottled stems of *Arisaema nepenthoides* thrust their way through the low vegetation bearing dense orange-red fruiting spikes. Red fruits also appeared on *Daiswa polyphylla (Paris polyphylla)* where they formed a dense terminal cluster above a ruff of seven to nine slender-pointed leaves, the whole carried on a stem 8-9in. (20-23cm) above the forest floor. The rhizome of this plant contains certain alkaloids and has been used to get rid of intestinal worms. Creeping about nearby was a miniature bramble – *Rubus calycinus* – which formed carpets of kidney-shaped leaves 1-2 in. (2.5-5cm) across. From the axils of many leaves small raspberry-like fruits were borne on 1-1½in. (2.5-4cm) stalks. It was a most attractive creeper and is now established in cultivation from this seed. It has even been used as a parent with the Chinese *R. tricolor* to produce several hybrids suitable as ground cover.

I was excited to encounter a shrub whose red berries were produced in pairs, apparently from the upper surfaces of the long-pointed leaves. It was *Helwingia himalaica*, a member of the dogwood family – *Cornaceae*. I remembered having seen the black-berried Japanese species – *H. japonica* – at the University Botanic Garden, Cambridge, when a student and remember also the then Director, John Gilmour, demonstrating that the apparent abnormality is due to the fusion of the peduncle with the petiole and midrib. We found more *Holboellia latifolia* and collected its purple pods, and there was more of the climbing gentian – *Tripterospermum volubile*. Growing in the shadiest parts of the forest was a peculiar brown fruiting spike belonging to a parasite – *Hymenopogon parasiticus,* whilst another *Cautleya (C. spicata)* colonised the moss-capped boulders.

Just before returning to camp we discovered several scattered trees of a whitebeam which I thought was *Sorbus vestita (cuspidata),* but which was later identified as *S. hedlundii* by the Armenian authority Eleonora Gabrielian. They were trees of 60-70ft. (18-21m) with large leaves varying in shape from elliptic to rotund elliptic. The leaves were white tomentose beneath with rust-coloured midrib and veins, resembling in this character a tree grown under this name in the Hillier Arboretum. We collected a number of fallen fruits the size of small crab apples coloured green or russet with brown speckles. Several young trees from this seed are now established in the Hillier Arboretum and elsewhere.

By now the sky was clear and the sun shone on the hills around highlighting the snow-capped peaks to the north which included Makalu. The turf around the campsite was full of *Satyrium ciliatum*, a small orchid, the majority of whose relatives are found thousands of miles to the south in South Africa. This species was a charmer showing its pretty pink flower spikes a few inches above the short grass and colouring the open ridge as far as the eye could see. Growing as a companion, though less spectacular, was a miniature annual elsholtzia – *E. strobilifera* – with elongated pale pinky-purple flower cones in branched heads (Colour Plate 43).

That evening, after de-leeching, we spent several hours pressing specimens and cleaning seed whilst the Sherpas played a game of handball outside in the moonlight. One of the Sherpa porters from Sedua poked his head into our tent, and after watching us for a while retreated, but not before he had picked up some cast-away *Arisaema* fruits which he popped into his mouth. Something I would not recommend gardeners emulating!

The following morning was one of the most enjoyable awakenings I have ever had. It began as usual with a loud rasp as the tent was unzipped. As I freed

Plate 22. Joseph Hooker examining plants and flowers collected by his Lepcha porters during his famous expedition to the Sikkim Himalaya 1848-1850. He collected and introduced numerous new plants to Britain including thirty *Rhododendron* species. As a result of this experience he wrote the classic *Himalayan Journals*, an account of his travels as well as the exquisitely illustrated *Rhododendrons of the Sikkim Himalaya*. Not surprisingly many Himalayan plants commemorate his name, amongst which *Berberis hookeri*, *Rhododendron hookeri* and *Pleione hookeriana* are amongst those still grown in cultivation

myself from my sleeping bag I saw Pema's smiling face, returned his greeting and watched hot tea being poured from a tin kettle into an enamel mug. The rays of the rising sun pierced the steam illuminating the interior with a warm orange glow. By the time Morris was awake the porridge had arrived and this we ate after first stirring in a large helping of syrup. By the time we had washed and dressed the sun was up and on the northern horizon Makalu and its attendant peaks glistened from a fresh fall of snow. We left Pema and the others to pack up the camp and followed the track up a grassy slope until it entered once again the *Rhododendron arboreum* forest. Conditions were so gloomy here that we had difficulty in keeping to the track which resembled one of several nearby gullies gouged by floodwater from the recent heavy rains. Occasionally the canopy high above parted to allow in a long shaft of sunlight which showed several stems swaddled in moss and lichens. In this soft, moist, vertical strata many epiphytes had found a comfortable home; these are plants which, tired of the eternal rat-race on the forest floor, have taken the 'elevator' to the upper 'floors' (branches) of the tree and now earn for themselves, with a few adaptions, a relatively easy living.

After a long steep climb we emerged into the light and saw the track winding up through open scrub with scattered deciduous trees and rhododendrons. Amongst the latter *R. cinnabarinum* and *R. barbatum* were now prominent with the plum-coloured flaking bark of the latter species particularly pleasing. Both these species were amongst those discovered and introduced to Britain by Joseph Hooker between 1848 and 1851.

A few words about Joseph (later Sir Joseph) Hooker (1817-1911), are perhaps not out of place here, for although he was widely travelled and had an immense knowledge of the world's flora, it is for his achievements in making known to the botanical and horticultural world the riches of the Sikkim Himalaya that he is most readily remembered (Plate 22). One of the most distinguished of nineteenth century scientists and a friend and close confidant of Charles Darwin, he spent two remarkable years (1848-1850) in the Sikkim Himalaya as part of his Indian travels studying the distribution and evolution of plant species. During this time he discovered many new plants including some thirty *Rhododendron* species, all of which were introduced to British cultivation. In 1865, on the death of his equally eminent father Sir William Jackson Hooker (1785-1865), he succeeded him as Director of the Royal Botanic Gardens, Kew, continuing with his travels, his studies and his writing well into old age. He died in 1911 in his ninety-fifth year. He wrote numerous books and learned papers but will mainly be remembered, by Himalayan plant enthusiasts certainly, for his *Rhododendrons of the Sikkim Himalaya* and *Flora of British India 1872-97* in seven volumes.

Stachyurus himalaicus and *Enkianthus deflexus* appeared, both with individual specimens up to 18ft. (5.5m) high. There were several large trees of *Populus jacquemontiana* variety *glauca,* their leaves on long petioles fluttering constantly in the breeze. The evergreen clumps of *Pieris formosa* now became dominant reaching 18-20ft. (5.5-6m) high pierced only by the stout trunks of many whitebeams – *Sorbus hedlundii* – up to 70ft. (21m) tall. Then one of my favourite trees turned up. This was the Himalayan birch – *Betula utilis* – an extremely variable species in leaf, shoot and colour of bark, which is not surprising considering its distribution along the Himalaya from Afghanistan to China. Its status is hotly contested by the rival factions of the 'splitters and lumpers' club, the latter seeing it as one variable species, whilst the splitters divide it into at least three species – *B. jacquemontii* in the west, *B. utilis* in the Himalaya and *B. albo-sinensis* in China. The white-stemmed birch of Kashmir, by the way, is now regarded as *B. utilis* variety *occidentalis.* There are several creamy-barked forms of *B. utilis* in cultivation, whilst those we found on the Milke Danda ridge and elsewhere in east Nepal possessed orange-brown or coppery bark, peeling in tassels and curls, especially below the main branches where they often formed ragged bunches. The bark apparently is sometimes used as an antiseptic in infusions as well as to cover wounds. It sometimes falls from the stem in sizeable sheets and I remember once receiving from Tony Schilling, then in Nepal, a letter written on just such a sheet which he had sealed in an envelope.

More *Lyonia ovalifolia* and *Piptanthus nepalensis* appeared as scattered shrubs, and then we discovered two 25ft. (7.5m) trees of *Sorbus insignis.* I was familiar with this species from a tree in the Hillier Arboretum grown from seed collected by Kingdon Ward in the Naga Hills, Assam, in 1928. I was unaware, however, that it occurred in Nepal. The handsome, large, pinnate leaves were composed of fifteen broad leaflets whose polished dark-green upper surfaces shone in the morning sun (Plate 21). I climbed into the branches in order to grasp the small, deep red, unripened fruits produced in dense corymbs. Sitting in this tree looking out over the surrounding rhododendrons I felt a tremendous satisfaction. Surrounded by plants which previously I had known only in cultivation, I found it hard to believe my good fortune and took a few deep breaths of Himalayan air to reassure myself that it was real. I now realised that at last the dreams of my youth were coming true and I began to sing at the top of my voice. My singing, however, was heard only by a pair of White-cheeked bulbuls who flew from a nearby rowan to disappear further down the ridge. I then looked around but Beer and Morris were nowhere to be seen and my gaze was met by a heavily laden porter who had stopped in his tracks and now stared incredulously in my direction. Laughing, I climbed out of the tree and set off up the track in pursuit of my colleagues. It was not long before I caught up with them as they had stopped to collect the fruits of a small rowan – *Sorbus kurzii*. The fruits were white, flushed pink, whilst the glossy-green pinnate leaves, borne in tight rosettes, were already turning crimson and orange. It was quite new to me and as far as I knew unknown in cultivation. W.S. Kurz (c.1833-1878) was a German botanist who collected plants in the East and was at one time Curator of the Calcutta Herbarium. Beneath this tree we found *Skimmia laureola*, a yellowish-green flowered shrub with shining black fruits on female plants. As with most, if not all, skimmias, the flowers are sweetly scented which is more than can be said for the leaves which emit a pungent aroma when bruised. It became quite common by the track, stunted in the open, reaching 4ft. (1.25m) or more in shade and undoubtedly belonged to subspecies *multinervia* (Colour Plate 44) which is capable of making a small tree up to 30ft. (9m) in optimum conditions whereas the typical form (subspecies *laureola*) is a low, often creeping shrub.

We found red fruits in abundance on *Cotoneaster linearifolius* which formed low mounds and mats of densely packed stems on grassy banks and hillocks. The tiny evergreen leaves were a dark polished green, and so tightly did these mounds knit together that one could stand on them without damaging their symmetry. This species was previously known in cultivation as *C. microphyllus* forma *thymifolius*.

At 9,800ft. (2,987m) we found another *Sorbus* with bold pinnate leaves and conspicuous stipules on the young shoots. It was a tree 18ft. (5.5m) high but unfortunately with no fruits.

The ridge narrowed and boulders crowded the track as we picked our way through low scrub which consisted of dwarf rhododendrons, *R. anthopogon* being the most common with its greyish-green leaves, followed by *R. lepidotum* with tiny sage-green leaves. Amongst these we found two isolated specimens of *R. ciliatum* and *R. glaucophyllum*. Flowering herbs peppered the turf and I was pleased to see the trailing slender growths of the annual *Cyanthus inflatus* whose bright blue flowers protrude from hairy inflated calyces. In places it contrasted with the yellow flowers of *Corydalis juncea,* another annual. At one point where the ground sloped steeply into a gully, a company of *Aconitum*

Plate 23. East Himalayan Silver fir *Abies densa* in the mist at 10,500ft. (3,200m) on the Milke Danda ridge. (October)

spicatum appeared in the undergrowth. This handsome monkshood bore 2½-3ft. (76-91.5cm) stems crowded with blue-purple helmeted flowers (Colour Plate 46) and would be a worthwhile addition to any herbaceous border or island bed in the garden, though I have not heard that seed we then collected has resulted in this plant becoming generally grown. It is claimed to be the most poisonous of the Nepalese species and is said to contain no less than fourteen different alkaloids.

We were now above 10,000ft. (3,048m) and still the track continued upwards, now into a mist which had stealthily crept along the ridge (Plate 23). Beer and I became separated from the others and we decided to move a little more quickly, ignoring the plants – we could not see them anyway. At a height of 11,000ft. (3,353m) I suddenly felt dizzy so I told Beer to go on whilst I sat down to catch my breath. I am glad that I did because growing in the turf at my feet was *Gaultheria trichophylla*, a choice little suckering shrublet 3-4in. (7.5-10cm) high with tiny ciliate leaves and sporting oblong to ovoid fruits ½in. (1.25cm) long, coloured a deep blue. It was quite plentiful on these open slopes and must have presented a pretty sight with the sun on the fruits. After a while I felt better and proceeded up the hill in Beer's wake to find myself almost immediately at the camp which had been pitched on a level area. The voices of Witcombe and Morris guided me to the kitchen where I found the group chatting over mugs of hot tea. It was a good campsite with water nearby and plenty of fuel (Plate 24). It always caused me grief, each time we established camp, to hear the sound of chopping in the forest and to see the Sherpas and porters emerging dragging branches and logs for the several fires. At this camp we were surrounded by rhododendron thicket in which grew *R. barbatum, R. hodgsonii, R. campanulatum, R campylocarpum* and *R. cinnabarinum.* To see these being cut, albeit in a limited way, set me to wondering what would have been the reactions of those Edwardian owners of the great rhododendron collections in Cornwall where a visiting enthusiast needed a passport to *see* the treasures let alone touch them! *R. hodgsonii* was certainly a handsome species with attractively flaking, pinky-brown stems up to 18ft. (5.5m). The leaves of young specimens measured 10-15in. (25.5-38cm) and their shining deep-green upper surfaces had a sprinkling of hoar-like indumentum (Colour Plate 47). On older specimens the leaves were reduced in size. The undersurface of the leaf was clothed with a pale buff indumentum

Colour Plate 43. *Satyrium ciliatum*, a ground orchid with relatives in South Africa, is a common flower of the Nepalese alpine pastures in autumn. Here it grows at 11,500ft. (3,505m) on the Milke Danda ridge accompanied (bottom right) by the annual herb *Elsholtzia strobilifera*. (October)

Colour Plate 44. The black-fruited *Skimmia laureola* subspecies *multinervia,* an evergreen shrub growing in a wood below the Milke Danda ridge. Its flowers are greenish-yellow and fragrant, contrasting with the foliage which is pungently aromatic when crushed. (October)

Colour Plate 45. The trail continued above camp 6 following the ridge whose eastern slopes were covered with Silver fir (*Abies densa*) and Himalayan birch (*Betula utilis*) with *Rhododendron* species as an understorey. The dark low patches in the foreground belong to *Berberis erythroclada*. (October)

which became silvery on exposure to the light. On a springtime visit two years later I saw this species bearing tight rounded heads of magenta-purple flowers, while in the sheltered forest lower down on the Milke Banjgang I found forms with larger looser trusses of pink flowers. *R. hodgsonii* was certainly valued by the hill people for its hard wood which was used for cups, bowls and other implements and made the best fires. The leaves too were used for lining baskets and for carrying food within the village or camp. We also later found them useful as fans on warm days. This notable rhododendron was named by J.D. Hooker after his friend B.H. Hodgson (1800-1894), a British resident in Nepal and an amateur naturalist of some repute, his main interest being mammals and birds (Hodgson's pied wagtail). Accompanied by Dr. Thomson he greeted Hooker and Campbell on their release from captivity by the Sikkim Bhotias in 1849.

R. arboreum had now been left behind down the ridge but the other species which replaced it proved equally dominant, forming almost impenetrable thickets up to 15ft. (4.5m) high. Through these thickets grew two trees, *Betula utilis* and the East Himalayan Silver fir – *Abies densa* (Colour Plates 45 and 50). The latter is the cause of much discussion, even argument, in botanical circles. It has been called *A. spectabilis,* and before that *A. webbiana,* but in *An Enumeration of the Flowering Plants of Nepal,* vol. l, published in 1978, the Spanish botanist J. do Amaral Franco distinguishes three species of *Abies* in Nepal. *A. pindrow* in the west, *A. spectabilis* in the west and central Nepal and *A. densa* in the east. According to Franco, *A. densa* differs from *A. spectabilis* mainly in its bark soon becoming scaly, its brownish (not yellowish) twigs and its broader leaves. Our trees certainly had brown shoots and scaly bark, but their most striking feature was the dark glossy-green leaf with two broad bands of chalk-white stomata beneath. These were densely crowded in two ranks along the branches. Young trees of this fir raced up to the ridge from sheltered gullies and were of conical shape, strong and virile (Colour Plate 49). Meanwhile, stout-stemmed older trees occurred as isolated individuals on the ridge itself, blasted by a hundred years or more of winds and storms, their once fine raiment now tattered and torn, hanging in long streamers (Colour Plate 50). Their boughs sagged from the vegetable encrustations of countless decades of epiphytes. Some trees were in fruit, the sloe-black, barrel-shaped cones lining the upper sides of the top branches like midnight candles.

These thickets, where tracks if any belonged to small creatures, were the haunt of beautiful birds like the Blood pheasant which went mostly unseen. However, one of these birds, a male, was killed by a stone thrown by a porter who brought it triumphantly into camp. It was grey and green above with blood-red throat, tail, legs and eye patch. Several times we heard the Impeyan pheasant but only once did we see it. I was leading a small contingent of porters one day through bamboo and rhododendron thicket when a large bird flew on to a branch some 15ft. (4.5m) to my left. We froze and watched fascinated as it turned slowly round as if on a pivot. A shaft of sun acting as spotlight highlighted the multitude of colours in the bird's plumage – blue, green, purple and chestnut. It reminded me of one of those magical birds from a child's storybook, because as suddenly as it had appeared it was gone, its silent glide carrying it from our view back into the shadows.

The next morning the sun was shining and our eyes saw a wonderful sight. It

Plate 24. Camp 6 at 11,400ft. (3,474m) on the Milke Danda. During the morning when the sun shone the green turf was spangled with blue gentians which by late afternoon had closed. (October)

was as though a piece of sky had fallen into our camp overnight because our hands and knees sank into a turf full of blue gentians belonging to two species *Gentiana prolata* and *G. sikkimensis*. Both grew no more than 3in. (7.5cm) high and bore tubular flowers, the former in groups of three, the latter in heads of five to nine. We decided against taking photographs of blue flowers so early in the day, due to the quality of the light, and agreed to do it later. Breakfast finished, Morris and I walked back along the ridge to where the previous afternoon the mist had intervened in our plant collecting. A breeze blew our hair and the views were magnificent. To the north-west Makalu and Everest dominated the skyline, whilst Kanchengjunga appeared in the north-east. Large carpets of trailing reddish stems on banks and boulders proved to be *Polygonum vacciniifolium*. The multitude of short erect flower spikes were a deeper pink than those normally encountered in cultivation and coloured the sides of the track for some distance (Colour Plates 52 and 53). Trailing down a wet rock face was another species – *P. emodi*, with long woody stems and long narrow leaves with revolute margins. The flower spikes were even more slender than those of *P. vacciniifolium*, and the individual flowers were crimson. Of the two, *P. vacciniifolium* is the better garden plant because of its hardiness, freer flowering and tidier habit. It is also more adaptable to different situations and will take sun or shade. To complete a trio of polygonums we then found *P. millettii* growing on boulders and rock ledges. Its leaves were heart shaped, much larger than those of the others, and the dense blunt-tipped spikes of deep rose-red flowers were carried aloft on 9-12in. (23-30.5cm) stems. The name commemorates Charles Millett (fl.1820s-1830s), an official of the East India Company during the early nineteenth century and an amateur botanist. In the same rocks grew *Codonopsis dicentrifolia* forming 9-12in. (23-30.5cm) clumps of slender-stalked prettily divided leaves. The blue flowers 1-1½in. (2.5-3.75cm) long were borne in long terminal panicles creating delightful fountains from a distance. Most plants grew on the south-west or south-east faces of the rocks, their roots deeply entrenched in vertical crevices. At the foot of these and other rocks, in the moist shady spots, occurred numerous rosettes of *Meconopsis napaulensis* with pale green, densely hairy, pinnatisect leaves. One plant supported a 3ft. (91.5m) central stem carrying a few late, nodding, lilac-blue flowers. First discovered by Nathaniel Wallich and introduced to British cultivation by Joseph Hooker around 1850 it was eagerly sought after by

Colour Plate 46. *Aconitum spicatum* growing amongst scrub at 10,200ft. (3,109m) on the Milke Danda ridge. This is one of several tall perennial species found in woods and scrub throughout the Himalaya. (October)

Colour Plate 47. One of our young porters with the foliage of *Rhododendron hodgsonii* which formed thickets around camp 6 at 11,400ft. (3,474m). The leaves are a contrasting silver beneath. (October)

Colour Plate 48. *Bergenia ciliata.* This specimen in the author's garden is of Nepalese origin and shows the short hairs on the leaf upper surface and along the margin. (August)

84

Colour Plate 49. *Abies densa,* the east Himalayan Silver fir, occupied the eastern slopes of the Milke Danda ridge around 10,600ft. (3,231m). Beer is seen here admiring the silver undersides to the leaves. Note the comparatively treeless ridge above and the tiny white flowerheads of a pearly everlasting *Anaphalis busua.* (October)

Colour Plate 50. Forest on the eastern flanks of the Milke Danda ridge at 11,500ft. (3,505m). *Abies densa* stand proud of birch *Betula utilis* and rhododendron thicket. (October)

Colour Plate 51. *Bergenia ciliata,* a large leaved perennial, was frequent in woods on the Milke Danda ridge. The bell-shaped flowers in spring have white petals and contrasting reddish calyx. A plant of Nepalese origin in the author's garden. (April)

gardeners. The famous dendrologist, sportsman and naturalist H.J. Elwes considered this 'the most beautiful herbaceous plant in the world' but that was before *M. betonicifolia*.

Clumps of *Anemone polyanthes* were scattered over the hillside, but in fruit they gave little indication of their merit when in flower. This robust perennial throws up one to several erect downy stems to 2ft. (60cm), bearing several large white or pink-tinted flowers in June and July. It is highly desirable and should be in every garden in England but regretfully it is not often seen in cultivation.

I was keen to reach a *Sorbus* species which hung its clusters of pink, turning to white, fruits in the denser parts of the rhododendron thicket. Its small neat leaves with numerous tiny leaflets identified it as *S. microphylla*, a charming small tree as yet rare and little known in general cultivation. We later saw this species in many places and it appeared to be the most commonly occurring member of its genus above 10,000ft. (3,048m). We discovered that many plants preferred the company of rocks and cliffs and we examined every outcrop within easy reach. On one of these a handsome purple-flowered onion with three-cornered stems – *Allium wallichii* – occupied a grassy ledge and its acquisition caused us considerable trouble. According to a recent report by J.F. Dobremez, this species is an important medicinal plant containing steroids, flavonoids and polysaccharoids. It is used for altitude sickness and as a stimulant.

It was whilst we were clawing our way along a particularly tricky rock ledge that we noticed the sun no longer warmed our backs, and when we looked around it was to find that the mist spewing up from the valleys had joined with cloud from above. For the next hour we ignored the rain which rushed in from the south-west, but gradually conditions became worse and we returned to camp where to our consternation the disappearance of the sun had caused the gentians to close and become virtually invisible in the grass.

Towards the end of the afternoon, the weather cleared and the sunshine persuaded Beer and me to explore the hillside above camp where a dwarf *Berberis* species formed colonies no more than 1ft. (30cm) high. It was a densely branched shrub with suckering reddish shoots and obovate spine-toothed leaves ½in. (1.25cm) long which were a polished dark-green above and a contrasting glaucous beneath. The single yellow flowers give way to oblong or obovoid deep red fruits ½-⅔in. (1.25-1.70cm) long (Colour Plates 54 and 55). It reminded me of *B. concinna* and in the event proved to be the closely related *B. erythroclada*, a species named by the Rev. W. Ahrendt, though it is regarded by many authorities as belonging to *B. concinna*. Ahrendt had based his name on a herbarium specimen collected by F. Kingdon Ward in south-east Tibet and the abundant seed which we collected constituted its first introduction into cultivation. Plants are now growing quite happily in the Hillier Arboretum and elsewhere. We called on two Sherpa boys to continue picking seed whilst we did a reconnaissance along the ridge. Returning as dusk settled on the ridge, we stopped and turned around before descending to our camp. To the north-west Mount Everest and her attendant peaks riding on a sea of cloud were painted a rich gold from a setting sun and appeared like ships in a Turner painting. To the north-east lay the pale massive of Kanchengjunga bathed in moonlight. The contrast was at once startling and humbling and for some time after returning to camp the experience occupied our thoughts. The night remained calm and we sat around the camp fire talking and working. A last look at the outside world before going to bed revealed a moon-washed landscape in which the only movement was clouds rising like goose-down from the valleys below.

Another day began with the sun and a blue sky to cheer us. Meanwhile six porters had decided to return to their farms and this necessitated several of their colleagues having to carry loads of 90lb. for which they were paid extra. Even so, two loads had to be left behind with Namgyal until we could send porters back from the next camp. All day we walked along a gently rising ridge track, our view into the valleys obscured by rising mist. By mid-afternoon it was drizzling and we became steadily soaked, our toes squelching in waterfilled boots.

Anaphalis species shared the hillsides with *Cremanthodium* species, whose nodding, yellow, daisy heads were as charming as they were characteristic. *C. reniforme* with its basal tuft of small kidney-shaped leaves was the most commonly seen. Occupying sizeable areas of bank was *Gaultheria pyroloides* forming close mats and carpets of prostrate stems and evergreen, obovate to elliptic-obovate leaves ½-2in. (1.25-5cm) long bearing an attractive reticulate venation (Colour Plate 58). In other areas the tufted growths of *Cassiope fastigiata* were found, though unfortunately long past flowering. Rosettes of *Primula petiolaris* shared the banks with the peculiar moss-like *Saxifraga brachypoda*. We crossed a wide stretch of pasture where clumps of *Euphorbia himalayensis* were turning fiery-red and orange (Colour Plate 57). We then realised what it was we had seen several times already that day. Occasionally, through breaks in the mist and cloud, we had caught glimpses of distant hillsides apparently alight, and had puzzled over this each time. The autumn display of the euphorbia was certainly a sight to be remembered and provided us with the only hint of warmth on an otherwise cold wet day's trek.

Passing through a region of rocks and boulders I spotted a small deciduous *Cotoneaster* species which reminded me of the Chinese *C. adpressus*. Its leaves were possibly smaller but they had the same shape (broad-ovate to obovate) and shine. Bertil Hylmo, the Swedish authority on the genus, has since pronounced this a new species – *C. milkedandai*. Specimens of a similar but taller species collected on a later occasion have been identified as *C. cavei* and this shrub is now in cultivation from introductions by my Dutch friend Harry van de Laar and Tony Schilling whose plant is a larger fruited form of superior garden merit.

Rhododendrons continued to be the dominant shrub cover. A colony of *Bergenia ciliata* appeared beneath trees on a wet slope, the leaves orbicular and clothed with short stiff hairs, like a cat's tongue to the touch (Colour Plates 48 and 51). I was surprised to see this species so far east where it is supposedly represented only by its smoother leaved subspecies *ligulata*. It was near this point that we found a 5ft. (1.5m) specimen of *Daphne bholua* with leaves striped creamy-white. It was quite acceptable as variegations go but there was no way that we could have introduced it to cultivation successfully.

The continuing rain and mist were such that we were forced to spend the next two days in camp, each day hoping for a change in the weather. Indeed, the weather became the main topic of conversation, a peculiarly British pastime. The slightest change, real or imagined, was discussed at length. The wind direction, density of mist, rainfall and temperature. There was also the question of casualties. A porter with his face swollen from an abcess on his

Colour Plate 52. *Polygonum vacciniifolium* growing in a garden in Devon. This charming carpeting perennial with its tapered pink flower spikes is common in the mountains of east Nepal. (August)

Colour Plate 53. *Polygonum vacciniifolium* carpeting a rock at 10,000ft. (3,048m) on the Milke Danda ridge. The leaves have coloured richly before dying. (October)

Colour Plates 54 and 55. *Berberis erythroclada* formed dense low colonies on the slopes around camp 6. Here, Beer is collecting its seed (B.L.&M. 41). A dwarf shrub, *B. erythroclada* is closely related to, and regarded by some authorities inseparable from, *B. concinna*. (October)

Colour Plate 56. *Rhodendron thomsonii*. Unseasonal flowers on a plant growing in the Asian Garden at the University of British Columbia Botanic Garden, Vancouver, Canada. This plant, one of a group, was raised from seed collected on the Milke Danda ridge. (October)

gum, a Sherpa with a festering sore on his ankle and another with 'wobbly legs Sahib'. Even Beer had failed to shake off a bad chest cough he had developed above Chainpur. Pema, our cook, meanwhile talked of becoming a monk next year. He was becoming disenchanted with the trekking business and the alternative, the army, only paid first-year recruits 75 rupees a month out of which food and clothes had to be bought. Now that we had left behind areas of cultivation, Witcombe and Mortimer decided that they would be going no further along the ridge and began scouting around for a track leading west. Some of the time we spent drying paper for the presses. This had to be done over the fire in the kitchen shelter and here the conditions were very difficult. The wet fuel caused clouds of acrid smoke to fill the shelter, necessitating a hasty retreat every few minutes. The Sherpas and porters on the other hand seemed untroubled, merely averting their faces when the smoke came their way, or at worst screwing their eyes tight until it changed direction.

An occasional search in the vegetation below the camp brought further trophies to the press or seed bag. In the valley, where the porters had taken up residence, a group of 50-60ft. (15-18m) Bird cherries – *Prunus cornuta* – bore long fingers of red, turning to black, fruits. The elliptic leaves were glaucescent beneath and up to 6in. (15cm) long. A small tree from this collection is now growing strongly in the Hillier Arboretum. Two bushes of *Potentilla fruticosa* were found and on the same slope a rather nibbled hummock of *Juniperus communis* variety *montana*. The rhododendrons had been joined by another species – *R. thomsonii*. In fact, this one species excluded all others in the area immediately below the camp and their flaky reddish-brown bark and dark blue-green orbicular leaves were made even more attractive when wetted by the rain. The seed capsules still retained their characteristic cup-like, fleshy, green calyx, though the deep red bell-shaped flowers were now but a memory (Colour Plate 56). This beautiful species was first introduced to cultivation from Sikkim by J.D. Hooker in 1850 and is a parent of many lovely hybrids. It is named after Thomas Thomson (1817-1878), a Scots doctor, and one time Superintendent of the Calcutta Botanic Garden (Plate 25) and the other member, with B.H. Hodgson, of the welcoming party who greeted Hooker and Campbell on their release from captivity by Sikkim Bhotias in 1849. It is interesting to note that these three people, Campbell, Hodgson and Thomson, all had rhododendrons named after them by Hooker. Other friends were likewise honoured, including Dr. H. Falconer (1808-1865), M.P. Edgeworth (1812-1881), Major E. Madden (1805-1856), R. Wight (1796-1872) and Lady Dalhousie (1786-1839). Hooker himself was likewise honoured by Thomas Nuttall with the naming of *R. hookeri* discovered in 1849 in Assam by T.J. Booth.

On 9 October we parted company with Witcombe and Mortimer who were anxious to visit the hill farms and similar areas of cultivation to the west. The members of the Horticultural Project then set off up the ridge, anxious to leave the camp and its memories of rain and mud, of smoke and coughs, swollen legs and leeches, yes, leeches at 11,500ft. (3,505m)! The mist was now so thick that one could barely see the man in front and every so often the porters would call to each other to maintain contact. I stopped at one point to readjust my rucksack and when I continued I could not see the porter ahead of me. I hurried to catch him up and followed the track which had suddenly narrowed along the hillside to a point where it disappeared into a bamboo thicket. I could hear my heart thumping rapidly as I realised I had missed my way. I just stood and listened and thought I heard shouts coming from below, so downhill I went, crashing through the bamboo, tripping and tumbling several times in my hurry to reach the others. I eventually cleared the bamboo and my heart dropped when I found the ground falling in a series of steep cliffs into what looked like a vast smoke-filled cauldron. It was a deep ravine from which mist spewed and I knew then that the calls I had heard were tricks of the mist, echoes maybe, and I was now lost. I sat down and thought it out carefully. The first thing I must do was to retrace my steps through the bamboo thicket. This I did slowly and painfully because the slope was steep and the broken bamboos sharp and lethal. At last I was back where I started and I then slowly followed the track back to the ridge. In an area of low scrub I noticed another track veering away to run steeply into a narrow ravine. I noted also the large imprints of Morris's boots in the mud and followed the track all the way down to where my colleagues waited at the base of a huge cliff. I was not the only one to go astray and it took the rest of that day for the porters to arrive, padding down the ravine in dribs and drabs until all were accounted for. There was no sense in our continuing that day so we simply made our camp by the cliff, erecting a screen to keep out the worst of the rain.

Whilst waiting for Pema to cook the supper we watched one of our porters preparing his. In one dish he made a tacky substance, deldo or tsampa, by mixing millet flour with water. In another dish, chillies were boiled in water to make a soup. All mixing was done with a spatula made on the spot from the wood of *Rhododendron hodgsonii.* He then took a pinch of the deldo and dipped it in the chilli before popping it into his mouth. During the day the porters chewed on cobs of corn and it was common to find discarded cobs on tracks even in remote areas. Porters provided their own food which they carried in a sack or, when available, in a plastic bag. Their main meal would be tsampa or rice, curried or otherwise, with chillies. When passing through villages they can and usually do supplement their diet with whatever they can buy – fruit, vegetables, eggs or a chicken being the usual fare.

That night a thunderstorm broke and attacked our position with full force. As we lay wedged at the base of the cliff in a deep ravine, thunder cracked in loud peals and lightning came in jagged fingers. All night long we heard branches and whole trees crashing around us in the forest. Eventually we dropped off and when we awoke at breakfast it was difficult to decide whether or not we had all suffered the same nightmare. Beer was lying in a pool of water which had accumulated from the cliff face whilst Morris on the outside was soaked from the rain driving in from the ravine. As for me, I had lost the previous night's draw for sleeping positions and had ended up sandwiched between the other two, as a result of which I had been warm and dry. A bowl of hot porridge and a mug of scalding sweet tea put new life into us and we needed it to face the now inevitable mist and drizzle (Plate 26). We picked a bagful of dark blue fruits from a carpet of *Gaultheria pyroloides* capping a large boulder and more fruits of *Sorbus kurzii.* A small, loose-limbed currant – *Ribes laciniatum* – provided us with a number of red berries and accompanying this shrub as an epiphyte on several trees was *Vaccinium nummularia* – a small evergreen with slender, pendulous, densely rusty-hairy stems crowded with small obovate leaves and bearing terminal clusters of black berries.

Colour Plate 57. *Euphorbia himalayensis,* an herbaceous perennial whose stems and leaves turn a rich orange and red before dying in autumn. Here on the Milke Danda ridge it is growing in a patch of *Potentilla peduncularis,* a relative of the European Silverweed *(P. anserina).* (October)

Colour Plate 58. *Gaultheria pyroloides,* a large colony of this creeping evergreen on a boulder at 10,000ft. (3,048m) on the Milke Danda ridge. Its dark blue fruits are being gathered by Morris. Above him are the smooth plum-coloured stems of *Rhododendron barbatum.* (October)

Colour Plate 59. *Delphinium viscosum* at 10,000ft. (3,048m) in the Jaljale Himal. Seeds collected from this location produced plants of inferior quality in cultivation. (October)

Colour Plate 60. *Aconitum gammiei*, a scrambling slender-stemmed perennial monkshood growing in scrub at 13,000ft. (3,962m) on the Jaljale Himal. (October)

Plate 25. Thomas Thomson, Scottish doctor, botanist and author, was employed as a surgeon by the East India Company. He led a busy and adventurous life before being appointed in 1854 Superintendent of the Calcutta Botanic Garden. He studied and collected plants whenever opportunity allowed and spent over a year exploring and botanising in the Sikkim Himalaya with Joseph Hooker. Like so many before him, however, ill health brought about by the rigours of a life spent in wild places forced an end to his activities. His work is commemorated in the names of several plants, most notably the blood-red flowered *Rhododendron thomsonii* (Colour Plate 56)

The track moved steeply uphill and we followed puffing and sweating in our waterproofs and cursing until new plants caused us to linger. One such was a rather pretty blue sowthistle – *Cicerbita macrantha* – with stems 12-18in. (30.5-45cm) high clothed with pinnatisect leaves and bearing nodding powder-blue flowerheads. Unfortunately, in cultivation this plant proved to be coarse in growth and unsuitable even for the border. We then came upon a rhubarb with large cordate leaves and dense 3ft. (91.5cm) panicles of red flowers. It grew on a rock ledge where we had rested awhile. It was later named *Rheum acuminatum* (Plate 27). *Juniperus squamata*. appeared in increasing numbers, forming scrubby patches 4-5ft. (1.25-1.5m) high, with spreading branches and shoots nodding at the tips. The awl-shaped leaves were greyish-green and the fruits black. A superb red form of *Polygonum vacciniifolium* turned up but regrettably no seed was available.

Plate 26. Morris and the author polishing off their porridge as Beer looks on. Because of the persistent rain and mist the previous day, the party spent the night beneath an overhang at the base of a rock face. (October)

We moved through a zone of low scrub in which dwarf rhododendrons, *Potentilla fruticosa, Berberis* species and a *Spireaea* species dominated. Many herbs now put in an appearance and we were particularly taken with a dwarf *Delphinium – D. viscosum (trilobatum)* – with three-lobed leaves and 6-9in. (15-23cm) downy stems bearing several large, pale-yellow downy flowers (Colour Plate 59). Attractive as it was on these alpine slopes, this was another plant which proved ineffectual in cultivation. A plant grown from this seed in the Hillier Arboretum was rather weedy with small greenish flowers on taller stems. A yellow flowered saxifrage – *S. hookeri* – vied with the comparatively large deep-blue bell-shaped flowers of *Cyananthus lobatus,* whose slender trailing stems were clothed with small deeply lobed or fingered leaves. Trailing too, were the long growths of a climbing monkshood – *Aconitum gammiei* – which rambled over junipers, producing its slate-blue helmeted flowers in profusion (Colour Plate 60). The Scot George Gammie (1864-1935), after whom this plant is named, was Botanist and Superintendent in turn of the Saharanpur and the Lloyd Botanic Gardens before being made Curator of the Calcutta Botanic Garden.

Several louseworts – *Pedicularis* species – were common here and an *Androsace* species whose tight green mounds had long since flowered. The plant that pleased us the most, however, was the fabulous *Corydalis cashmeriana* with its sky-blue flowers sprinkled in the grass. It seemed to grow best in the competition provided by grass and other low herbage and extended over a large area of hillside. A long-time favourite with alpine plant enthusiasts despite its frequent dislike of cultivation, *C. cashmeriana* has been eclipsed in recent years by the more amenable *C. flexuosa* from western China.

Plate 27. A lunch break in the mist at 13,000ft. (3,962m) on the Milke Danda ridge. Morris checks a map reference whilst Beer contemplates the journey ahead. Note the leaves of *Rheum acuminatum* on the left. (October)

Colour Plate 61. *Saussurea gossypiphora*, the so-called Snowball plant at 14,000ft. (4,267m) in the Jaljale Himal. Nearby grows *Rhododendron anthopogon*. (October)

Colour Plate 62 (right). *Saussurea gossypiphora:* note the narrow, deeply-lobed leaves protruding from the woolly head. (October)

Colour Plate 63 (far right). *Saussurea gossypiphora* showing the protective woolly cocoon open to reveal a terminal thistle-like seed head. (October)

5. RHUBARB HILL

All that night I tossed and turned and could not get warm. Cold dampness seeped up through the groundsheet and the tent seemed damp inside. When dawn came at last, we found that we were camped in the middle of a bog. Pema, anxious to establish a camp and hampered by mist, had assumed the wet ground to be rain soaked as elsewhere. Little wonder that the night had been so frustrating. The conditions now, however, were bright and blue sky was evident in patches. The bog, a soggy area of grasses and sedges, was spattered with the rosettes of at least three different *Primula* species, two of which we were able to have named. The most obvious was *P. obliqua*, a striking plant forming stout clumps of finely toothed, strap-shaped leaves, covered beneath with a yellowish farina. The fruiting capsules were borne in umbels terminating stout 1-1½ft. (30-45cm) scapes. Although past flowering these plants were made attractive by the rich butter colour or golden-yellow suffusion of the leaves as they left their summer green behind them. It was a common species which occurred throughout these mountains between the 13,000 and 14,000ft. (3,962-4,267m) contours, often colouring the hillsides from afar (Colour Plates 64 and 65). The second species – *P. dickieana* – was much smaller with oblanceolate leaves 1-2¼in. (2.5-5.5cm) long, distantly toothed in the upper half. The umbels of seed capsules were carried on a 6in. (15cm) slender scape. Seed of both species was plentiful and we filled several paper packets. Beer had seen both species in flower elsewhere during his reconnaissance and described those of *P. obliqua* as nodding, cream in colour and 1in. (2.5cm) or more across, whilst those of *P. dickieana* varied from white to lavender with a yellow eye and measured over 1in. (2.5cm) across. The last named was first found by Joseph Hooker in Sikkim in 1848.

Our campsite was situated a few hundred feet below the ridge at 13,500ft. (4,115m) and our route now lay north-eastwards through the range of mountains known as the Jaljale Himal (Plate 28). We scanned the ridge above and noticed a narrow col whence poured a small stream. The sun seemed imminent and we decided to climb the hillside to see what lay on the other side. Following the line of the stream we soon found many new plants amongst which *Bergenia purpurascens* was the most noticeable because of the bright crimson of its fleshy leaves. These were obovate to elliptic in shape. Large patches of this excellent plant were found in damp places, especially by the water's edge as well as on rock ledges (Colour Plate 68). Most forms of this species I have seen in cultivation colour well in winter, the evergreen leaves turning to red sometimes with a burnished purple tint. The purple flowers were long finished and we were able to collect lots of seed.

Competing with the bergenia for late colour was *Aster himalaicus*. This splendid alpine daisy formed patches of obovate leaves with clasping bases. It occupied drier, better-drained situations than the bergenia and enjoyed full sun and wind. The flowerheads, 1½-2in. (3.75-5cm) across, comprised a yellow disc surrounded by purple ray florets (Colour Plate 69). They were carried singly on

Colour Plate 64. *Primula obliqua* colonising a bog at 13,000ft. (3,962m) in the Jaljale Himal. (October)

Colour Plate 65. *Primula obliqua,* a bold clump of this lovely species, its autumn foliage quite as attractive as its cream-coloured flowers in early summer. (October)

Colour Plate 66. *Rhododendron setosum* (above) and *Euphorbia himalayense* growing at 14,000ft. (4,267m) in the Jaljale Himal. The former is a dwarf spreading, densely twiggy shrub with small densely scaly leaves. (October)

Colour Plate 67. *Salix lindleyana* variety *microphylla* forming extensive carpets of creeping stems on banks and over rocks in the Jaljale Himal. The narrow leaves turn pale yellow before they are shed in autumn. (October)

Colour Plate 68. A bold colony of the evergreen perennial *Bergenia purpurascens* growing at 14,000ft. (4,267m) in the Jaljale Himal. This species is renowned for the rich colouring of its winter foliage. It grows here with *Rhododendron anthopogon*. (October)

Colour Plate 69. *Aster himalaicus*, a carpeting perennial frequent on the exposed slopes of the Jaljale Himal, its flowers attracting late flying insects. (October)

Plate 28. The rocky slopes above Camp 9 at 13,600ft. in the Jaljale Himal. The yellow and red clumps of *Primula obliqua* and *Euphorbia himalayense* are scattered throughout the area, whilst the higher reaches between 14,000ft. and 14,500ft. are where we found the peculiar Snowball plant – *Saussurea gossypiphora*. (October)

erect hairy stems, in some instances their numbers hiding the leaves beneath. After a while we could spot this plant from a distance as purple patches on the hillside. Plants raised in the Hillier Arboretum from this seed have proved vigorous and hardy though taller in the stem and with slightly smaller flowers.

A prostrate willow *Salix lindleyana* variety *microphylla* with small, narrow, rosemary-like leaves formed large mats, its leaves turning yellow creating golden splashes in the grass (Colour Plate 67). *Cassiope fastigiata* was plentiful on hillocks and banks, but as we approached the col *Rhododendron anthopogon* and *R. setosum* (Colour Plate 66) took over, their dense low clumps occupying large areas and swamping lesser plants. One bush of the former species still sported a late cluster of reddish flowers, darker even than those of the Award of Merit clone 'Betty Graham' raised from Ludlow & Sherriff's seed by the Coxes of Glendoick.

The sun broke loose from a bank of cloud just as we breasted the col at a height of 14,000ft. (4,267m). The spine of the ridge was relatively narrow and the ground fell away steeply to the north. Stretching across the horizon to the north-west we saw a series of snow-clad peaks and ridges. Six superb mountains dominated our vision from west to east – Chamlang 24,183ft. (7,371m), Baruntse 22,150ft. (6,751m), Lhotse 27,885ft. (8,499m), Everest 29,029ft. (8,848m), Makalu 27,790ft. (8,470m), and Chomolonzo 22,150ft. (6,751m) (Plate 29).

Suddenly a thick mist descended and obliterated the view along with Beer and Morris, so I sat down on the nearest rock. An hour later it began to clear, draining from the steep slopes like some ghostly double tide in retreat, leaving the ridge isolated like a whale in the foam. I rose to my feet and walked to the edge of the northern escarpment peering down a gully which revealed a single silvery vein of water. Something then caught my eye which caused my heart to race. Less than a hundred yards away there appeared a dozen snowballs lying in the grass. I moved quickly in their direction and the nearer I approached the less they resembled snowballs, and more balls of cottonwool. It was only on close examination, however, that I discovered these strange objects were living plants. It was one of those curious members of the *Compositae* known as *Saussurea gossypiphora,* a bizarre species of a large and variable genus of plants related to the thistles but without prickles. I was able to photograph and examine the plants in some detail. The short stem was provided with long, narrow, sharply cut and toothed leaves and carried at its summit a single, or sometimes several, thistle-like flowerheads. The entire plant was densely clothed with long, silky, white hairs which took the form of a cottonwool-like mass, completely enveloping all but the tips of the leaves (Colour Plates 61, 62, 63).

The cottonwool is a protective measure, like a fur coat, insulating the flowers from the extremes of heat and cold common at such altitudes. But the saussurea has a secret to reveal. In the top of the cottonwool ball is an aperture just large enough to allow a bumble-bee access to the flowers. Even when the plant is covered by snow, which it sometimes is at flowering time, the bee can still carry out its task because the process of respiration within the cottonwool creates just enough warmth to melt a passage through to the outside world down which the bee finds its way. This observation was first made by A.F.R. Wollaston (1875-1930) during the 1921 British Everest Expedition. Wollaston watched the bees entering and leaving the snow-holes then scraped away the snow to reveal the saussurea. We collected seed from several specimens but none of our shareholders reported successful germination, and so this strange and remarkable plant retains its reputation as being virtually impossible to cultivate, a fact not altogether surprising considering the combination of growing conditions in its native environment. Wollaston, who was medical officer and naturalist to the Everest Expedition survived many perils in the wild only to be murdered by a student in Cambridge.

I had been so enthralled with the saussureas that I had not noticed Morris's arrival. When the mist blanketed the ridge he had gone back to camp where he had lunch before returning to look for me. Beer was also in camp so I accompanied Morris down the slope still talking about the latest find. We picked our way through alpines whose late flowers gave lie to the opinion of those pundits in England who had doubted that we would see much in flower. *Cremanthodium ellisii (plantagineum)* with obovate, toothed, plantain-like leaves and a single nodding yellow daisy on a 6-9in. (15-23cm) stem; *Saussurea uniflora* with solitary erect stems 6-8in. (15-20cm) high clothed with conspicuous purple-flushed bracts and bearing a single terminal, blue, thistle-like flowerhead (Colour Plate 70); a gentian species, possibly *Gentiana depressa,* with pale-blue trumpets, white and green speckled within, dark striped and speckled without; *Polygonum vacciniifolium,* clothing rocks with leafy trailers and a myriad pink or red miniature spear-like flower spikes; *Tanacetum atkinsonii (Chrysanthemum atkinsonii)* with finely divided leaves and yellow daisy flowers; blue *Swertia* species and *Cyananthus lobatus.* These and several others, including *Aster himalaicus* and *Delphinium viscosum,* created colourful tapestries of a kind one normally associates with the European Alps in June. At intervals, often on the

Plate 29. Famous peaks of the Everest region seen from the Jaljale Himal at 14,000ft. (4,267m). A snow-topped Mt. Everest (29,029ft./8,848m) appears in the centre background with the steep buttress of Lhotse's south face to its left (27,885ft./8,499m). Dominating the right skyline is Makalu (27,790ft./8,470m). The far left peak is Peak 6. (October)

Colour Plate 71. *Polygonum molle,* a far creeping herbaceous perennial, here growing on the edge of a low colony of *Rhododendron campanulatum* at 14,000ft. (4,267m) in the Jaljale Himal. (October)

Colour Plate 70. *Saussurea uniflora* at 13,000ft. (3,962m) in the Jaljale Himal. This is an attractive plant with blue flowerheads above red-bracted stems. (October)

Colour Plate 73. A breakfast time boil-up at 14,000ft. (4,267m) in the Jaljale Himal. The porters had tremendous reserves of breath and a few minutes' steady blowing soon had the faggots crackling into flame

Colour Plate 72. A *Rhododendron* species, probably *R. campanulatum,* colonising an east facing slope at 14,000ft. (4,267m) in the Jaljale Himal. At the time its sea-green leaves put me in mind of *R. aeruginosum,* but this proved to be little more than wishful thinking. The dwarf, dark-leaved rhododendron on the left is *R. anthopogon.* (October)

Colour Plate 74 (right). Dorje, one of our young Sherpa porters negotiating a steep slope at 14,000ft. (4,267m) on the Jaljale Himal. He is carrying one of the kitchen boxes constructed by Morris in Bangor. (October)

edge of rhododendron patches we found *Polygonum molle*, its panicles of white flowers almost at their best (Colour Plate 71). This is a bold perennial in leaf and flower though its creeping rootstock can make it a thug in the garden.

The next two days were long and frustrating. We continued to follow the ridge keeping to the 14,000ft. (4,267m) contour, heading first in an easterly then in a northerly direction. In one place the track diverged and neither porters nor Sherpas knew which one we should take. Then someone spotted a cone of rocks nearby and on taking this apart we discovered a message left by Dawa with instructions to follow the left-hand track. The mist stayed with us for most of the time usually accompanied by rain or drizzle. Once the mist parted and we gazed into a deep valley where *Abies densa* forest gave way to alpine rhododendrons, their dark carpets enlivened by the gold splashes of *Primula obliqua* foliage.

Seed collecting was restricted to the few bright periods when the mist cleared or thinned out. Interesting plants continued to appear but the weather conditions made certain that we missed many more. On one east facing hillside grew a rhododendron which in its sea-green foliage put me in mind of *R. aeruginosum*. The intensity of colour, however, did not quite compare with this species and after ruminating on the identity of this plant for many years I finally agreed with rhododendron guru Peter Cox who, having seen the same or similar plants on the Jaljale Himal, concluded that they belonged to *R. campanulatum*, approaching *R. aeruginosum* but not close enough to be included in that species (Colour Plate 72).

The two most fascinating flowering plants we encountered during this period were *Corydalis meifolia* and an *Aconitum* species close to *A. staintonii*. The first was a strikingly glaucous plant with deeply divided leaves and racemes of black and yellow flowers. We only ever found it growing in running water and beneath waterfalls. The aconitum reached no more than 3in. (7.5cm) high, bearing one or two large blue-helmeted flowers. It occurred on grassy slopes in some profusion and grew from a small tuber. A willow species with narrow leaves formed carpets and mats and may have been *Salix lindleyana*, but the abundant seed we collected, being of short viability, failed to germinate. Elsewhere grew another willow, *S. calyculata*, a low creeping shrublet with larger leaves than the other whilst some plants bore clusters of red seed capsules (Colour Plate 75).

At the end of one particularly tiring day we climbed up a scree where boulders, loosened by the porters' feet, hurled downwards so that we were forced to seek refuge beneath a rock outcrop. It was not a pleasant experience to hear but not to see rocks tumbling towards us and we were thankful when we had attained the ridge above. All that day it had poured with rain and our route had taken us across screes, through streams and bogs, up cliffs and narrow gullies, and all this in dense mist. Our maps were of little help and only our compass and the experience of our porters had kept us on the right track. It was frustrating knowing that we were passing through superb terrain with mountain peaks and valleys and yet unable to see and appreciate it.

Now the rain had turned to sleet as we continued along the

Plate 30. Camp 11 at 14,000ft. (4,267m) on the Jaljale Himal. On the eastern horizon the majestic peaks of Kangchengjunga (28,208ft./8,597m). (October)

Plate 31. Early morning at Camp 11 at 14,000ft. (4,267m) on the Jaljale Himal. We awoke to find overnight snow had transformed the landscape (October)

ridge. A party of birds flew from a large slab-like rock and their rufous tail feathers and the white patch on their backs identified them as Impeyan pheasants. They called both on the wing and when stationary with something like a curlew's cry, but shorter. On the same ridge we saw a covey of Himalayan snowcocks, the males with grey-spotted plumage. About the size of guinea-fowl, they appeared on the track ahead of us and rather than fly simply ran away into the mist.

With the light fading fast, we decided to camp amongst a jumble of large boulders at 14,000ft. (4,267m). It was several hours before the last porter staggered in and as each one arrived I gave him a generous pinch of tobacco and a sheet of British Rail lavatory paper to make cigarettes. This had become a daily ritual, and considering the appalling conditions in which the porters carried it was small reward. Still barefoot they tramped through ice-cold rivers and torrents, across sharp-edged screes dressed in little more than loincloths, with just a blanket to sleep in (Colour Plates 73 and 74). The last porter to arrive, a small and sickly looking man, was so tired he crawled under a nearby rock and, wrapping himself in his blanket, fell fast asleep. The wood carried from lower altitudes was wet and took a long time to burn, by which time Beer, Morris and I had climbed into our sleeping bags, but even they were wet. Somehow we got to sleep but we were awoken at 5.30a.m. the next morning to the sound of something or someone banging hard on our tent. We unzipped our bags and flap to investigate the cause of the disturbance. The scene which met our gaze as we looked through the tent entrance was like something from a Christmas card. Snow had fallen heavily during the night and one of our Sherpa boys, Dorje, had gone round beating it from the tents (Plates 30 and 31). There was no question about continuing our journey that day so we set about looking for firewood which we found after tramping some distance downhill in the fallen dead branches of another rhododendron we had not come across before, forming thickets at the base of a cliff and below the snow-line. The leaves were elliptic to elliptic-obovate, 5-8in. (13-20cm) long including the stout grey petiole, acute, broad cuneate to almost rounded at base, covered beneath with a thin, smooth, shining, buff indumentum. The flower buds were stout and coloured the same grey as the petioles and last year's shoots. It proved to be *R. wightii* named after Robert Wight (1796-1872), an assistant surgeon in the East India Company and Superintendent of the Madras Botanical Garden. Wight was an energetic and industrious collector of botanical specimens. From his first tour of duty in India (1819-1831) he returned to England with 100,000 specimens. After three years he

Colour Plate 75. *Salix calyculata*, a dwarf creeping willow common in Nepal, here growing at 13,700ft. (4,175m) in the Jaljale Himal. Note the red fruiting clusters of this female plant. (October)

Colour Plate 76. *Rheum nobile* growing above carpets of *Rhododendron anthopogon* at 14,000ft. (4,267m) in the Jaljale Himal. The impressive column of overlapping bracts can reach 3-3½ft. (90-100cm). This is a mature fruiting specimen. When in flower the inflorescence is squatter and more conical than columnar, whilst the bracts are milky white. (October)

Colour Plate 77. *Rheum nobile,* a fruiting column with bracts removed to show the dense clusters of triangular red seeds not unlike those of a dock *(Rumex)* to which *Rheum* is closely related. The young stems of this plant are sometimes eaten raw or cooked by the Bhotias. (October)

106

Colour Plate 78. *Delphinium nepalense* growing among rocks at 14,000ft. (4,267m) in the Jaljale Himal. All parts of this plant are hairy, including the hooded flowers. (October)

Colour Plate 79. *Aconitum staintonii:* a slender scrambling monkshood here growing through the leaves of *Potentilla peduncularis* at 14,000ft. (4,267m) in the Jaljale Himal. (October)

Colour Plate 80. The green-stemmed *Ephedra gerardiana* variety *sikkimensis* and the white flowerheads of an edelweiss *Leontopodium jacotianum* on a slope in the Jaljale Himal. (October)

was back and continued were he had left off. It is said that when he finally retired in 1853 Wight took home with him a herbarium in excess of 4,000 species.

Growing on the edge of the snow we found a delightful little *Cremanthodium* species with the usual nodding yellow daisy head on a 3-4in. (7.5-10cm) stalk and a rosette of small deeply divided dandelion-like leaves. We saw it on many subsequent occasions and it proved to be *C. pinnatifidum.* A flash of colour then caught our eyes and we saw a wall creeper quartering the rock-face above our heads. The red wing feathers and white spots in an otherwise greyish attire were quite outstanding.

We watched for a time the mist alternately forming and dispersing in the valley below before retracing our steps up the hillside. The sun in the meantime appeared and warmed our backs, throwing our shadows across the snow. On returning to camp we found Pema carrying a large and curious plant. It was cone-shaped, 3ft. (90cm) long and composed of large pale-green overlapping bracts. Beer recognised it as *Rheum nobile,* the noble rhubarb, which he had seen during his reconnaissance. The rhubarb is eaten raw or cooked by the Tibetans but gives the westerner stomach ache and in no way can it compare with that familiar companion of custard. Beer and I climbed the rocks above the camp to a place pointed out by Pema and there found many more. They towered through the snow like green rockets ready for blast-off. We collected several specimens, breaking the stems away from the basal rosette of large orbicular-cordate leaves. The typical triangular dock-like fruits were carried in crowded fingers at intervals along the stout 3-3½ft. (90-100cm) stem, each cluster arising in the axil of a large, conspicuous, scallop-like, apple-green bract which concealed and protected the fruits, collectively forming a dense column. Beer told us that at flowering time in June/July, these columns are squatter, more conical and a startling milk-white. The plant appeared to be monocarpic, as those which had flowered seemed spent. We found many non-flowering rosettes, however, and it appeared fairly common on the grassy slopes of the hill (Colour Plates 76 and 77).

Like most of the slopes we had crossed this one had water moving freely through the surface layers but never lingering long enough to cause waterlogging. Only in a normal autumn would it in any way become dry, and then only comparatively so. It struck me that the rich flora of these alpine slopes was blessed with that near mythical condition oft quoted in nurserymen's catalogues as 'a moist but well-drained soil'.

Back in camp we found Morris trying to persuade the porters to go and collect wood. They grumbled about the snow but eventually moved off leaving behind the small sickly porter and another who was lame. We sat around the fire bagging seed of the rhubarb, stopping only once to observe a large raptor gliding across the hillside above camp. From its size, comparatively long tail, heavy wings and rufous-coloured neck we guessed it to be a Himalayan golden eagle.

When we awoke the next morning the snow was still lying around but the sun was out and the views were breathtaking. During breakfast we looked eastward across a series of ridges and valleys to the massive of Kangchengjunga (28,208ft./8,597m), whose several peaks seemingly supported the sky. Only once has this holy mountain been climbed, by a British team in 1955, and even then it had stopped short of the main summit in deference to the wishes of the Indian, Nepalese and Sikkim governments. To Tibetans, Kangchengjunga is known as 'Five Treasures of the Eternal Snows'. They believe that the god of wealth lives there, storing on its five peaks the five treasures of gold, silver, copper, corn and sacred books.

The porters were still concerned about the snow so Morris, Beer and I shared our spare boots and plimsolls between them and we set off down the hill. It was not long before we cleared the snow-line and walked through the undergrowth. In these hills the dwarf rhododendrons carpet the ground like heather on a Pennine moor and our boots crunched through dense aromatic scrub. We splashed through shallow streams and torrents whose sparkling waters ran on smooth stones to leap headlong into space. It was one of those days when it felt good to be alive.

The track in places ran across grassy hillsides spangled with sky-blue *Gentiana depressa,* dark-blue *Aconitum staintonii* (Colour Plate 79), yellow *Delphinium viscosum* and the lovely blue *Cyananthus pedunculatus.* Here also two dwarf junipers were rife. *Juniperus squamata* occurred as a dense, low spreading bush, some forms actually hugging the rocks, whilst a few individuals were more open, even scraggy, in growth. All, however, had the characteristic orange-brown peeling bark and sage-green foliage on nodding shoots. The other species has been identified as *J. indica.* Known as the Black juniper it has long been considered by some authorities as conspecific (the same as) *J. wallichiana.* Judging by descriptions I have read of the last named and a photograph (Figure 149) in Adam Stainton's book, *Forests of Nepal,* the two, as found in the wild, could not be more different and this view has since been confirmed by Keith Rushforth and others who point out the columnar or tree-like habit, spring flowering characteristic and larger fruits of *J. wallichiana,* whereas *J. indica* is a low growing and spreading shrub flowering in autumn.

J. indica reminded me of some forms of *J. sabina,* only without the characteristic savin smell. It too, like the accompanying *J. squamata,* was variable in habit, one form making compact mounds 2ft. (60cm) high and several feet across, whilst others, more open in habit, reminded me of a small Pfitzer juniper. It differed most noticeably from *J. squamata* in its rich green colour and densely clothed, densely packed branches and branchlets which were straight rather than nodding at the tips. Leaves were a mixture of the adult-scale and juvenile-needle types. Both species bore ovoid, shining black, single-seeded fruits ⅓in. (.85cm) long (Colour Plates 81 and 82).

That evening we camped in a deep glaciated valley above a cold, still, alpine lake whose surface mirrored the progress of the sun across the sky until it passed behind the mountain, leaving a trail of gold and orange flotsam in its wake. The sky was overcast next morning as we packed bags and rucksacks. A visit to the lake flushed a pair of white-capped redstarts whose red tail feathers and creamy-white caps created a bright flash of colour in the cold grey dawn. We climbed out of the valley as snow began to fall and were soon on the ridge where we found a small lake partially covered with thin ice (Colour Plate 83). The height was 14,000ft. (4,267m) and we were surprised to see a dipper swimming on the surface of the water, looking like a miniature waterhen with a white breast. A shallow layer of snow covered the ground, punctuated by tiny stains which on close examination proved to be the nodding flowers of *Cremanthodium pinnatifidum* pushing through their chill blanket, just like crocus and soldanellas do in the European Alps. A gentian relative – *Swertia multicaulis* – in seed with several depressed stems radiating from a basal rosette occurred both on the track and on the slopes above. Gradually the snow

Colour Plate 81. *Juniperus indica* growing on a rocky slope at 14,000ft. (4;267m) in the Jaljale Himal. This is a variable, low-growing shrubby species found in the dry inner valleys of the Himalaya. (October)

Colour Plate 82 (above). *Juniperus squamata* (above) and *Rhododendron lepidotum* were common companions on the Jaljale Himal. Both are dwarf wide-spreading shrubs often forming dense low thickets. (October)

Colour Plate 83 (left). A bleak brown and grey landscape with lakes at 14,000ft. (4,267m) in the Jaljale Himal. Our route led through the mountains to the right. (October)

Colour Plate 84 (below left). The valley bottom above the village of Topke Gola. The black shelter of a Bhotia family has been pitched in a grazed area while all around grow junipers *(J. recurva)*, berberis (mainly *B. angulosa*), rhododendrons of several kinds and tall Silver fir *(Abies densa)*. (October)

Colour Plate 85 (below). Bhotia children outside the family shelter in a valley above Topke Gola. Cut branches of *Juniperus recurva* provide a soft and aromatic carpet and bedding while the framework for the shelter is provided by *Betula utilis* (*utilis* meaning useful). The children's father was away tending his yaks and their mother collecting fuel for their fire. (October)

thickened and visibility decreased to a few yards but still the track was discernible as it threaded its way through a huddle of dark crags. Then we found ourselves in a narrow defile and looking up we perceived dim shapes, solitary or in groups, which seemed to be watching our progress like squat inhabitants of some alien realm into which we had stumbled. Some of the 'inhabitants' appeared on rock ledges near at hand and we discovered to our amusement that they were merely columns of the noble rhubarb – *Rheum nobile*. Another *Cremanthodium* was found – *C. ellisii,* with obovate leaves and nodding flowers on robust 6-8in. (15-20cm) stems.

About midday we stopped for lunch where a long low cliff afforded us shelter from the wind-blown sleet. The crevices of the cliff supported several interesting plants including *Tanacetum gossypinum* (*Chrysanthemum gossypinum),* a 2in. (5cm) tall, white, woolly plant with a tight terminal head of yellow flowers, also a fern which looked to be the parsley fern – *Cryptogramma crispa.* Another creeping willow carpeted the rock, its slender, interlacing, reddish stems closely following the contours in the manner of an ivy. Its leaves were small and narrow and already turning yellow. This may have been *Salix lindleyana* variety *microphylla.*

At the base of a waterfall we discovered a group of *Primula capitata* subspecies *crispata* in seed, and a plant from this collection flourished in the peat garden at the Hillier Arboretum for several years. Each year in July or August it sent aloft several 4-6in. (10-15cm) scapes bearing dense terminal rounded heads of blue-purple, yellow-eyed flowers. The leaves were liberally powdered with farina. On our climb up a long rocky gully we twice disturbed groups of the chukor, similar to but larger than the partridge and more colourful. Usually when disturbed they launched themselves from rock or crag to fly rapidly downhill rather like the British red grouse. Another bird seen on several occasions by lakes and torrents was the Hodgson's pied wagtail, in general aspect similar to our native species and named for B.H. Hodgson of *Rhododendron hodgsonii* fame.

We suddenly came upon a large lake hemmed in by vast, steep, snow-covered slopes where several landslips had recently occurred. The track traversed one of these slopes and we all followed moving slowly and with great care. Some of our porters were still barefoot and seemed ill at ease, understandably so in these difficult conditions. Half-way across, those in the lead stopped to allow everyone to catch up and I took the opportunity of distributing lavatory paper and tobacco amongst the porters, most of whom tucked their supply into their inner garment preferring to wait until they reached safer ground before enjoying a smoke.

Whilst sitting on a rock attempting with cold fingers to retie my bootlace I spotted a cluster of smokey-blue hooded flowers with coal-black anthers peeping from beneath the rock. They belonged to *Delphinium nepalense,* a choice alpine species which had only comparatively recently been named by Andrew Lauener, an authority on the genus, at the Royal Botanic Garden, Edinburgh. The palmately cut leaves, as well as the 3-6in. (7.5-15cm) stems and 1-1½in. (2.5-3.75cm) long flowers were densely and softly hairy. It was a most exciting find which led to a successful search for further plants. Invariably they had chosen dry sheltered pockets beneath rocks and seemed quite unperturbed by prevailing conditions. Indeed it was amazing that plants not only grew but flowered in this seemingly hostile terrain (Colour Plate 78). Sharing the slopes with the delphinium we found a Himalayan version of the familiar edelweiss – *Leontopodium jacotianum* – and a tiny creeping shrublet forming dense tufts of stiff green rush-like stems 3-4 in. (7.5-10cm) high which proved to be *Ephedra gerardiana* variety *sikkimensis* (Colour Plate 80). As seen in the wild on these alpine slopes this is a most acceptable subject for the rock garden, especially when bearing its bright red currant-like berries. Unfortunately, once in cultivation it waxes fat in the fertile soil and benign conditions and grows into a coarse mound up to 2ft. (60cm) high, rarely if ever fruiting as the flowers are unisexual – male and female born on separate plants. The species *E. gerardiana*, and no doubt its variety, is used in native medicine. The ephedrine it contains is useful as a cardiac tonic. The plant is also utilised in asthma attacks and for respiratory affections.

On these same slopes we saw a party of Rose finches, mainly brown females with a few rose-coloured males for company. Continuing our march we plodded up to the pass at 15,000ft. (4,572m) where a chorten of stones had been constructed to support a cluster of poles bearing white prayer flags. The driving snow and gathering mist, however, dissuaded us from resting here so we pushed on through an area of fallen rocks and down the other side. Soon we had left the pass with its cold grey slabs and walked down a steep hillside where the snow had almost cleared. Before us stretched a large green valley with a river and flanking forest. The entire north-facing side of the valley was covered by a dense tangled growth of *Rhododendron wightii* which would have presented a spectacular effect in May when the trusses of pale-yellow flowers appear. We descended the hillside moving through a mixed deciduous and evergreen forest which was a relief after several days in the heights. We then broke into a large glade in the middle of which stood a small tent-like shelter made from a heavy black woollen material. From out of this emerged two small children, a boy, barefoot and urchin-like, and a girl, their black woollen garments, her striped apron and long black greasy hair identifying them as Bhotias, originally from Tibet (Colour Plates 84 and 85). They spoke to Pema who told us that their father was away bringing their yaks down from the high pastures. The clearing was surrounded by tall firs whose heads seemingly supported the clouds, the lower branches providing both fuel and bedding for these nomads who wander in the high border regions with their herds of yak, sheep or goats until winter forces them into the valleys. The dense firs created beneath them a gloomy world relieved only by the colourful mounds of a *Berberis* species, probably *B. angulosa*, whose foliage had turned orange and red.

Leaving the glade behind, we continued through an area of rhododendron and juniper scrub in which many plants of interest caught our attention, but we were tired and hungry and anyway we could return here another day. The track surfaced on an open hillside and we saw below us a collection of dark wood and stone houses whose ragged occupants came out to meet us as we descended the slope. The Bhotia village of Topke Gola consisted of twenty occupied houses plus a small stone gompa (temple) presided over by a lama. Our first contact however was brief since our camp was situated some 500ft. (152m) above the village at a height of 12,500ft. (3,810m). Wearily we plodded up a steep boulder-strewn slope to emerge at last on to a deep green pasture running gently down to a still lake. A hundred yards above the water's edge our first base camp had been established and with renewed energy we strode towards the orange tents to be greeted by Dawa and Da Norbu. A large meal was prepared and after much talking and consumption of chang (mountain beer) we retired to our tents for a long sleep.

Colour Plate 86. Our base camp by the sacred lake above Topke Gola. The camp is at 12,500ft. (3,810m) whilst the snow covered ridge above lies between 15,000 and 16,000ft. (4,572 and 4,877m). Rhododendrons of several species cover the slopes joined below by Silver fir (*Abies densa*). (October)

Colour Plate 87 (right). In Topke Gola a makeshift structure serves as a pedestal for juniper twigs which are burned as an incense to placate the goddess in the lake above. (October)

Colour Plate 88 (far right). The village of Topke Gola looking south down the valley of the Mewa Khola. In winter the Bhotia inhabitants live at lower altitudes returning with the melting of the snow in spring. (October)

114

Colour Plate 89. The Sacred Lake at 12,500ft. (3,810m) above Topke Gola. According to the local people, here dwelt a beautiful goddess. The hills around are covered with rhododendron and Silver fir. (October)

6. TOPKE GOLA AND THE SACRED LAKE

The lake below our camp was believed by the lama and villagers to contain a beautiful goddess, and in deference to their beliefs we had promised not to wash or swim in its waters, nor to camp within 100 yards (91.5m) of its shore (Colour Plates 86 and 89). A rhododendron-covered knoll by the lake's edge supported a small temple dedicated to the goddess and each morning the lama would toil up the hill from the village to conduct a lone ceremony during which he rang various bells and sang incantations. A metal trident protruded from the water close to the shore and a small dish attached to its stem was a repository for money and food offerings to the goddess. Each morning in the village small heaps of dry juniper twigs and foliage were ignited on several birdtable-like structures, the air carrying the resultant incense up the hill to please her (Colour Plate 87).

The villagers, all of Tibetan origin, spend the summer months above the village grazing yak, sheep and goats, from which they obtain milk and wool (Plates 32 and 33). The wool is woven on crude wooden looms to make various articles of clothing including a poncho-style garment which is worn by shepherds. It is thick, oily, warm and virtually waterproof When winter threatens they migrate down the Mewa Khola to villages where the snow does not reach, leaving the lama to keep a long lonely vigil (Colour Plate 88).

Plate 32 (right). Bhotia boy of Topke Gola carrying home milk from the yaks grazing on our campsite by the sacred lake

Plate 33 (far right). A Bhotia woman returning to Topke Gola with a load of fuel gathered in the hills above our camp. This was a regular task for women and children alike

We arrived at Topke Gola on 15 October and stayed for twelve days, during which time we explored the forests, valleys and hillsides around, finding innumerable plants and collecting a great deal of valuable seed. The seed we generally dried in the sun on plates and in dishes before cleaning and bagging (Plate 34). Linen bags were used for the final drying process, these being hung on a line stretched between the various tents. Small collections of dried seeds were placed in stout paper envelopes and stored in wooden crates or polythene-lined kitbags. We found cleaning of the various seeds the most tedious business and were delighted therefore to find that the Sherpas and porters, especially the women, had a natural ability in this often delicate operation. Obviously their dextrous hand movements had been perfected when as children they had helped their parents to sort and clean the year's grain supply. It was fascinating to watch the way they shook the dish with trembling movements causing the chaff and debris to leap over the edge, leaving the seeds behind. Supervision was however required when changing seed batches. It was no use leaving the Sherpas alone with several separate collections to clean, and we gave them one collection at a time taking care not to produce the next until the last was safely bagged or packeted and labelled with its collection number.

Pressing of specimens continued and Beer had long since organised the porters into drying teams, the damp drying sheets being held over the camp fire to dry or laid out on the grass when weather permitted. Our arrival at Topke Gola signalled the end of unsettled weather and the majority of our days there proved warm and sunny, much to our delight and relief and gave us the welcome opportunity to sort out, dry and reorganise our equipment (Plate 35).

Our duties fell into three main categories. Beer assumed responsibility for the pressing and recording of specimens, whilst I compiled the field notes to accompany each seed collection. I also kept a plant diary into which all interesting information concerning plants found but not necessarily collected was entered. Morris was responsible for the seed cleaning and bagging as well as for the overall camp organisation, for which he possessed just the right mixture of patience, authority and common sense.

During the reconnaissance, Beer had built a little nursery garden at Topke

Plate 34. The author sorting seed in camp above Topke Gola. All seed collected was cleaned and set out to dry except on wet or windy days. The fruits here include *Rosa sericea, Sorbus foliolosa* and *S. vestita.* (October)

Plate 35. One member's selection of clothing and equipment for the expedition. The umbrella provides protection from the sun as well as the rain. A down-filled duvet jacket and sleeping bag are essential for cold nights whilst (bottom right) heavy climbing boots contrast with walking (trekking) boots and plimsolls or trainers for camp wear

Gola to accommodate some of the interesting plants he had brought from further afield. Unfortunately little now remained due to the ravages of yaks and goats. The yaks and their calves shared our campsite having been brought down from their summer grazing at 16,000-17,000ft. (4,877-5,182m). One night we were woken by the ground vibrating and heard the sound of many running hooves. Morris and I threw ourselves out of the tent, still in our sleeping bags, and crawled to the nearby slope where Beer and some of the others had already gathered. At that moment stampeding yaks reached the camp knocking things over, including our tents, and rushed on to the lake. Despite this incident we co-existed with them until they were moved on down the valley to pastures new.

The hillsides above the village and lake were steep and clothed with fir, juniper, rhododendrons and various deciduous shrubs in autumn colour. They presented a vast rolling tapestry of green, brown, red and gold, far richer in colour than anything I had ever seen before (Colour Plates 90 and 91).

All around on slopes, paths, amongst bushes and beneath rock over-hangs occurred the over-wintering rosettes of the fabulous Himalayan poppies – *Meconopsis* – and we found a total of six different species within an hour's walk of the camp. By far the most common was *M. paniculata*, whose dense rosettes measured as much as 20in. (51cm) across. Its leaves were deeply and pinnately lobed and densely covered with golden bristles which caught and held drops of dew or rain, making of them mirrors to reflect the sun into one's eyes (Colour Plates 93 and 95). This is a monocarpic species, the plant dying after seeding, and there were many seeding panicles 5-6ft. (1.5-1.85m) high clothed, like the leaves, with golden bristles which when disturbed came away in clouds like fibreglass. It made seed collecting an uncomfortable task. Occasionally we saw a few late yellow flowers 1½-2in. (2.5-3.75cm) across. However, Beer told us that during his previous visit in July, this poppy was at its peak and coloured the hillsides as far as the eye could see. Although in full sun, these poppies received their share of underground moisture, and judging by the number of lush rosettes growing on and by tracks, the amount of running surface water during the monsoon must be beneficial if not essential to their well being. The young shoots are sometimes eaten by the Tibetans and Sherpas. Some years later I saw a drift of this species flowering in the Royal Botanic Garden, Edinburgh, grown from seed we had collected from this location in 1971 (Colour Plate 94). *M. paniculata* was first discovered and introduced by Joseph Hooker around 1850.

Meconopsis napaulensis, by comparison, produced pale or lime-green

Colour Plate 90. Stream above Topke Gola at 12,500ft. (3,810m). This was a paradise for plant lovers with Silver fir (*Abies densa*), rhododendrons, berberis, cotoneasters, spiraeas and shrubby honeysuckles together with juniper and rust-coloured carpets of *Polygonum vacciniifolium.* (October)

Colour Plate 91. Hillside above Topke Gola covered in shrubs of many kinds. The rust-red patches are the dying leaves of *Polygonum vacciniifoliium.*(October)

Colour Plate 92. Overwintering rosettes of *Meconopsis napaulensis* were common throughout the Jaljale Himal and the Lumbasumba Himal further north. When mature these send up in June a stout many branched inflorescence of red, blue, purple or occasionally white flowers. (October)

Colour Plate 93 (far left). Our campsite above Topke Gola and the screes and hillsides around were notable for the golden hairy overwintering rosettes of *Meconopsis paniculata*. (October)

Colour Plate 94 (left). *Meconopsis paniculata*: plants flowering in the Royal Botanic Garden, Edinburgh, grown from seed collected above Topke Gola in October 1971. This species is monocarpic, dying after flowering and seeding. (June)

Colour Plate 95. *Meconopsis paniculata*, a large overwintering rosette of this glorious Himalayan poppy covered with golden bristly hairs. (October)

rosettes with paler bristles (Colour Plate 92). Late flowers all proved to be in the blue-lilac range, though from seed of B.L.&M.37 grown at Longstock Gardens near Stockbridge in Hampshire, a plant with breathtaking ruby-red flowers was produced. It is or was being maintained by careful seed selection as this species also is monocarpic. By contrast the stout clumps of *M. grandis* which we found in the vicinity of the lake are perennial with oblanceolate, dark-green, bristly leaves to 12in. (30.5cm) or more in length. Beer described having seen in July the single purplish-blue nodding or inclined flower atop a 3-4ft. (91-122cm) stem, a well-flowered plant creating a striding splash of colour amongst its native scrub and boulders. *M. grandis* is variable in flower colour, the most sought after forms being those with blue flowers. It was first discovered in 1881 among the ruins of some stone huts south of Kanchengjunga by George Watt (1851-1930), the Scottish Professor of Botany at Calcutta.

Under a large boulder on the hillside at a height of 14,500ft. (4,419m) we found the monocarpic *M. discigera* forming a dense tuft of oblanceolate leaves slightly lobed towards the tips. The seed capsules were barrel-shaped, 1in. (2.5cm) long with a conspicuous club-shaped style projecting for ½in. (1.25cm). They were borne in a few-branched panicle 12in. (30.5cm) tall and the whole plant was clothed in silky brown hairs. This is a handsome species when sporting its blue flowers and is well worth growing in one of its better colour forms. *M. sinuata*, another monocarpic species, we found only once on a rather wet patch of hillside. From a tuft of withered leaves arose several 2ft. (60cm) stems each bearing a single, elongated, bristly capsule. There were several plants in a limited area, and like so many of these hillside plants it enjoyed having its 'head' in the sun and its roots in a well-drained medium, liberally supplied with water at the critical time of growth. During his earlier recce in the Iswa valley Beer had seen this species with several purple flowers to each stem. The leaves he described as being curiously blotched with brown. During his previous visit to Topke Gola, Beer had found a single plant of *M. simplicifolia* growing beneath a rock face close to our campsite but there was now no sign of it.

Potentilla peduncularis formed extensive patches on the hillside. It looked very much like our native silverweed – *P. anserina* – with pinnate leaves, silvery silky (especially beneath), turning a rich reddish-brown in autumn. The flower too, according to Beer, resembles that of *P. anserina* being yellow, 1in. (2.5cm) across, borne several together at the top of a 9-12in. (23-30.5cm) stem. Another species, *P. cuneata,* was equally common on grassy banks and by streams, often on moist ground. Compared with the other this was a diminutive creeping plant forming pads of tiny trifoliolate leaves, the leaflets three-toothed at the apex. The yellow flowers too were smaller, ½in. (1.25cm) across, but produced in sufficient numbers to make the whole plant conspicuous, which is why it is a favourite with rock gardeners in Britain. Under a large boulder above the camp we found a peculiar withered plant with fruits that resembled small green tomatoes, except that they were almost enclosed by the five-lobed calyx and borne singly on an elongated fleshy stalk. Beer remembered having found it in July when it bore small greenish flowers. It later proved to be a Himalayan mandrake – *Mandragora caulescens,* a relative of the famous European mandrake of the ancients. Growing in some quantity on these slopes was *Primula calderiana* subspecies *strumosa.* In July Beer had found it covering our campsite in full flower, when it presented a heartening sight, the orange-eyed yellow flowers, ½-¾in. (1.25-2cm) across, borne in a many-flowered umbel atop a stout 10-15in. (25.5-38cm) scape (Colour Plate 97). At the time of our visit, however, the stems and leaves were withered and all that remained to indicate a living plant was a large, plump, pointed, green bud. We gently teased aside the outer scales to reveal the inner scales covered with a bright yellow farina. It resembled more a bulb than a resting bud.

Anemone polyanthes was frequent amongst the boulders strewn about the hillsides and Beer told us that in July he had found both white and apple blossom-pink flowered forms of this desirable perennial. Many of the banks by tracks and above the river which fed the lake were clothed with the creeping carpets of *Gaultheria trichophylla* and the carpeting stems of *Cotoneaster glacialis*. The two were often mixed and the comparatively large sky-blue fruits of the former contrasted with the red fruits of the latter (Colour Plate 96) to create a colourful, almost jewel-like, effect. Lots of *Primula capitata* was found in seed, and in wet ground by the lake and along the river banks two other species were fairly plentiful. The first of these, *P. hopeana*, seemed happy in either sun or shade and formed dense rosettes of oblanceolate, toothed, green leaves 6-10in. (15-25.5cm) long. The scapes were 12-18in. (30.5-45cm) high and at the time of Beer's arrival at Topke Gola in June bore umbels of nodding, bell-shaped, creamy-white flowers. This is closely related to *P. sikkimensis* and is regarded as the same by some authorities. It was named after J. Hope (1875-1970), a Yorkshireman who began his career at the University Botanic Garden, Cambridge, moving to the Royal Botanic Garden, Edinburgh, before joining A.K. Bulley as gardener at Ness in Cheshire. In one area *P. hopeana* formed drifts, even entering the shallow water at the edge of the lake. Accompanying the above species and sharing its sunnier locations was *P. megalocarpa (macrophylla* variety *macrocarpa)*, its stout clumps of lanceolate, fleshy, finely toothed leaves 6-10in. (15-25.5cm) long, covered beneath with a white farina. Beer described the flowers as being 1in. (2.5cm) long, lilac or purple in colour with a conspicuous calyx borne in six to twelve loose flowered umbels, terminating a 9in. (23cm) scape in June and July. In the same boggy areas as the primulas grew a delightful little alpine lousewort – *Pedicularis longiflora* variety *tubiformis* – whose tiny tufts of deeply cut leaves gave birth to the most delicate yellow, two-lipped flowers with corolla tubes 1½in. (3.75cm) long. It is an everlasting pity that the lousewort tribe are semi-parasites and difficult if not impossible to grow in cultivation. Our two British species give no clue to the immense variety to be found in the mountains of Europe and Asia.

When Beer had left Topke Gola in July the banks of the river above the lake had been lined with a deep-pink frothy cloud of *Myricaria rosea* in full flower. This dwarf shrub, a relation of the tamarisk *(Tamarix)*, formed dense clumps and mounds of slender plumose stems, the tiny leaves densely clustered along the purplish shoots, turning from summer green to red then rusty brown. As far as I am aware this species is not in general cultivation and although we collected abundant seed I have not heard of any success with its germination. Maybe, like the willow, its seed is of short duration and needs to be sown immediately on ripening. It would certainly repay someone to introduce a living plant into cultivation where it would surely be hardy and an excellent dwarf flowering shrub for exposed places, especially by the sea.

Colour Plate 96. *Cotoneaster glacialis* forms close carpets on slopes and over rocks above Topke Gola. This effective ground covering evergreen is rare in cultivation. (October)

Colour Plate 97. *Primula calderiana* subspecies *strumosa*, here growing in Bhutan. This species was frequent on and around our campsite above Topke Gola. The green resting buds are large and plump. (April)

Colour Plate 98. A glorious tangle of shrubs and conifers on a hillside at 12,500ft. (3,810m) above Topke Gola. Junipers, *Juniperus recurva* and *J. squamata,* dominate with berberis, cotoneasters, shrubby honeysuckle and a lone Silver fir (*Abies densa*) left of centre. (October)

Colour Plate 99. A fine stand of Silver fir (*Abies densa*) with *Juniperus recurva* in the foreground on a hillside above Topke Gola. The brownish-orange deciduous shrub is a *Berberis* species. (October)

Colour Plate 100. *Clematis montana*, here growing in a garden in Derbyshire. This well-known and hardy vigorous scrambler was originally introduced from northern India by Lady Amherst in 1831. It was common in thickets and woodlands throughout our journey in the mountains of east Nepal. (May)

On grassy rock ledges above the lake we found a dwarf tap-rooted member of the carrot family – *Umbelliferae*. No more than 8in. (20cm) high, the many radiating branches terminated in a dense cluster of fruits with a ruff of conspicuous bracts. The whole seed head was dome-shaped and several inches across, whilst the pinnate leaves formed a basal rosette. The entire plant possessed a strong smell of fennel and we were delighted to learn later from the British Museum (Natural History) that this plant was *Pleurospermopsis sikkimensis* and new to Nepal.

In the shelter of the deciduous forest beyond the lake grew large quantities of *Cremanthodium reniforme*, its nodding daisy heads seeding on 6-12in. (15-30.5cm) stems above the long-stalked, boldly toothed, kidney-shaped leaves. The monotypic *Megacodon stylophorus* also occurred here, its bold hosta-like basal leaves supporting a 3ft. (90cm) leafy stem. A member of the gentian family, it bears a 10-12in. (25.5-30.5cm) raceme of eight to ten pendant yellowish-green flowers in July. This rare species would be much in demand if it were in cultivation, its foliage alone being worthy of inclusion on the rock garden, scree or in the peat garden.

The shrubby flora of these hillsides mainly consisted of spiraea, juniper, berberis and cotoneaster. *Spiraea arcuata* reached 6-8ft. (1.85-2.5m), its arching, angled stems, densely clothed with obovate leaves, toothed in the upper half. The pink flowers which Beer had seen in June were now brown seed capsules borne in tight corymbs all along the upper sides of the branches. It was common in scrub, and plants are now established in the Hillier Arboretum and elsewhere. Its most frequent companions were *Berberis angulosa* and *Cotoneaster staintonii*. The former shrub, with its erect reddish, ribbed stems and dark green clustered leaves, is not one of the most desirable species except in autumn when the deciduous leaves turn a brilliant crimson, creating an effect of flames on the hillsides visible for some distance. I have since seen numerous pictures taken of autumn scenes in the Himalaya and the rich colour of this berberis can be detected in many of them. Unfortunately it rarely colours as well in English cultivation where it remains an uncommon shrub, mainly grown for its comparatively large orange-yellow flowers and scarlet fruits. In Nepal these fruits vary in shape from rotund to oblong and are eaten by Sherpas and Tibetans. The erect branches of the cotoneaster attained greater heights – 6-8ft. (1.85-2.5m) – with hairy, elliptic, pointed leaves to 2in. (5cm) long. The oblong red fruits ⅔in. (1.70cm) long were borne singly in the axils of the leaves.

A small shrubby honeysuckle – *Lonicera myrtillus* – formed occasional mounds of tangled branches 3½ft. (1m) high with small narrowly oblong leaves, turning bright yellow. The red fruits, though freely produced, were rather small. *Ribes luridum* was in the same category, its small red currants being no compensation for the untidy habit and small three to five lobed leaves. It was, nevertheless, common in mixed scrub in sun or shade.

The junipers, however, were the most noticeable members of the hillside community (Colour Plate 98). Three species were involved *Juniperus recurva, J. squamata* and *J. indica*. The first of these made a tree with a single main stem up to 25ft. (7.5m) high, though there was evidence that larger specimens had been felled in the past and there remained on one hillside a few decrepit trees of large girth. It varied enormously in appearance, some specimens being open branched and gracefully drooping, whilst others were as dense and compact as many Lawson cypresses seen in cultivation. All forms had brown flaky bark and the characteristic nodding or drooping branchlets. The colour too, was variable and we found forms with rich-green, sea-green and silvery-green foliage. The black fruits, ½in. (1.25cm) long, contained a single seed. As seen at Topke Gola, this juniper is a variable species with many forms of high ornamental merit, far more so than the trees one normally encounters in cultivation in the British Isles. *J. squamata* seems closely connected in the field with *J. recurva*. Both species showed similar variations in foliage, form and colour. However, even in young specimens, the latter possessed a single leader whilst the former was multi-stemmed and shrubby.

J. squamata in the Topke Gola area encompassed a wide assortment of forms. There were those of low, dense and compact habit, similar to certain named forms in present cultivation, whilst at the other extreme were those taller, often gawky forms of less ornamental merit. The majority had ascending branches, developing a vase-shaped habit similar to the Pfitzer juniper (*J.* 'Pfitzeriana'). Foliage varied in colour through several shades of green to grey and blue. Some forms had long slender branchlets, others were short and congested. Seed of many forms was collected and resultant plants are now established in many collections including the Hillier Arboretum. In some locations these two species were present in such great numbers that the spectacle would have daunted or else delighted a taxonomist. In contrast, *J. indica* formed dense low patches of rich deep-green foliage. It rarely mixed with the other two.

Abies densa grew to a large size in the valley above Topke Gola (Colour Plate 99). One venerable specimen had a huge bole containing a hole large enough for a man to pass through, caused no doubt by fire. An unfortunate habit of the hill people, especially herdsmen, is the lighting of fires at the base of large trees. The tree, of course, offers a measure of shelter, but it was distressing to see the number of trees damaged in this way. One day I climbed up a small specimen of this fir in order to pick the cones from the upper branches. Later that same day I wandered beneath a grove of superb giants of around 150ft. (45.5m) high, their boles clothed with moss and polypody ferns. Some large specimens had been felled using the fire method and we were able to pick cones in some quantity. Despite the intentional and accidental destruction of these firs it was gratifying to see a great deal of regeneration taking place, the young saplings forming dense thickets in some places.

Rhododendrons occurred in quantity especially *R. campanulatum* which formed dense thickets, often with *R. wightii,* whilst *R. campylocarpum* and *R. cinnabarinum* were nearly as common. The large leaved *R. hodgsonii* was conspicuous though only as scattered large individuals.

Clematis montana (Colour Plate 100) was in fruit, its silky seed tassels flaunted all along the stems as they scrambled into trees and over shrubs. *Aconitum spicatum* was present in several clearings in the fir forest, and on our way back to the camp one day we found the seeding capsules of *Parnassia nubicola* scattered through a lakeside bog. This species, widespread in the Himalaya was first introduced to cultivation by Countess Amherst (Plate 36).

The villagers were most inquisitive and looked upon our presence as something the gods had arranged. They regularly visited our camp simply to

Plate 36. Countess Amherst (1762-1838) wife of Lord Amherst, Governor General of India 1823-1828. Lady Amherst collected many Indian plants while accompanying her husband on his travels. Some at least were procured from the back of an elephant. The genus *Amherstia* is named after her. She was the first European to introduce *Clematis montana* and *Anemone vitifolia* to Europe (England)

Colour Plate 101. *Picrorhiza scrophulariifolia*, a creeping herb of the figwort family *(Scrophulariaceae)*. Its roots were seen in Topke Gola laid out on mats to dry in the sun. They contain a bitter substance called picrorhizin used medicinally as a stomatic tonic and as a febrifuge. This specimen was photographed in the mountains of Kashmir. (July)

Colour Plate 102. Valley at 12,500ft. (3,810m) above Topke Gola. This is a botanist's paradise full of Silver fir, juniper, rhododendron, berberis, cotoneasters, clematis, with gentians and meconopsis in season. A fitting last resting place for a plant explorer! (October)

Colour Plate 103. *Soroseris pumila:* a curious composite, its woolly rosette well camouflaged amongst the rocks and grit at the edge of a scree above Topke Gola. (October)

stand and stare. Predictably the children were the least inhibited and they followed our every move, sometimes to our embarrassment (Plate 37). The Tibetan child is expected to take its share of the family chores just as soon as it is able to walk. Little girls carried even younger brothers and sisters on their backs, and every day a small band of urchins of both sexes would stop off at the camp on their way to collect firewood in the hills. Several carried sharp kukris tucked into their cummerbunds and a coil of rope over their shoulders (Plate 38). The children looked sticky and dirty but were possessed of the most disarming smiles. One small boy helped milk the yaks each day by binding the yaks' back feet together so they could not escape.

One day we were invited to visit the panchayat leader at his home in the village, and this was our first social contact with the Bhotias. The night before had witnessed a storm in the hills to the south, and although we caught only the edge of it, the campsite was running with water and the kitchen tent had blown down. We arrived in the village in good time anxious not to displease the panchayat leader. Our host bade us climb up the steps of his home and we immediately entered a dark passage-way full of pungent and unfamiliar smells. We moved slowly forward stumbling over pigs, goats, cats, dogs, chickens and children, in that order, all intent on leaving. Finally we sensed ourselves in a much larger space and our fingers searched urgently for signs of contact until at last they touched and were held by a warm hand. The hand belonged to our hostess who then led us gently to a place where a fire spluttered on a stone flag set into the wooden floor.

We sat down with our backs against the planked wall and as our eyes strained to take in our surroundings we saw faces gradually materialising from the shadows around. There were long faces, fat faces, old faces, young faces, faces etched with age and experience, faces with the shine of innocence. Yet all the faces had one thing in common – they all smiled and nodded as if to reassure us that we were among friends.

We were handed tompas (wooden containers like steins without handles) and urged to drink the contents – chang or mountain beer. This we did by sucking at a wooden 'straw' which entered through a hole in the lid of the vessel. The warm milky-white liquid seemed immediately to enter the blood stream and all memories of the recent storm receded to be replaced by an increasing desire to

Plate 37 (right). A lovable little urchin from Topke Gola who came to our camp most days to see what we were up to

Plate 38 (far right). Bhotia girl from Topke Gola pausing on her way to gather fuel for her family's fire. Note the kukri for cutting branches and a rope to bind them

laugh and sing. The faces smiled encouragingly and our hostess immediately topped up our tompas from a hot kettle, ignoring our mild protestations.

Chang is made by fermenting any one of several grains, mainly rice, maize or millet. Our current brew originated from the latter source and each draw on the 'straw' filled the mouth with a myriad of tiny seeds which, if one was not to offend, had to be swallowed without trace of displeasure. Those westerners who do not like caraway cake would not have enjoyed the experience.

Whilst we sat thus, drinking and smiling, my eyes wandered around the room taking in the shadowy corners, the corn-cobs hanging from the low ceiling and the dull glow of pans and containers. They then came to rest on the fire which struggled beneath a heap of green juniper wood and leaves. This unhappy combination gave off a dark acrid smoke which spiralled to the ceiling where, unable to escape, it billowed out in an ever-threatening blanket. It then occurred to me that this chimneyless abode contained no windows either and, as a result, the smoke and occupants were prisoners together. I looked again at the ceiling and realised to my horror that the smoke was fast descending in an all-enveloping cloud. We shrank to the floor as the smoke settled and then we were struggling to our feet, shaking numerous hands, gasping sounds of thanks. Down the passage we staggered, pursued by the smoke, stumbling over children, chickens, dogs, cats, goats and pigs all trying to get in. Down the steps we tumbled, eyes streaming, chests heaving, gulping the cool mountain air.

When we were still in the foothills at Side Pokhara and had already tasted several meals in which dried potato had formed the main ingredient, Pema had met our grumbling with the solemn promise: 'When we get into the mountains Sahib, where it is cold and they grow many potatoes, I will make you chips.' Accordingly, when we reached the mountains at Topke Gola where it was cold, Pema was despatched in search of potatoes. He returned one afternoon with a small basket of them, each no bigger thin a pigeon's egg (Plate 39). To a Sherpa, however, a promise is a promise and he prepared each and every one and we had chips with our evening meal. The main course was a kind of pasty called moma by the Sherpas. It was a pastry case stuffed with chopped vegetables and a meat which was far more tasty and tender than the scrawny chickens we had been used to. It was not until we had eaten the last pasty that

Plate 39. Pema our Sherpa cook with a plate of local potatoes at Topke Gola. They were our first in over a month and tasted delicious when fried

Pema told us that the source of the meat was the lovely Blood pheasant, a brace of which he had purchased from a villager. Fresh yak milk is rich compared with cow milk but was welcome after the dried milk we had been using. But, pheasant and chips apart, far from living on local fare, we found that few villagers were in a position to sell food, let alone share it, and we relied on our dried meals, though sugar and rice were two commodities in reasonably plentiful supply and on two occasions Dawa and two assistants were sent down the Mewa Khola on shopping expeditions.

On our arrival in the camp at Topke Gola we had found two new Sherpa porters, both girls in their late teens. Berma was a plump girl with an active imagination and a tongue to match. Mile was by contrast slender and of shy disposition. Both came from the village of Sedua in the Upper Arun valley and had accompanied Beer on his reconnaissance. Berma and Mile were sisters of Dorje and Tende respectively, both of whom we had engaged as porters in Dharan. Apart from these Sherpa porters, nearly all the others had been paid off and had returned to their villages in the valleys.

One day Morris and I decided to explore the valley which we had travelled down on the day we entered Topke Gola. On our way to the village with the Sherpa Da Norbu, we encountered the lama on his way to the temple by the lake. He possessed a wonderful face, as brown as a date. His black hair he had plaited into a pigtail and he wore a long claret woollen gown.

A family group was sitting outside its village house spreading plant material on a bamboo mat to dry in the sun. The man of the house told us that the plant was collected in the mountains and was a powerful medicine against stomach troubles. On closer examination it proved to be *Picrorhiza scrophulariifolia (kurooa)*, a humble member of the *Scrophulariaceae* (Colour Plate 101). It is a creeping plant forming tufts of spoon-shaped toothed leaves 2-6in. (5-15cm) long and dense racemes 4-6in. (10-15cm) long of small pale-blue flowers with conspicuous protruding stamens in July and August. According to B.O. Coventry, *Wild Flowers of Kashmir,* the root and rootstock contain a bitter substance called picrorhizin. The crude drug appears on the market in the form of short dry pieces of root and is used medicinally as a stomatic tonic and as a febrifuge.

We left Da Norbu to wash the expedition laundry in the village stream and proceeded up the valley and into the trees which were a glorious jungle of fir, juniper and birch (Colour Plate 102). We first found a plant which reminded me of our native golden rod – *Solidago virgaurea,* with its narrow elliptic leaves and slender raceme of widely spaced, nodding, yellow flowerheads. It turned out to be *Youngia racemifera,* presumably named after Alfred R. Young (1841-1920) who collected plants in Kashmir. We reached the open hillside at a place where a long narrow landslip had recently taken place. Here several trees attracted our attention beginning with *Acer caudatum (papilio),* a small tree with a handsome grey or brownish-grey flaky bark. Several of these trees had been damaged by fire at some stage in the past and strong basal sucker growths were already well developed. The deeply five-lobed irregularly toothed leaves were a rich green in colour and carried on rhubarb-red petioles which, like the young shoots, were finely pubescent. There were tufts of greyish hairs in the axils of the main veins

Colour Plate 104. *Sorbus foliolosa (ursina)*. This tree, here growing in the Hillier Arboretum, Hampshire, was the first introduction of the species to western cultivation. Its seed was collected in Nepal by Col. Donald Lowndes in 1950. We found it common in the woods around Topke Gola. (September 1973)

Colour Plate 105 (right). *Betula utilis*: the orange-brown peeling papery old bark of a young tree growing in a valley above Topke Gola. The Himalayan birch is widely distributed along the mountains of northern India from Kashmir in the west to Bhutan and China in the east. (October)

Colour Plate 106 (far right). *Prunus rufa*, a little known Himalayan cherry with attractive peeling bark, frequent in the hills above Topke Gola and now in cultivation. (October)

Colour Plate 107. *Sorbus foliolosa (ursina)*. The same tree as seen in Colour Plate 104, but showing its autumn colour. (October 1974)

beneath. The bunches of red winged fruits were mostly empty of seed and as far as I am aware only one seedling resulted from this collection. *Sorbus foliolosa (ursina)* was our next find, a small spreading tree 15ft. (4.5m) high with pinnate leaves, the leaflets covered beneath with a grey rufous-tinged tomentum. The few fruits which remained were coloured a dark crimson and would no doubt turn to white eventually (Colour Plates 104 and 107). Several trees of *Betula utilis* were conspicuous by their rich orange-brown peeling bark (Colour Plate 105), and we collected the seed of a particularly fine specimen. Accompanying these trees was a small cherry up to 18ft. (5.5m) high with a spreading head of branches. The leaves were elliptic, toothed and long acuminate, 3-4in. (7.5-10cm) long, rounded at base and with glands on petiole and leaf base. It was the bark, however, that caught our attention, varying between individuals from blackish-brown to a warm amber and peeling in the best *Prunus serrula* tradition. It was as ornamental as this well-known Tibetan cherry, having the same polished shaggy appearance. Some trees were single stemmed, whilst others had several stems from a common base. Only a few small fruits could be found on the branches. These were ellipsoid, ½in. (1.25cm) long, green at first turning to red and finally shining black, borne singly on a 1-2in. (2.5-5cm) drooping stalk. We scratched around in the debris beneath several trees without success and came to the conclusion that the fruits are eaten by birds before they have chance to fall. We argued about the identity of this cherry for the rest of the expedition, but not until the British Museum (Natural History) examined our specimens did we hear that it was *Prunus rufa* (Colour Plate 106). This species is present, though rarely, in cultivation and a form has been grown by Hilliers for many years but with a close unimpressive bark. According to Bean, the Nepalese tree is forma *trichantha*. From the few seeds we collected only one germinated. This now grows in the Hillier Arboretum, whilst plants grafted from this specimen have been sent to Wakehurst Place, Sussex, and to Maurice Mason's collection at Fincham in Norfolk. As we stood admiring the cherries on the hillside we saw a flash of white and looked up just in time to see a flock of Snow pigeons coming in to land on the cliffs above, their white underparts sharply contrasting with the dark upperparts.

The next day was a lovely sunny morning which augered well for our collecting on the screes. These vast seas of broken rock and rubble seemed almost to be moving beneath one's feet. From the high crags which gave them birth they stretched for almost a mile before emptying into the belly of the valley. It was surprising that plants survived in this terrain let alone flourished. The cruel winds from Tibet came howling over the fanged ridges to pounce on animal and plant alike. They swept across the screes cutting down to size anything that dared to rise above a certain height. Within the body of the scree ran long depressions of larger rocks where plants had managed to establish themselves and live what was at best a precarious existence.

Leontopodium himalayanum was fairly common here and seemed little different from the edelweiss of Europe. *Soroseris pumila* was another composite but very different from the last. Its leafy stem, 3-4in. (7.5-10cm) long, was concealed by the dust and grit in which it grew so that the slightly domed inflorescence, 1½-2in. (3.75-5cm) across, rested on the ground and appeared stemless (Colour Plate 103). The inflorescence was surrounded by greyish-brown hairy leaves, and when not in flower was difficult to distinguish from the surrounding ground. The individual flowers possessed four yellow-ray florets each with a single style. They opened first along the margin, gradually moving in towards the centre. It was a peculiar plant, not without merit, but probably not worth cultivating. Our old friend *Saussurea gossypiphora* turned up again and we were later told that it was collected and dried by the lama at Topke Gola who burned it on special occasions in honour of the lake goddess.

A tiny catchfly – *Silene setisperma (Lychnis inflata)* – grew very commonly between the stones, a delicate plant for such a hostile place as this. Its slender 3-4in. (7.5-10cm) stem bore a terminal nodding flower ⅔in. (1.70cm) long. This consisted of an inflated calyx, parchment-white and slightly transparent, with ten narrow brown ridges. The tips of the five free purple petals protruded from the mouth of the calyx and were similarly coloured (Colour Plate 111).

Tanacetum gossypinum (Chrysanthemum gossypinum) occurred in some quantity, growing with the slender-stemmed white-flowered *Arabidopsis himalaica*. In an area of shifting grit we came upon *Delphinium glaciale* forming tufts of deeply cut palmate leaves, from out of which the comparatively large blue-purple flowers protruded (Colour Plate 110). It looked very similar to the *D. nepalense* we had previously seen, and we were still debating this similarity when a wind swept across the screes bringing with it a blinding sleet. We were so caught by the suddenness of the wind that we could only crouch close to the ground in a huddle and wait for it to pass. We waited no more than ten minutes and when we rose to our feet the entire scree was white with powdered snow. We continued on our way across the shattered boulders and rocks until a long deep depression opened up before us. The first thing to attract our attention was an animal the size of a hare and dark bluish-grey in colour. We saw only the back end of it as it darted out of sight beneath a large boulder. This sudden disturbance flushed an Impeyan pheasant from its hiding place and as it glided on outstretched wings down the depression we had an excellent view of its upper parts. The iridescence of its purple wings and cinnamon-coloured tail were breathtaking, and with the distinctive snow-white patch on its back it is one of the Himalaya's most beautiful birds.

A stream ran along the depression, tumbling in miniature waterfalls down steep rocks. Colonising the streamside for a considerable length was a most striking and unusual perennial which we later identified as *Saussurea obvallata*. Although it thrived by the streamside we also later found it established on the open scree where, however, its stems were invariably broken and shattered. It begins life as a stout basal clump of lanceolate to oblanceolate toothed leaves 12in. (30.5cm) or more long. From the centre of the clump emerge several stout leafy stems 18-24in. (45-61cm) tall, each bearing at its summit a dense cluster of large shell-like creamy-white bracts which collectively form a hemispherical cocoon around the cluster of thistle-like flowerheads (Colour Plates 108 and 109). What an intriguing species this is, related to the cotton wool plant *S. gossypiphora,* having the same basic thistle flowers, yet in totally different guise. We collected lots of seed and though much of this germinated I never heard that plants had successfully flowered in cultivation.

The depression proved rich in species, because of its comparatively sheltered and stable condition. Stout 4-5in. (10-13cm) clumps of the small leaved *Rhodiola quadrifida* occupied moist shady pockets, and the terminal clusters of red flowers shone in the darkness. This species would enjoy similar places in

Colour Plate 108 (right). *Saussurea obvallata*, a curious short-lived perennial, was common on the screes above Topke Gola. (October)

Colour Plate 109 (far right). *Saussurea obvallata*: the creamy-white cocoon of large shell-like bracts protect a terminal cluster of thistle-like flowerheads. (October)

Colour Plate 110. *Delphinium glaciale*, a choice pale blue-violet flowered monkshood eking out a living amongst the rocks on the screes above Topke Gola. (October)

Colour Plate 111 (far left). *Silene setisperma*, formerly known as *Lychnis inflata*. This diminutive alpine catchfly with its parchment coloured red striped and inflated calyx was plentiful among the rocks on the screes above Topke Gola. (October)

Colour Plate 112 (left). Vast screes like moving seas of rock and rubble at the head of a valley above Topke Gola. The author standing with Beer and the Sherpa Da Norbu debating the merits of a creeping willow – *Salix lindleyana*. A surprising number of fascinating plants find a home in this inhospitable terrain. (October)

Colour Plate 113. The cottonwool seed masses of a creeping alpine willow – *Salix lindleyana* – looked from a distance like the remains of a dead sheep. The seeds have a limited viability. (October)

the garden as our native roseroot *Rhodiola rosea*. A charming find was *Thalictrum elegans,* a delicate plant with finely divided glaucous green leaves and 3-6in. (7.5-15cm) panicles of tiny purple fruits. The desirability of this plant in fruit is misleading as the flowers are small greenish-purple and of little or no ornamental merit. Crowding the streamside for as far as the eye could see was a saxifrage with clumps of erect fleshy stems 6-8in. (15-20cm) high, clothed with obovate fleshy leaves 1½-2in. (3.75-5cm) long turning purple or red as winter approached. The flowers were yellow, ½in. (1.25cm) across, each petal with two orange spots on its inside base. It was identified by the British Museum (Natural History) as *Saxifraga moorcroftiana*, named after William Moorcroft (1765-1825), a Lancashire man and a veterinary surgeon in the East India Company who collected plants with Nathaniel Wallich in Nepal.

On many parts of the scree we encountered large patches of cotton wool which looked from a distance like dead and decayed sheep. On closer inspection they proved to be prostrate willows – *Salix lindleyana* – in fruit (Colour Plates 112 and 113). In certain exposed stony areas we discovered groups of the delicate *Primula buryana* with rosettes of ovate, toothed, hairy leaves 1-2in. (2.5-5cm) long. The 3-4in. (7.5-10cm) stems carried white flowers ¾in. (2cm) long. We grew a few plants at the Hillier Arboretum from this seed but they did not thrive.

The depression developed into a narrow gully which we climbed down disturbing at one point a pair of Sooty wrens who flew further down the gully and out of sight. After a while we encountered dense scrub in which *Rhododendron campanulatum* and *R. wightii* predominated, and feeling too tired to retrace our steps, and with the light diminishing, we were obliged to force our way through the thicket for several hundred yards before reaching the valley track, along which we trudged wearily back to camp.

We spent the next morning sitting on the hillside above camp collecting seed and writing up our notes. Da Norbu had been down to the village and returned with small blocks of stone-like material which he assured us was Tibetan cheese. It was yellow-brown in colour and appeared remote from my favourite creations from Caerphilly, Wensleydale and Lancashire. In fact I have several times since shown a piece of this material to audiences describing it as a dinosaur's toe-nail and many have believed me until told the truth. The cheese is made from yaks' milk and when first formed is packed into linen bags and strung up under the rafters in the main living area. In time, and influenced by warmth and smoke, the cheese solidifies and when required needs to be chopped into pieces with a kukri. Small pieces are popped into the mouth and sucked rather like a caramel but harder and longer lasting. I remember my grandfather telling me how, in Mesopotamia, as a soldier on the march, he would suck a pebble or small smooth stone to keep the salival glands active. Tibetan cheese was used similarly by travellers in the hills, and we found it quite refreshing once we had grown used to the idea. There was very little taste and if I had been given a piece to try whilst blindfolded I would have imagined I was sucking a piece of flint.

On the lake we could see a family group of six surface-feeding ducks. They had been there for several days and occasionally called to each other in a goose-like manner. Once, when they flew we saw their striking pattern, consisting of a pale biscuit-coloured back and under-parts, creamy-brown head, white upper wings and black tail and wing primaries. They were Ruddy shelducks and seemed quite at home in their mountain fastness, very different from the maritime habitat of the common species.

Da Norbu helped me clean seed and talked in a slow uncertain English, using his hands and facial expressions to emphasise a particular point. He was a short, strong, stocky fellow and I was surprised therefore to learn that some years ago he had damaged his back in a climbing accident and had spent much of the time since then in various hospitals in Nepal and India. This was his first expedition since his recovery and I had many occasions on which to ponder this fact with amazement and disbelief. Da Norbu's father, Ang Norbu, had been a high altitude porter for several expeditions including the Swiss Everest Expedition of 1952 and the successful British Everest Expedition the following year. Twice for the British he carried to the South Col, 26,200ft. (7,985m), and was awarded a Coronation Medal by the Queen. Sadly he died in an avalanche on Cho Oyu (26,000ft./7,925m) whilst with the British Women's Expedition to Nepal in 1959.

Morris had headed towards the ridge above and after lunch I explored the cliffs on the same hillside. I disturbed a variegated Laughing thrush whose plumage appeared mainly greenish with a black and white face. It called continuously and seemed in a bad humour, belying its common name. I felt the sun warm on me and lay on the ground staring at the sky. A noise of birds calling came to my ears and twisting my head I saw a flock of Alpine choughs floating and wheeling in the air currents above the cliffs. They behaved like a troupe of clowns, flying first in formation then breaking up and weaving about, all the time calling as jackdaws do. Occasionally two would break away and a mock battle would ensue as they tumbled through the air always disengaging and sweeping to safety just above the ground.

Scents both sweet and earthy drifted up to me from the pastures, and far below in the valley I could see the orange tents of our camp, and below that the village houses blurred every so often by wisps of smoke escaping through the many cracks. I must have lain thus for some time because I was suddenly aware of the temperature cooling and a change in the light intensity. Climbing to my feet I followed a circuitous route back to camp collecting on my way seed of *Fritillaria cirrhosa* and *Morina nepalensis*.

Beer had returned from a seed-collecting trip in the village area where he had previously marked several plants in flower. These included a pale-yellow flowered form of *Rosa sericea* and a prostrate member of the *Leguminosae* called *Gueldenstadtia himalaica*. This pretty little alpine formed mats of tiny pinnate leaves plastered with purple pea flowers 1in. (2.5cm) long borne singly on short erect stalks. *Aster stracheyi* was another of his finds, a tufted perennial with long-stalked, elliptical basal leaves and 24in. (61cm) hairy reddish stems bearing a single purple-rayed flowerhead 1in. (2.5cm) across. The name commemorates Sir Robert Strachey (1817-1908) of the Bombay Engineers who collected in north-west Himalaya and adjacent Tibet. On the way up the hill Beer had collected a large amount of small shining red berries ¼in. (.65cm) across which belonged to *Hemiphragma heterophyllum*, a perennial member of the *Scrophulariaceae*, whose loosely trailing pubescent brown stems were to be found throughout the Topke Gola area. The toothed ovate to rounded leaves ¼in. (.65cm) long occurred in opposite pairs and were very different from the tiny linear leaves which occurred in bunches on the numerous axillary branches.

Colour Plate 114. The Giant Himalayan Lily *Cardiocrinum giganteum* here growing at Wakehurst Place in Sussex. This group is part of one of the largest drifts in cultivation containing upwards of a thousand individuals. (June)

Colour Plate 115. *Cardiocrinum giganteum* at Wakehurst Place in Sussex. The striking creamy-white trumpet-shaped flowers are stained purple within and possess a delicious fragrance. (June)

Colour Plate 116. *Cotoneaster integrifolius,* here growing in a garden in Durham, was abundant on hillsides around Topke Gola. Commonly cultivated under the name *C. microphyllus*, it is stronger growing than *C. glacialis* with which it often grows in the wild, forming mounds and hummocks of tiny dark almost blackish-green shining evergreen leaves. (May)

7. THE GOLDEN EDELWEISS

Many times during our journey across the Jaljale Himal we had listened to Beer's stories of the plants he had seen on his reconnaissance. One of these, the giant lily, *Cardiocrinum giganteum,* he had found in June amongst boulders and trees in the Mewa Khola valley, a day's march below Topke Gola. It was then in full flower with 5-8ft. (1.5-2.5m) sturdy leafy stems bearing a terminal raceme of six to eight large, pendant, creamy-white trumpets (Colour Plates 114 and 115). It was because of this and other finds that Beer and I decided to spend a couple of days seed collecting down this valley. Leaving Morris and the others in camp, and taking Da Norbu with us, we climbed down the hill to Topke Gola and followed a track leading from the village into the woods below. It was a gorgeous morning and we were in high spirits singing our favourite melodies in between discussing the interesting plants we might see. The river tumbled and crashed a few yards below us and its sound was a constant companion as we followed the track through Himalayan Silver fir and birch and beneath archways of rhododendron. Passing between two steep banks we found *Cotoneaster integrifolius* (Colour Plate 116) covering one side and *C. glacialis* equally common on the other. Further on we found both species growing together in a tangled carpet. *Cotoneaster congestus* with duller green, more pointed leaves was also present on the slopes above.

A berberis species was frequent, its leaves just beginning to turn orange and red. It was a robust shrub with erect stems 8-10ft. (2.5-3m) high, the young shoots bearing obovate, slightly spinose leaves 1-1½in. (2.5-3.75cm) long. The dark red oblong fruits were borne in long clusters. Which species this was I have been unable to discover and all attempts to have the herbarium specimens named have so far proved futile. It would seem that the very mention of berberis defeats most botanists, although in recent times Dr. David Chamberlain of the Royal Botanic Garden, Edinburgh, has made a brave attempt. There is a story told by gardeners about one of their kind who marched into a well-known herbarium on a busy mid-week morning clutching a bagful of unnamed berberis specimens collected from his garden. Unfortunately for him he made the mistake of announcing the reasons for his visit in a loud voice, at which the department emptied as a dozen athletic botanists sought out those corners and hideaways so plentiful in such places.

To be fair, it is well known that berberis, like willows, are promiscuous, and cultivated berberis can be a nightmare even to one familiar with their goings-on. I remember Harold Hillier telling me about a visit paid to his nurseries many years ago by Camillo Schneider, the German botanist who named and described many of E.H. Wilson's Chinese berberis introductions. Schneider had asked permission to collect specimens in the Hillier nurseries and, aware of the reputation of both botanist and berberis, Hillier was puzzled therefore to see Schneider cutting specimens he knew to be seed grown from cultivated sources. At the end of the day Schneider thanked Hillier profusely for his generosity and left carrying a large hamper stuffed with berberis specimens of

Colour Plate 117. *Ribes himalense*, a Himalayan red currant, was common in the Mewa Khola valley, its ruby like berries hanging in strings from the leaf axils. (October)

as mixed an origin as could be devised, a veritable Pandora's box. What became of the specimens no one seems to know. Hillier heard no further from Schneider who died in 1951. His manuscript on the genus *Berberis* and presumably his specimens as well were apparently destroyed by fire during the allied bombing of Berlin in the Second World War.

Prunus rufa occurred in the valley as scattered individuals, its dark burnished peeling bark contrasting with the orange-brown peeling bark of *Betula utilis*. Some of the firs – *Abies densa* – reached heights in excess of 150ft. (45.5m), most of them clothed with epiphytes. Lower down the valley the branches of old firs were almost entirely encased in a yellowish-green, cushion-like moss, whilst several burned-out shells remained as evidence of indiscriminate burning. Da Norbu told us that in the Solo-Khumbu region of Nepal, this habit is prohibited, fines of 100 rupees being exacted from proven offenders. *Sorbus microphylla* was quite plentiful above the river, its canopy a cloud of orange and yellow as the leaves turned. *Viburnum nervosum (cordifolium)* occupied similar locations, forming a large multi-stemmed shrub 18-20ft. (5.5-6m) high with stellately hairy young shoots and buds. On several specimens the heart-shaped, toothed, hairy leaves, 4-7in. (10-18cm) long, had turned a deep crimson, whilst the shining black fruits were borne in dense corymbs. Clambering 18ft. (5.5m) into the branches of a cherry were the rope-like stems of *Clematis connata*, with its large trifoliolate leaves. The leaflets were ovate-acuminate, rounded at base, three-lobed and sharply toothed, each on a long stalk. It was then in seed but a month or more earlier it would have been showing its bell-shaped soft yellow flowers in panicles, rather like a larger edition of the Chinese *C. rehderiana*. Few alpine currants are decorative enough for gardens but *Ribes himalense* looked most becoming on the rocks above the river. It reached 6-8ft. (1.85-2.5m) in height with palmately lobed leaves 2-3in. (5-7.5cm) across and long pendulous strings of red currants which glistened in the sun (Colour Plate 117).

Acer caudatum became frequent, especially in the several clearings through which our track ran. In these clearings the Himalayan Bird cherry – *Prunus cornuta* – had been planted as orchards, some trees quite old with rounded crowns and gnarled trunks (Colour Plate 118). In one such place we found a wooden house occupied by a Bhotia family from Thudam. We decided to have lunch here and whilst Da Norbu was preparing a fire we watched a colourfully dressed old woman spinning wool so fast that the eye could scarcely follow. She sat on the grass surrounded by heaps of variously dyed wools, including some of a beautiful deep blue which had stained her hands.

Over lunch we followed the activities of a pair of White-capped redstarts that flitted about on the rocks below us. After lunch we continued down the valley which now became deeper and narrower and more of a steep-sided gorge, into which the vegetation crowded in dense masses. *Rhododendron hodgsonii* and *R. campylocarpum* were joined by *R. barbatum*, and the giant fir was now replaced by the equally giant Himalayan hemlock – *Tsuga dumosa*. It is a pity that this conifer is tender in the British Isles as it makes such a lovely symmetrical tree, quite the equal of the hardier western North American *T. heterophylla*. There was a zone, around 10,000ft. (3,048m), where both fir and hemlock mingled before separating into their respective territories.

The large-leaved evergreen *Berberis insignis* appeared by the track carrying axillary clusters of ellipsoid black fruits ⅔in. (1.70cm) long (Colour Plate 119), and many ferns now occupied the banks and other shady places above the river. The berberis is rare in cultivation, where it requires plenty of space in which to develop. I have a young plant from Beer's second Nepal expedition and it attracts by its large glossy leaves and few-spined stems. Much larger specimens I have seen at Exbury Gardens, near Southamton, and at Clyne Castle near Swansea. We could tell from the gradual change in vegetation that conditions were becoming more amenable to plant life and we were not surprised to find *Rhododendron arboreum, Acer pectinatum, Osmanthus suavis* and an evergreen *Symplocos* making an appearance. *Carpinus viminea* was also frequent here. If ever there was a tree I should like to introduce into cultivation it is this beautiful Himalayan hornbeam. Its leaves are attractively toothed, parallel veined and coppery-red when newly emerged. I have seen it several times since in Nepal, Bhutan and Kashmir but never in fruit (Colour Plate 120).

At one point the track skirted the foot of a wet moss-covered shady rock-face on which a colony of *Primula geraniifolia* was well ensconced. The long-stalked, rounded, hairy leaves 3-3½in. (7.5-9cm) across were sharply toothed and bore numerous small pointed lobes. Although now in seed, when Beer had passed this way in June the rosettes had carried 9-12in. (23-30.5cm) hairy scapes bearing loose umbels of mauve-purple flowers ½-¾in. (1.25-2cm) across. The rock face at that time must have presented a pretty sight. On the damp banks alongside the track we were surprised to see *Primula glomerata* still in flower. The blue-purple flowers were densely crowded into globular heads, unlike the flat-crowned heads of the related *P. capitata,* and some particularly fine specimens approached in size those of the drumstick primula, *P. denticulata,* a species we had seen only once on the Jaljale Himal.

The track meanwhile crossed a log thrown over a narrow gully and along the margin of the stream below grew a giant perennial. The huge thrice-divided angelica-like leaves and tall 6ft. (1.85m) panicles of crowded brown seed capsules announced the presence of *Astilbe rivularis* whose appearance in cultivation is an all too rare occurrence. It is a stately suckering plant which requires plenty of space in a sheltered streamside or woodland site, and I remembered having seen a well-established specimen in the garden of Tom Spring-Smyth's parents at New Milton, a plant collected by Spring-Smyth in east Nepal.

Eventually at around 9,000ft. (2,743m) we entered a small pasture by the river and decided to spend the night there in a wooden shepherd's hut with a thatched bamboo roof. Da Norbu soon had a fire going and whilst he busied himself cooking, Beer and I wandered about in the rocks by the river. Apart from a single specimen of an erect, red-stemmed, yellow flowered spurge – *Euphorbia pseudosikkimensis* – the only other plant to attract our attention was *Rubus nepalensis*. This small plant sent out long, trailing, hispid stems which covered a great deal of ground between the stones, bearing small, trifoliolate, hairy leaves with toothed leaflets. The single, slightly nodding flowers were carried on erect stalks. They measured ¾in. (2cm) across and consisted of five white petals backed by a contrasting purplish calyx. These were succeeded by conspicuous shining red raspberry-like fruits which were rather insipid but pleasant enough to the taste. We collected two bags full and ate half as many in the process. Plants from this seed are now well established in cultivation, where

Colour Plate 118. *Prunus cornuta,* a plant of wild origin growing in a Dutch nursery. This lovely, but strong-growing Bird cherry was frequent in woods and glades below Topke Gola. The flowers give way to shining black fruits. (May)

Colour Plate 119. *Berberis insignis,* probably the largest leaved of any species, here growing in the woods of the Mewa Khola valley below Topke Gola. It is also noted for its smooth non-spiny shoots contrasting with the regularly spine-toothed leaves. The berries mature a glossy black. (October)

Colour Plate 120. *Carpinus viminea*. Scrubby growth on the stem of a large tree in the Upper Arun valley. The beautifully veined and taper-pointed leaves are coppery-red in colour when young. (April)

Colour Plate 121. Da Norbu with the bold foliage of *Rhododendron grande* found in the woods in the Mewa Khola valley below Topke Gola. (October)

Colour Plate 122. *Rhododendron grande* flowering in the woodland garden at the Hillier Arboretum in Hampshire. We found a fine group in the valley of the Mewa Khola below Topke Gola (April)

Plate 40. Something to sing about – the author in the Mewa Khola valley celebrating the finding of *Rhododendron grande*. (October)

they should be given a dry sunny situation to encourage plentiful flowers and fruit. In shady moist situations it becomes rampant and flowers sparingly. Although hardy on the whole, it is occasionally damaged by severe frosts. Since our introduction (1976), *R. nepalense* has been crossed with *R. tricolor* by Peter Dummer of Hillier Nurseries, the resultant hybrid a vigorous carpeting evergreen with leaves varying from ovate, three-lobed to trifoliolate. It makes an excellent ground cover.

In the early hours of the next morning I awoke with stomach pains. I blamed the rubus fruits but as they had not affected Beer I could only assume that I had a more sensitive stomach. All the rest of that day I felt rough and our return up the Mewa Khola was for me a slow and wearying experience. After breakfast, Beer slipped down the gorge to where he had previously seen the giant lily, returning shortly afterwards with a bag of fat seed pods and a few bulbils. He told me that the bulbs of recently flowered plants seemed exhausted and produced subsidiary bulbs as a result. The first discovery of the giant lily is accredited to Nathaniel Wallich in about 1824. It wasn't introduced to western cultivation, however, until 1848 when Major Edward Madden sent bulbs to the National Botanic Garden, Glasnevin, Dublin. The first flowering from this introduction occurred at Lamorran Rectory, near Truro, Cornwall. I always enjoy seeing this lily in gardens and one of the best displays I remember was in the famous Longstock Water Gardens near Stockbridge in Hampshire. Nor can I ever forget the photograph of it in Gertrude Jekyll's book *Wood and Garden* in which, curiously, a monk, his face partially concealed by his cowl, is seen admiring its flower spikes which tower above him. Jekyll greatly admired this lily which she referred to as one of the great flower events of the year, and her description of it and its cultivation in the book cannot be bettered.

Whilst Beer was away I collected the fruits of the small evergreen shrub *Sarcococca hookeriana* which grew in quantity around the hut. The rounded fruits, purplish-black in colour and ⅓in. (.85cm) across, contained three seeds. I then found a Himalayan holly – *Ilex dipyrena* – a small tree of 15ft. (4.5m) with angled young shoots and ovate to elliptic or oblong leaves, entire or with a few spine-tipped teeth. The leaves of young or sucker shoots were more densely spine-toothed. The juvenile green fruits were rounded to oblong, slightly laterally compressed and borne in axillary clusters. Scrambling into a nearby tree were the blanketing growths of a climbing ragwort – *Senecio scandens* – with toothed and lobed, lanceolate, long-pointed leaves and large terminal panicles of yellow daisy flowers. This is sometimes encountered in British cultivation but it is not normally hardy or persistent there.

The most exciting find, however, was *Rhododendron grande*. Several specimens grew in the thicket above the hut, all loosely branched trees of 20-30ft. (6-9m) with stout, green and glabrous young shoots. The terminal bud was large and rounded with tightly adpressed scales contrasting with those of

Colour Plate 124. *Rhododendron camelliiflorum,* flowering at Holly Cottage in Hampshire. This plant was collected in Nepal by Major Tom Spring-Smyth. It was common as an epiphyte on stumps and boulders in the woods of the Mewa Khola valley. (May)

Colour Plate 123. *Helwingia himalaica* in the Mewa Khola valley below Topke Gola. A member of the dogwood family *Cornaceae*, this deciduous shrub is more curious than ornamental and is principally known for the fruit (and flower) stalk being fused to the leaf stalk and midrib, the flower and fruit appearing to sprout from the leaf upper surface. (October)

Colour Plate 125. *Stachyurus himalaicus,* here photographed in the Hillier Arboretum, is distinct in its red flowers, those of most other species being yellow. It was frequent in the woods of the Mewa Khola valley below Topke Gola, but unfortunately is not reliably hardy out of doors in Britain. (February)

145

R. hodgsonii which are long-pointed with scales free at the tips. The huge leaves 10-18in. (25.5-45cm) long were elliptic to elliptic-obovate, acute, rounded at base, dark glossy green above, covered by a thin silvery indumentum below. They were carried on stout petioles 2in. (5cm) long, forming magnificent rosettes (Colour Plates 121 and 122 – and Plate 40). I could only wish that I had been here in the spring to see the purple-eyed, ivory-white, bell-shaped flowers in dense terminal trusses. We later discovered that Spring-Smyth had found this very same grove in 1961 and had introduced seed which is now represented as plants in several well-known collections in Britain. Sir Joseph Hooker, who first introduced this species from Sikkim in 1850 under the name *R. argenteum*, considered it a magnificent rhododendron, stating: 'I know nothing of the kind that exceeds in beauty the flowering branch of *R. argenteum*, with its wide-spreading foliage and glorious mass of flowers.' Perhaps the tallest recorded *R. grande* is one seen by the plant explorers Frank Ludlow and George Sherriff in the Black Mountains of central Bhutan in 1937 which they described as being at least 70ft. (21m) high. In cultivation it is best seen in the great woodland gardens of the western parts of the British Isles, though I have seen excellent examples at Borde Hill in Sussex and several other collections in the south.

We travelled slowly up the valley for several hundred yards where the vegetation was full of new and ornamental individuals. The curious were well represented and we again collected fruits of *Helwingia himalaica* (Colour Plate 123), while the yew *Taxus wallichiana* occurred as several large spreading specimens on the hillside above. Several maples appeared and we recognised *Acer sterculiaceum, A. campbellii* and *A. pectinatum* from previous encounters. A fourth maple was found growing above the river, a small tree of about 30ft. (9m), its leaves three or occasionally five lobed, in the latter case the basal lobes small, each lobe doubly serrate and with a tail-like point. They measured 5-6in. (13-15cm) across, glabrous above, sparsely rufous pubescent on the veins beneath, petioles bright red. At first I thought this belonged to *A. acuminatum,* which is mainly found in the western Himalaya but I now believe it to have been a juvenile phase of *A. pectinatum.* Indeed, I have since seen *A. pectinatum* showing a wide variation of leaf form as a young tree in Bhutan.

At one point a stream tumbled down a steep rock-face and the banks on either side proved particularly rich in shrubs. A bramble – *Rubus splendidissimus* – formed dense clumps of arching, silvery-hairy stems up to 6ft. (1.85m). The leaves were made up of three, almost sessile, broad elliptic, long-pointed leaflets which were doubly serrate, green above, covered beneath with adpressed, silvery, silky hairs. The orange-red, raspberry-like fruits were borne in downy branched corymbs. A plant grown from this seed and planted in a sheltered place in the Hillier Arboretum later perished after a severe frost. Of similar size and habit was *Neillia thyrsiflora,* whose strong, non-flowering, rich brown shoots bore three-lobed leaves 4-5in. (10-13cm) long. The peculiar green fruits borne in terminal panicles, consisted of a bulbous based calyx, covered on the outside with gland-tipped hairs and containing a small capsule. In denser parts of the vegetation, often in deep shade, we found a *Hypericum* species with slender arching stems 4-5ft. (1.25-1.5m) high, bearing opposite leaves 2-2½in. (5-6.5cm) long, ovate tapering to a blunt point, green above, glaucous green beneath. The fruits were conical with an irregular surface, borne in threes. The calyx was two-thirds the length of the capsule with lanceolate sepals. Although we guessed this shrub to be in some way related to *H. hookeranum,* we were pleasantly surprised when Dr. Norman Robson of the British Museum (Natural History) identified it as *H. choisianum,* our seed representing possibly the first introduction of this species into cultivation. It is now well established in several collections and is a most elegant shrub with yellow cup-shaped flowers and nodding tips to the shoots.

The most exciting aspect of this location, however, was the preponderance of ericaceous shrubs, of which the most interesting was an evergreen blueberry, *Vaccinium glaucoalbum.* It formed dense clumps and patches of branching stems 1-2ft. (30-60cm) high clothed with elliptic, finely toothed leaves 2½-3in. (6.5-7.5cm) long. These were tapered at both ends, dark green above and vividly glaucous beneath. The leafy-bracted racemes were produced on the previous year's wood and bore pruinose black fruits in great quantity. One occasionally sees this species in gardens on acid soils and a most handsome evergreen it is, but the pink-tinted young growths are liable to damage from late frosts and the plant is best given light tree cover.

Another evergreen – *Gaultheria semi-infera* – produced clumps of arching, shortly strigose hairy stems 4-5ft. (1.25-1.5m) high, clothed with elliptic-lanceolate leaves 3-4in. (7.5-10cm) long. These were acuminate, cuneate at base, serrulate, dark glossy-green above, pale below. The small fruits, ¼in. (.65cm) across, were borne in dense racemose clusters along the previous year's shoots, varying in colour and on different plants from white to lavender-blue. *Gaultheria nummularioides* was also plentiful, creeping and forming dense carpets in the moss, its small, neat, double-ranked leaves carried on densely brown, hairy, arching shoots. I had only once before seen this species in cultivation, at Caerhays Castle in Cornwall, where a thriving colony occupied a low shady bank by the footpath. Sadly, this colony has since perished. Plants raised from seed collected in Nepal died in the Hillier Arboretum after the 1976 drought following spring frosts.

Vaccinium nummularia formed drooping clumps on the wet rock face, and to complete the representation we found *Gaultheria griffithiana,* a much larger species than others we had seen with robust, arching, green and glabrous stems 5-6ft. (13-15m) high. One individual sent its stems 9ft. (2.75m) into the lower branches of a tree. The elliptic to obovate leaves, 4-5in. (10-13cm) long, were serrulate, ending in a slender point, dark green above, paler below. The fruits were jet black ⅓in. (.85cm) across, carried in dense axillary racemose clusters. This is a bold species quite unlike any other I know and is now in cultivation from our seed at the Royal Botanic Garden, Edinburgh. William Griffith, after whom this plant is named, was an assistant surgeon in Madras and one-time Superintendent of the Calcutta Botanic Garden. He travelled extensively in Bhutan and Afghanistan and accompanied Nathaniel Wallich in Assam. He died aged thirty-five in Malacca in 1845 (Plate 41).

By the river grew a large spreading bush of *Stachyurus himalaicus,* its leaves beginning to turn orange and pink, its branches strung with short drooping clusters of small rounded yellowish seed capsules which we collected (Colour Plate 125).

We crossed the river by way of a rough unstable arrangement of planks and slowly climbed the steep slope beyond. It was here above the track that we found our second *Magnolia* species – *M. globosa.* It was a small, multi-stemmed, spreading tree 20ft. (6m) high by 30ft. (9m) across with obovate

Colour Plate 126. Bhotia porters loading a yak in the valley of the Syamjung Khola in the Lumbasumba Himal. (October)

Colour Plate 127. *Meconopsis horridula*: a prickly handful seen between Topka Gola and Thudham. (October)

148

Colour Plate 128. *Rhododendron campanulatum* sprouting from an old fir stump in the Mewa Khola valley below Topke Gola. It was here in one of the dwellings that I was given delicious yoghurt to quell my upset stomach. (October)

leaves 6-8in. (15-20cm) long. Both buds and the leaf veins beneath were densely covered with a pelt of ferruginous hairs. There was no sign of its having flowered and equally no sign of seedlings. Still somewhat elated by this find we progressed further up the gorge until a huge fallen boulder some 25ft. (7.5m) high blocked our passage. Then we discovered that the track by-passed the obstruction, which was by no means a recent happening, and continued up the slope beyond. We made to follow the track but Beer suddenly pointed to a rhododendron sitting on the mossy top of the boulder. It was a large clump with stems 5-6ft. (1.5-1.85m) high, the older stems with reddish peeling bark. The young shoots, buds and leaf undersurface were densely covered with small brown scales. The leaves themselves were elliptic, 2-3in. (5-7.5cm) long tapering to a blunt tip with a small mucro, cuneate at base, dark green above. The seed capsules were borne singly, or occasionally in pairs, shortly stalked

Plate 41. William Griffith (1810-1845). Described variously by his contemporaries as a man of genius, extraordinary ability and as the greatest botanist ever to set foot in India, this Scottish naturalist, explorer and botanist died tragically young. His life, however, was packed with action and adventure and he achieved more than many other travellers and botanists did in a lifespan twice his. He not only collected and described plants but drew them as well, and despite bouts of sickness and dangerous living he amassed an enormous collection of specimens of the Indian flora. Among the plants named after him *Larix griffithiana, Euphorbia griffithii* and *Gaultheria griffithiana* are all native to the east Himalaya

(½in./1.25cm), oblong (⅔in./1.70cm) long with a short (¼in./.65cm) bent style, densely brown scaly. We later identified this species as *Rhododendron camelliiflorum* whose small white wide open flowers I saw in the spring of 1973 on the Milke Banjgang. It is frequent in the moist woods below 10,000ft. (3,048m) and is invariably an epiphyte on rocks or trees (Colour Plate 124).

Gradually we climbed the gorge, my stomach and legs still weak, and Da Norbu, as a result, carrying far more than he had expected to. A last stop was made to collect seeds of an extraordinary evergreen holly growing beneath trees above the track. It was a low growing bush up to 3ft. (90cm), its tough wiry branches forming a dense thicket sprinkled with small elliptic, toothed leaves ⅓in. (.85cm) long, glossy dark green above. The red fruits were none too plentiful, rounded ¼in. (.65cm) across, occurring singly in the leaf axils. It proved to be *Ilex intricata*.

All the way up the gorge we passed yaks and zobyaks browsing as they were driven down from the heights. The zobyak is a hybrid between a yak and a cow, differing mainly from the yak in its shorter coat and longer, more upswept, horns. It is a hardy beast and unlike the yak is equally happy at low altitudes. These herds are taken down to altitudes of about 7,000ft. (2,133m) until spring when the snows melt and recede, at which time the herds and herdsmen return to the heights. This usually takes place in March and is eagerly awaited by all

concerned. During summer a yak will give between one and two litres of milk a day. It is a valuable beast, for apart from its milk it provides a dense oily wool, a tough hide, good meat and, more important, it is a tough and reliable pack animal (Colour Plate 126). It is wilder and more unpredictable in its habits than the domesticated cow and it is unwise for a stranger to approach it too close. Generally though it is docile when handled or approached by herdsmen, but even they have been known to receive an unexpected kick, so they tie the back legs together when milking. When on the move a yak caravan plods along at a steady pace, the lead yak feeling out the track like a giant mountain goat. When confronted by diverging tracks the lead yak is encouraged one way or the other by a stone thrown to its left or right side by a herdsman. They often wear colourful tassels around their horns or tails, and most if not all wear bells around their necks. A lost yak is invariably located by the sound of its bell, and equally the sound of a yak caravan in motion is one of those unforgettable experiences of the high Himalaya.

As we stopped to allow the passage of a rather splendid shining black betasselled yak, we were overhauled by two small Bhotia boys. They were returning from school at Dongan some twelve miles from Topke Gola and 4,000ft. (1,219m) lower down the valley. They stayed with us almost to Topke Gola, talking all the time, stopping when we did whether to collect seed or to take a breather. Due to my condition and slow progress we decided not to push ahead to the village that day and prepared to spend the night in the house in the clearing where the bird cherries grew (Colour Plate 128 and Plate 42). The women and children sat outside on the veranda watching our approach. The men were not at home but the women were quite happy for us to stay and one immediately began roasting corn for us. The grandmother, on being told of my upset stomach, gave me a mug full of dahl (curdled milk) from a wooden container. It tasted quite pleasant and had an immediate settling effect on my stomach, even giving me an appetite for supper. Just before dark the menfolk arrived driving their yaks before them into the clearing. They entered the house one at a time showing not the slightest concern at our presence. There were three brothers all in their twenties, one of whom had a small child and a baby. Eventually the whole family settled on the floor around the fire talking amongst themselves and occasionally asking Da Norbu questions about the sahibs. Soon their meal was ready, having been prepared by the grandmother and her daughter-in-law. First they ate roasted corn and then a huge pile of fresh green nettles were crammed into a small blackened

Colour Plate 129. *Leontopodium monocephalum,* the Golden Edelweiss, at 16,000ft. (4,877m) in the Lumbasumba Himal. As rare and desirable as Jason's fabulous fleece, this high altitude perennial has proved nigh impossible in cultivation. (October)

Colour Plate 130. *Cortiella hookeri (glacialis),* a curious stemless member of the carrot family, *Umbelliferae.* It was frequent on steep slopes around 16,000ft. (4,877m) in the Lumbasumba Himal. (October)

Colour Plate 131. *Anaphalis cavei,* one of several grey woolly alpines we found growing at 16,000ft. (4,877m) in the Lumbasumba Himal where it was common among rocks on steep slopes and scree margins. (October)

pot of boiling water. This was constantly stirred and beaten into a kind of thick spinach soup. During its preparation the grandmother produced small green limes from the folds of her gown and these were sucked silently by the others. When the daughter-in-law began to breast-feed her baby, Beer and I retired to the far corner of the room to sleep.

Next morning, my stomach was back to normal, thanks to the dahl, and ever since I have had the greatest faith in natural yoghurt and similar stomach mollifiers. The family were up and about, engaged on various tasks which we watched over breakfast. The two older brothers moved off down the valley whilst the small boy tugged the yak calves to a tying-up point which allowed his mother to milk the cows without difficulty. Her husband meanwhile struggled to cut wool from a large black yak. Wielding his kukri he made several attempts, dodging repeated kicks, before being caught on the ankle by a crafty double kick. In retaliation he struck the animal between the horns with the back of his kukri blade and followed this by tying its back legs together with rope. This done he quickly set to work slicing away great chunks of wool from the yak's ample coat. The baby then starting crying, at which the mother casually tipped a ladle of cold water on its head, bringing an immediate end to its tears.

The house in which we slept was typical for these parts, consisting of a rough stone base with a wooden superstructure, usually Silver fir – *Abies densa*. Neither mortar nor nails were used, and as far as we could judge these structures stood for many years with just the occasional patching and repairs.

On our return to Topke Gola we were greeted by Dorje and his sister Berma and Tende's sister Mile who brought large tompa's of cold chang to quench our thirst. From the folds of her tunic Berma withdrew a bamboo comb and proceeded to attack Beer's hair and ended by plaiting a little pigtail in his beard to the accompaniment of much laughing from the others. The last 500 yards (457m) up the steep hill to camp was, as always, the most tiring and we arrived wheezing and panting.

Having long since paid off the porters, we had to hire yaks to carry our gear, and this needed time. Morris agreed to stay on another day whilst the yaks were rounded up, and so the next morning, Beer and I climbed up the side valley above Topke Gola on the track to the village of Thudam which lay two days distant to the north (Plate 43). After a stiff climb we found ourselves in a flat valley bottom with high cliffs on either side. A small group of men caught us up and we were pleased to see Pema the cook accompanied by Da Norbu, Namgyal and Dorje acting as porters. By the streams grew clumps of *Meconopsis grandis* in vast quantities, and we promptly filled many bags with its seed. Beer told us how, on the reconnaissance, he had seen the many streams in this area coloured by primulas of several kinds but especially *P. megalocarpa*. Their myriad rosettes remained as evidence of his story, those of the last mentioned often sitting in the shallow water. Our track continued upwards across a steep rock-strewn slope, most of which was snow covered. Before reaching the snow, however, we stopped to examine a new poppy which occupied the banks on either side of the track. The many rosettes were in seed, the capsules borne on several erect stems 6in. (15cm) high. The entire plant was armed with prickly bristles giving rise to the most apt name *Meconopsis horridula* (Colour Plate 127). Beer had seen it earlier in flower, when it looked most becoming with comparatively large blue crimpled flowers. It is yet another monocarpic species, fortunately easily grown from seed.

We were now approaching 15,000ft. (4,572m) and having slowly negotiated a narrow stream gully we rested whilst contemplating a thousand-foot snow slope leading up to a col at 16,000ft. (4,877m) Having decided that contemplation would not make our climb any easier, we set off on a zigzag course, making slow and laborious progress interspersed with numerous stops. At one point a line of footprints crossed our track originating apparently from the ridge above and heading towards a distant crag. The footprints were large and, inevitably, thoughts of the Yeti entered our heads. I suspect, however, that they were those of a Snow leopard. Eventually we reached the col and lost no time in pushing down the other side. A huge valley opened before us and we saw many great screes and hanging glaciers (Colour Plate 132). It was almost as hard plodding down through the snow as it was going up and we spent more time on our backs than on our feet, but finally we made it to the open stream, and after another mile of clearer walking located a suitable campsite for the night. It was still mid-afternoon and Da Norbu, Dorje and Namgyal set off on the return journey to Topke Gola. Beer and I climbed to a vantage point where we could watch the Sherpas' progress and by late afternoon they could be seen, ant-like, plodding through the snow towards the col. Soon after they had disappeared we returned to camp for a hot meal prepared by Pema.

Next morning after an early breakfast we climbed up the steep slope above

Plate 43. Pass above Topke Gola which we crossed on our way to Thudam. The lake feeds the Syamjung Khola, whose waters travel via the Bagang Khola and the Arun river to the Ganges and finally the Bay of Bengal. (October)

camp making for a high crag. The main woody vegetation on these slopes consisted of *Rhododendron setosum, R. anthopogon* and *Potentilla arbuscula.* The last named was a dense twiggy little shrub 9-12in. (23-30.5cm) high with relatively thick, short branches densely clothed with large brown, grey-hairy, papery stipules. The leaves, though fallen and brown were composed of five leaflets. This species is sometimes treated as a variety under the name *P. fruticosa* variety *rigida*, but whatever its status, it remains an excellent dwarf flowering shrub for the small garden and is especially pleasing during summer when its hummocks are plastered with the comparatively large yellow flowers of good substance. Nowadays, although uncommon in cultivation, its 'blood' may be seen in several first-rate hybrids, including 'Elizabeth', 'Dart's Gold Digger' and 'Hachmann's Giant'.

Both *Saussurea obvallata* and *S. gossypiphora* occurred, the latter in seed, the cottonwool ball opened revealing a tuft of thistledown.

Soon we were negotiating a large scree and we needed all our concentration to prevent ourselves from sliding across the unstable surface. *Eriophytum wallichii,* a relation of the common bugle *(Ajuga)* grew here, its large, dry, flannelly bracts being its main claim to fame. Most plants, having detached themselves from the ground, were blowing about in the wind like tumble-weed, which no doubt is how its seeds are spread. We left the scree just below the crags and crossed an awful desolate area of broken rocks laced with snow. Here we found a plant as rare and as desirable as Jason's fabulous fleece. Growing amongst the rocks, forming mats and cushions was the golden edelweiss – *Leontopodium monocephalum* – a boring name for one of the most lovely and fascinating alpines imaginable (Colour Plate 129). I had read somewhere about the elusive nature of this species and though I had momentarily wondered whether we should find it, the idea was quickly forgotten in the hurly-burly of preparations. Now I could hardly believe our luck and I took several photographs as proof to non-believers. Each mat was

Colour Plate 132. Having crossed the pass at 16,000ft. (4,877m) we entered a magnificent valley skirted by vast screes with snow spattered black rocks above. The low brown vegetation on the more stable screes belongs to *Potentilla arbuscula*. (October)

made up of pale green, densely woolly rosettes topped by a 2in. (5cm) stem bearing a golden, woolly inflorescence. Seed was in abundance and we quickly filled a linen bag. Although we produced two dozen seedlings in pots at Hilliers, they one by one wasted away within the space of a few weeks. I have never heard from any other shareholders about the fate of other seed or seedlings. To grow a flourishing pan of this species for exhibition at an Alpine Garden Society show would be a highlight even in that eminent Society's year. Cool conditions, high light intensity, excellent drainage and snow cover in winter combine to provide this edelweiss and its woolly companions with conditions difficult if not impossible to provide in British cultivation.

Several other plants occurred on the sheer walls of the crags above and included the delightful *Primula tenuiloba* which formed small pads on the moss- and lichen-covered rock as well as on the grit at the edge of the screes. Beer described how, during the reconnaissance, he had seen this delicate species showing its pale blue, or occasionally white, flowers on ½in. (1.25cm) stalks above the minute deeply toothed leaves. In the same area he had found *P. concinna,* its small, yellow-eyed, mauve flowers borne in short-stalked umbels above cushions several inches in diameter. This species was first discovered by Joseph Hooker in 1849 on a high pass between Sikkim and Tibet. On a grassy ledge we found an umbel, its domed heads of fruits 2-3in. (5-7.5cm) across actually sitting on the ground, the leaf rosette having withered. It proved to be *Cortiella hookeri (glacialis)* (Colour Plate 130).

Back on the screes again we found a small saxifrage – *Saxifraga pseudopallida* – forming tufts between the stones. Beer had seen it previously in flower, each white petal with two yellow spots, five to six flowers in a cluster atop a 4-5in. (10-13cm) stem. *Potentilla argyrophylla* variety *leucochroa* appeared with its silvery, silky, trifoliolate leaves and erect 6-9in. (15-23cm)

Colour Plate 133. A yak caravan in the snow after crossing a 16,000ft. (4,877m) pass between Topke Gola and Thudam. (October)

stems bearing comparatively small yellow flowers. For several years we had this plant successfully established in the Hillier Arboretum where it was admired for its foliage rather than its flowers. On the cliffs grew *Potentilla eriocarpa,* its 4-6in. (10-15cm) stems, with 'fingered' leaves, hanging in tufts from sunny crevices. It shared its exposed perch with the grey woolly tufts of *Anaphalis cavei* which we also found on the scree below (Colour Plate 131).

When we at last attained the exposed summit of the hill, all around us rose the peaks and ridges of the Lumbasumba Himal. We could see the valley of the Syamjung Khola, in which lay our camp, curving in a great arc to Thudam. Looking north across range after range of mountains glistening white in the sun we could see an enormous high plateau with brown dry-looking hills and my heart skipped a beat as I gained my first sight of Tibet.

A fall of stone beneath us diverted our attention and we looked to see Pema climbing towards us with flasks of tea and still warm chapattis. Happily munching our food and drinking the hot beverage, we gazed south, over and above the col, to the farthest distant ridge where our march had first begun over a month ago. We remembered our flight from Kathmandu to Biratnagar and our first sight of the white wall. Now we were sitting on the same wall and our minds dwelt silently on all that had happened in between. The rocks on which we sat we estimated to be at 17,000ft. (5,182m), and it was the highest point Beer or I had ever achieved. The only sign of vegetation here was *Potentilla microphylla* variety *depressa* which formed dense, hard hummocks, 6 in. (15cm) high and 2ft. (60cm) across of tightly packed rosettes. We scraped the hummocks with a knife to fill a bag with seed.

Eventually we made our way back down the hillside trotting and jumping in the wake of Pema whose rapid passage over the rocks and broken ground would have done a goat proud. We were expecting the arrival of Morris's yak caravan, but although we waited for several hours there was no sign of them and when darkness crept quietly into the valley we retired to camp for our supper. Being well above the tree-line Pema simply gathered heaps of dwarf rhododendrons with which to make a fire and the heat and sparks given out by this aromatic fuel kept us well at bay until supper was served.

We were filling bags with *Potentilla arbuscula* seed the following morning when Dawa arrived to tell us that the yak caravan was less than an hour behind. They had left Topke Gola at 11a.m. the previous day after spending two hours rounding up and loading the yaks. Unable to make the col before lunch they had decided to camp at the foot of the snow slope and wait until morning.

After an hour we were on the move again and what a sight and experience it proved to be. The yaks charged along the valley bottom, their tails curled over their backs like chows, urged on by the yak-men who whistled, shouted and clapped their hands (Colour Plate 133). After a while we allowed the yaks and yak-men to press on whilst we made a more leisurely progress in order to look at the plants and collect seed.

Many streams converged on the river and between their courses large areas of shingle and stones contained several interesting plants including *Waldheimia glabra,* a perennial plant of the daisy family with prostrate stems clothed with small obovate fleshy leaves, deeply lobed at the tips. The flowers, 1in. (2.5cm) across, had a yellow disc surrounded by reddish-purple ray florets. It grew in the grit close to the water's edge where also grew *Myricaria rosea,* forming long thin bands of rust-coloured seed plumes, marking the routes of the water courses for mile upon mile. In a small grassy pasture by the river we discovered a tiny monkshood – *Aconitum hookeri* – with creeping stems ascending 2-3in. (5-7.5cm) at their tips. The leaves were palmately lobed and each slender stem carried a downy seed capsule ½in. (1.25cm) long. It was abundant over a limited area. An hour later we were passing through a deep gorge, the cliffs so high that they blotted out the sun and everywhere was dark and cold. Beer and I were happy to press on but Morris dragged his feet looking longingly at the splendid precipices, no doubt wishing there was time to do a real rock-climb.

The track we were following now ran downhill and we found ourselves in a wooded area where birch, fir and rhododendrons of several species flourished. We then broke through the trees to find ourselves face to face with the Bhotia village of Thudam, a collection of houses huddled at the foot of a steep hillside and a few feet above the river.

8. LAND OF THE GHORAL

The village was situated above the confluence of the Syamjung Khola and the Lhesa Khola at a height of 12,500ft. (3,810m). Our camp had been set on a fairly level piece of ground on the opposite side of the valley (Colour Plate 134), and to reach it from the village a series of three bridges had to be crossed. These were no more than bundles of slender logs tied together and renewed when each melting snow flood swept them away (Plate 44).

The following day was quiet and we did our washing and seed drying, Morris again draping the tents with long strings of seed bags so that the camp appeared to be festooned with bunting.

The campsite was more or less covered in scrub, consisting of the red hipped *Rosa sericea, Berberis angulosa, Cotoneaster staintonii, Juniperus recurva* and *J. squamata* and a willow – *Salix disperma* (*wallichiana*) – a handsome shrub of 8-10ft. (2.5-3m), its white woolly fruiting catkins borne in some profusion along the erect twigs (Colour Plate 135). The synonym commemorates Nathaniel Wallich (Plate 16).

Abounding on a grass bank above the river was a peculiar saxifrage – *Saxifraga brunonis* – with small rosettes of narrow green leaves and numerous red thread-like stems (stolons) reminding me of a small, well-ordered dodder (*Cuscuta* species). The small clusters of yellow flowers on 2-3in. (5-7.5cm) stems Beer had seen previously. Indeed, he told us that it commonly grew on moss-covered boulders by rivers in these regions. *Primula glomerata* was again plentiful on moist slopes on both sides of the river and accompanying it in one

Plate 44. Bhotia father and son crossing the 'bridge' over the river at Thudam (12,500ft./3,810m). Early snow powders the roofs of the houses. (November)

Colour Plate 134. Our campsite in the valley of the Lhesa Khola north of Thudam. Low cloud hangs between the river and snowy crags. (November)

place, near to the camp, was a rather lower than normal form of *Polygonum amplexicaule,* its flowering stems no greater than 18in. (45cm), the slender spikes of red flowers drooping attractively. This plant, from seed collected at the time, has proved popular and distinct in cultivation, so much so that, in answer to several requests, I gave it the cultivar name 'Arun Gem' in recognition of its garden merit and its location in a branch of the Upper Arun valley. Botanically, it belongs to the variety *pendulum.*

Across the river from the camp and around the village grew a large branching plant which appeared to be annual. The flowers, seen earlier by Beer, were bell-shaped, greenish and produced singly in the axils of the large leaves. The rounded fruit capsules contained numerous small seeds and were themselves enclosed in a large bladder-like ribbed calyx. Pema told us that it was used as yak fodder. We have since identified the plant as *Scopolia stramonifolia,* a member of the potato family *Solanaceae.* Both birch – *Betula utilis* and the peely-barked cherry – *Prunus rufa* were plentiful on the surrounding hillsides, though many of the cherries had been mutilated in the search for firewood. The birch too was much in demand for occasional building, especially yak pens and temporary supports. Our Sherpas had used it for several structures in camp including supports for the kitchen tent and as props for the clothes line and it certainly lived up to its Latin name, *utilis* meaning useful.

For more permanent structures Silver fir was preferred, and of the remaining Silver fir forest in the vicinity of Thudam much was mutilated, as was the juniper – *Juniperus recurva.* The latter, however, was regenerating to a surprising degree and amongst the masses of seedlings and saplings we found several large old trees heavy with fruit.

Behind one of the village houses Beer and I found a superb specimen of *Rhododendron campylocarpum* 15ft. (4.5m) high growing with an equally impressive *R. hodgsonii* of 18ft. (5.5m) (Colour Plate 136). Other rhododendrons occurred in the vicinity but by far the most noticeable was *Rhododendron arboreum* subspecies *cinnamomeum.* Regularly cut by the villagers, it appeared as dense mounds 4-6ft. (1.25-1.85m) high scattered across the hillsides. The leaves, on being turned, exhibited a rich rusty pelt of woolly hairs which could be scraped away with the fingernail (Colour Plate 137). This rhododendron is, by some authorities, regarded as a species in its own right but it is undoubtedly a subspecies of *R. arboreum* and it would appear to represent this species at high altitudes. The flowers are usually white, though they may also be pink or crimson.

Looking up the valley above the village we could see the fiery red splashes of *Berberis angulosa* (Colour Plate 138) whilst closer to hand we collected seed of *Piptanthus nepalensis.* Sometimes called the evergreen laburnum, this robust shrub formed specimens 6ft. (1.85m) high by 12ft. (3.70m) through, the sprawling branches draped with flattened pods which rattled each time the wind blew. Three other shrubs were common on the hillside above Thudam and these were *Aster albescens, Spiraea bella* and *Potentilla fruticosa.* The last named was a small shrub 2-3ft. (60-90cm) high, the leaves with five leaflets. It is now well established in cultivation and produces the typical yellow flowers of this group. The aster also was a small shrub or subshrub but of sprawling growth with grey-backed toothed leaves and flattened clusters of seed heads. In cultivation it is normally only suitable for warmer areas but at Wakehurst Place in Sussex plants grown from our seed have proved most successful in the wall

Colour Plate 135 (above left). *Salix disperma*, a female shrub showing its silvery fruiting catkins by the Lhesa Khola (15,000ft./4,572m) north of Thudam. This Himalayan willow has also been known as *S. wallichiana*. (November)

Colour Plate 136 (above). *Rhododendron hodgsonii* growing on a ridge in the valley of the Bagang Khola below Thudam. The stems of this splendid species are covered with pink-tinted cinnamon bark which peels away with age to reveal the creamy-brown new bark. (November)

Colour Plate 137. *Rhododendron arboreum* subspecies *cinnamomeum*. This attractive form of the Tree rhododendron was common around the village of Thudam. The rich reddish-brown indumentum of the leaf undersurface is clearly seen in this cut specimen. (November)

Colour Plate 138. *Berberis angulosa*, one of several shrubs forming dense scrub and thicket around our campsite at Thudam. Note the shining red berries born singly in rows along the branches. Here it is growing with *Juniperus recurva*. (November)

Colour Plate 139. *Acer caudatum:* the thin papery flaking bark of a young tree. Older stems have a more permanent ridged brownish-grey bark. This maple was not uncommon as an understorey tree in the forest. (November)

Colour Plate 140. *Aster albescens*, a shrubby relative of the Michaelmas daisy, here growing in a garden in the English Lake District. This plant was common on the slopes above Thudam. (July)

garden where its grey-green foliage and wide heads of lavender blue daisy flowers are a familiar sight from summer into autumn. Indeed, this particular collection has flowers of a richer colour than normal. I have also seen a similar form in the relatively exposed garden of Allium 'Queen' Dilys Davies above Ullswater in the English Lake District (Colour Plate 140). It is still to be found in a few nursery catalogues, occasionally under the generic name *Microglossa*.

On descending the hillside to the village we came across a huge moss-covered boulder on which grew a *Pleione* species quite different from that which we had previously seen on the Milke Danda. Here the pseudo-bulbs were nice and plump and varying in shape from almost round to ovoid. In colour they were a lovely shining rose-madder turning to green with age. Neither leaves nor flowers were in evidence. Like the Milke Danda species this was in a dormant state, the moss in which it grew quite dry, yet during the monsoon period it would enjoy a thoroughly wet condition. Thudam is at approximately 12,000ft. (3,657m) and is covered in snow during winter which suggests that this was probably *P. hookeriana,* a species with a widespread distribution through the eastern Himalaya into south-west China. In general this is found at a higher altitude than most other species. Flowering takes place in spring, the flowers varying in colour from white to rose-pink with or without a yellow, orange or brown blotch on the lip.

There was another plant which caught the eye amongst the rocks of the hillside. This was an unusual small subshrub with a big name – *Boenning-hausenia albiflora,* a member of the buttercup family *Ranunculaceae* but most resembling a white flowered shrubby meadow rue – *Thalictrum* species. It is a charming plant for a border with its elegantly divided leaves and rather fluffy flower clusters, but it is unfortunately of borderline hardiness and those plants which we grew from seed in the Hillier Arboretum have long since perished.

As we made to leave the village our attention was caught by a man who appeared from the darkness of a doorway and called to us. It was the lama we had met at Topke Gola and who served both communities. He led us towards a new gompa built of stone with a wooden roof, barely two months old and we followed him through a bright-blue painted door into the dim interior. Before us stood a large cabinet packed with old books, and on either side a large prayer wheel – tall drums made of parchment colourfully painted and inscribed with Tibetan script and motifs. These the lama spun for our benefit and as they whirled around, a stick attached to the top of each drum struck the clapper of a bell positioned above. The rest of the room was bare save for a few tapestries on the walls.

Back in camp, Tende produced a tall wooden churn which he had borrowed from the village and announced that he would prepare for us Tibetan tea. Into the churn he placed yak butter which is white and tastes like a weak margarine, black tea, yak milk and salt. He then beat the ingredients with a long wooden pestle before pouring the liquid into a large kettle which he then placed on the fire to boil. The resultant 'tea' looked and tasted like a slightly salty soup which we found unusual but not very enjoyable.

The following morning at breakfast a group of nine men arrived from Baracula, a village in the Arun valley near Sedua. They had carried for Beer on his reconnaissance and had remembered that he would be returning this way. They were happy to wait until we were ready to leave Thudam in eight days' time and moved off to find food in the village.

Beer decided to climb up a steep gully above camp and took Da Norbu with him whilst Morris and I wandered downriver from camp to look for seed. It was a bright sunny morning and everything looked at its best including the snow cone of Makalu (27,790ft./8,470m) which we could clearly see from the camp. I was particularly impressed by the stems of a maple *Acer caudatum,* trees of 25-30ft. (7.5-9m) with deeply etched and furrowed brownish-grey bark, thin and flaky on younger stems (Colour Plate 139). We followed a track to where an old man stood in a clearing. He was busily beating milk in a churn and smiled a welcome as we arrived. Behind him stood a pile of neatly stacked newly cut planks. Our attention, however, was taken by a superb *Acer pectinatum*, a tree some 50ft. (15m) high, the young shoots as brilliantly coloured as the popular red twigged dogwood *Cornus alba* 'Sibirica'. The spreading branches were draped in long clusters of red-winged fruits, whilst the leaves had turned a clear yellow. This is a most handsome maple, lacking the attractive bark of *A. caudatum* which replaces it at higher altitudes but superior in every other department (Colour Plate 141). The tree in the glade rivalled anything I had ever seen at the Westonbirt Arboretum, and in this setting with a cloudless sky above, the air crisp and cool, and with the crashing of the river in our ears and the paddling of milk in the churn it gave us a lasting memory.

Of other trees seen that day, rowans, mainly the white fruited *Sorbus microphylla,* and the dark firs, were in the majority. On our way back to camp we found a parasitic plant – *Xylanche himalaica* – growing on the roots of *Rhododendron arboreum*. The brown fruiting spikes of this member of the broomrape family – *Orobanchaceae* – came straight from the ground and occurred singly or in clusters. Previously we had seen it on the roots of *Rhododendron hodgsonii, R. campylocarpum, R. wightii* and surprisingly, once, on *R. lepidotum*. By the river below camp we found a lone specimen of *Lyonia villosa,* a small tree, 15ft. (4.5m) high, with smooth, polished reddish-brown shoots. The leaves were ovate to elliptic, 2-3in. (5.7.5cm) long, unequal at the base, obtuse to rounded at the tip, green above whilst pale green to sub-glaucous beneath. The small seed capsules were carried in short leafy terminal racemes. At this season I could see little difference between this species and the closely related *L. ovalifolia*. The last named has a wide distribution from Kashmir eastwards through China to Taiwan and Japan. Bean comments on the tender nature of the Himalayan plant which is rare in cultivation. *L. villosa,* collected from a higher altitude may well be a more worthwhile introduction.

On our return we found two surprises awaiting us. First of all Dawa, after several attempts, had finally persuaded a jelly to set, no easy matter at altitude. Pema meanwhile, in answer to our request, had decided to bake a loaf of bread. To achieve this he first set a large pan on the fire. Into this he placed three stones to support a smaller pan containing the mixture. Replacing the two lids he then heaped on the top lid hot ashes from the fire. In two hours the bread was ready and it tasted delicious, crisp on the outside, warm and soft within, far better quality than Pema's previous effort – a cake which, when accidentally dropped, had shattered into a thousand pieces.

We had discussed the desirability of travelling up the Lhesa Khola to see if a more northerly valley might bring us a different range of plants. The lama was leaving the next morning to visit Walungchung Gola further to the east and it

Colour Plate 141. *Acer pectinatum*, photographed in Bhutan, is a handsome maple widespread in the eastern Himalaya. Variable in leaf depending on age, the leaves of a mature tree as shown here are typically three-lobed with two small basal lobes. They are edged with fine teeth with hair-like points and borne on red petioles. (October)

Colour Plate 142. *Rhododendron setosum*: a golden leaved form growing in the valley of the Lhesa Khola north of Thudam. (November)

Colour Plate 143. *Rhododendron wightii* photographed in Bhutan. This large leaved species was common on the slopes above Topke Gola and Thudam. Note the dark stain in the throat of each bloom. (May)

Colour Plate 144. *Gentiana ornata*, here growing with *Gaultheria trichophylla* and *Potentilla peduncularis*, is one of the most beautiful of the Asiatic autumn flowering species. It was not uncommon in the mountains above Thudam. (November)

seemed a good idea to accompany him for a little of the way. We left late morning accompanied by Dawa and Pema, with Dorje, Namgyal and Tende acting as porters. Da Norbu remained in camp to keep an eye on things until our return in three days. The weather was fine and sunny as we climbed away from the village and followed the river which tore over the rocks through a ravine below the track. The whole of the far north-facing hillside was covered by a dense growth of *Rhododendron wightii* which, beginning above the river at 12,800ft. (3,901m), surged upwards like a deep-green tide to the crest of the ridge at 14,000ft. (4,267m) (Colour Plate 143). By contrast the south-facing hillside, across which lay our track, was covered by a mixture of birch, fir and juniper above a crowded undergrowth of rhododendron, cotoneaster and berberis with *Rosa sericea* providing a thorny connection. Rhododendrons, *campylocarpum, cinnabarinum* and *campanulatum,* occurred in some numbers up to 13,000ft. (3,962m), at which point *R. hodgsonii* and *R. thomsonii* took over. *R campanulatum,* however, appeared as scattered individuals up to 14,000ft. (4,267m), whilst 300ft. (91m) higher we discovered a lone stunted *R. campylocarpum.*

The rhododendron population above 13,000ft. (3,962m), however, was dominated by the dwarf species *R. anthopogon, R. lepidotum* and *R. setosum* (Colour Plate 142) which formed a continuous carpet, shared in the lower reaches with *Spiraea arcuata, Cotoneaster integrifolius* and *Lonicera rupicola,* the last a dwarf shrubby honeysuckle related to the popular Chinese species *L. syringantha* but inferior in merit. It was in this 'moorland' zone that we collected the dry seed capsules of a bulbous plant – *Fritillaria cirrhosa* – whose nodding green bells would have graced the scene in June and July. Eventually we came to the parting of the ways and the lama took a track which moved north-east towards Walungchung Gola, whilst we continued north in the direction of Tibet (Colour Plate 145). The terrain became drier and more exposed and most plants seen were creeping or dwarf in nature and included the tiny green-stemmed shrublet *Ephedra gerardiana* variety *sikkimensis.* We made camp that evening by the river at a height of 14,600ft. (4,450m). A short pre-supper foray turned up two gentians – *Lomatogonium sikkimense,* a tiny annual with slender stems and pale-blue flowers 1in. (2.5cm) long by ½in. (1.25cm) across, and *Gentiana ornata,* a beautiful perennial species with rosettes of short trailing shoots with narrow leaves and terminal broad bell-shaped flowers of sky-blue with darker stripes on the outside and paler interior. These open wide in all weathers and measure 1in. (2.5cm) across (Colour Plate 144). This is the Himalayan counterpart to the Chinese *G. sino-ornata* and is just as easy in cultivation in a cool lime-free soil and an open sunny situation.

We awoke early the next morning to find a cold north wind blowing down the valley. The river, which here flowed shallowly between rocks and boulders, was partially frozen. Dorje was the first to awaken and shortly afterwards we saw him quartering the ground above the camp filling a bamboo basket with dried yak dung for the fire (Plate 45). After a quick breakfast we continued up the valley leaving Dawa and the others to break camp.

The waters reflected the sun which slowly climbed out of the east beyond the peaks of the Lumbasumba Himal. The river itself was bordered by the rust-coloured plumose growths of *Myricaria rosea,* a dwarf tamarisk which we had seen several times before. Some of the clumps and mounds now in seed had turned a rich scarlet and others a deep beetroot purple (Colour Plate 146).

Plate 45. Dorje in the Lhesa Khola valley collecting dried yak dung to use as fuel for the camp fire. It burns not unlike peat when fully dried though it gives off a pungent smoke. (November)

Occupying shingle banks, sometimes in company with the above, was a dwarf sea buckthorn – *Hippophae tibetana* – its stout grey spiny branches forming dense low carpets 6-9in. (15-23cm) high and many yards across. The small grey oblong leaves had already fallen and as we could see no sign of fruits we assumed that these were male plants. Sea buckthorn carries its male and female flowers on separate plants and both sexes need to be in fairly close proximity to effect pollination. A colony of female plants massed with bright orange berries must present a striking picture in these dry, brown, autumn valleys, but we did not see a sign of one.

About an hour out from camp we spotted what we thought was a sheep standing by the river's edge ahead of us. On closer examination however we decided against this identification and realised that it was a young ghoral, a Himalayan animal which looks like a cross between a sheep and a deer and is related to the latter. In colour it was grey and small straight horns protruded from its crown (Colour Plate 147). It was reasonably tame and allowed us to approach to within a few feet before moving away, sometimes stumbling in doing so. We came to the conclusion that this was a sickly individual left behind by the main herd, as the species is normally timid and fleet of foot and avoids contact with man.

Soon we were above 15,500ft. (4,724m). The only sound was of a nearby river and the only movement was a flock of Snow pigeons clearing a dark-faced cliff above us. The only woody vegetation appeared to be *Rhododendron anthopogon* and *R. setosum* with an occasional patch of *Potentilla arbuscula*, whilst large dark stains on the hillsides proved on examination to be patches of the Black juniper – *Juniperus indica* (Colour Plates 148 and 149).

At the head of the valley was a chorten (a type of cairn, with religious significance) built on top of a large rock slab. Here the track curved to the left and followed another valley whose steep sides appeared bare of vegetation. We stopped to watch a lone hoopoe which suddenly appeared and perched on a nearby boulder, flexing its strikingly barred crest. Another movement then caught our attention and we saw on the opposite hillside several puffs of dust and stones tumbling down the slope. At first we could not detect anything and then, through his binoculars, Beer spotted a party of ghorals, some thirty or more, motionless, watching us. Gradually we began to pick them out with the naked eye and there began one of those frustrating schoolroom games, each waiting to see what the other would do next. After a quarter of an hour,

Colour Plate 145. Hill above Thudam marking the parting of the ways. To the right of the hill passes the track to Walungchung Gola taken by the lama whilst the party continued on a track to the left up the Lhesa Khola. (November)

Colour Plate 146. *Myricaria rosea*, a dwarf tamarisk common along shingle banks and stony river courses in the valleys above Thudam. The rich rusty-red colour of the leaves and seed heads could be seen at a distance. (November)

Colour Plate 147. A young Ghoral in the Lhesa Khola north of Thudam. This normally shy animal is related to a deer and is usually found at middle altitudes in the Himalaya. This individual was probably sickly or injured as it stumbled on occasion and allowed us to get quite close. (November)

Colour Plate 148. Hillside between 15,000 and 16,000ft. (4,572 and 4,877m) in the Lhesa Khola north of Thudam. The dark patches in the otherwise brown landscape belong to the low growing Black juniper *Juniperus indica*. (November)

Colour Plate 149. *Juniperus indica* growing at 15,000ft. (4,572m) on a steep slope in the valley of the Lhesa Khola north of Thudam. (November)

however, we conceded victory as, impatient to be off, we turned away and climbed slowly up the track.

At a height of 16,000ft. (4,877m) we found ourselves looking along a wide shallow valley which travelled a mile or so to the foot of a steep slope whose crest almost certainly marked the border with Tibet. Two dark specks had appeared in the sky above the ridge and gradually loomed larger as they flew in our direction. They were ravens, and as though trained to do so they circled above our heads for a short while before returning from whence they came, having uttered no sound of alarm.

There was no sign of the Sherpas so we decided to wait for their arrival and having dropped our rucksacks in a pile on the track began to examine the nearby slopes. Beer and I were slowly searching on opposite sides of the river when we each found a *Rhododendron* species new to us. Our shouts were simultaneous and I crossed the water carrying a small twig of my find to match that which Beer was busy photographing. It proved to be *R. nivale* and formed low mounds 6in. (15cm) high of tangled stems with reddish scaly young shoots clothed with tiny, greyish-green scaly leaves ¼in. (.65cm) long. The whole plant was aromatic when bruised, in common with *R. anthopogon* and *R. setosum,* both of which accompanied it. Although we searched for some time these appeared to be the only woody plants at this height – 16,500ft. (5,029m) – and, apart from a few miserable shrivelled grasses, the only other plant to be seen was *Arenaria polytrichoides* which formed straw-coloured cushions up to 10in. (25.5cm) across. Each cushion was made up of numerous closely packed rosettes of sharp pointed narrow leaves and were hard enough to stand on without breaking them (Colour Plate 150). These seemingly indestructible high-alpine cushions seemed a far cry from the little sandworts of Britain, and even further removed from that curse of fine lawns, the creeping pearlwort, to which it is also related.

We had waited for over an hour with still no sign of the others, so reluctantly we picked up our belongings and retraced our steps down the valley. The sun was setting before we met Dawa coming up the track to find us. He explained that having had instructions from the panchayat man of Thudam not to go near the border, he had made camp some distance further down the valley and hoped that we would not be too angry. I <u>was</u> angry at having to give up the chance of a look into Tibet, but eventually acknowledged Dawa's good sense.

On 5 November whilst breakfast was cooking we found by the river *Polygonum affine,* a carpeting perennial with strap-shaped leaves and dense spikes of rust-coloured fruits (Colour Plate 151). I was pleased to see this plant in the wild as it is such a garden favourite when its rose-pink flowers are present. This form was the same as, or very similar to, that collected in central Nepal by Colonel Donald Lowndes in 1950 and with its shorter, thicker spikes, far superior to the thin-spiked forms from the western Himalaya of which 'Darjeeling Red', despite its name, is one.

After breakfast we decided to climb a steep hill above our camp, and leaving Pema and Namgyal as watchmen, immediately set off. At a height of 16,200ft. (4,937m) we stopped for a rest. Above us a rock stack soared to 17,200ft. (5,242m) and we made this our next objective (Colour Plate 152). The snow had frozen on the steep ground below the stack and we reached its base by cutting steps with our ice picks, the first occasion we had used them for this purpose. From the summit we could see Tibetan peaks covered in snow and to the north-west lay

Plate 46. A group of teenage girls and children in the Bhotia village of Thudam. Despite the cold, footwear is still optional

more snow-covered peaks, whilst to the west other ranges could be seen, their summits obscured by cloud. Whichever way we turned we saw mountains and valleys and hanging glaciers, a cold grey landscape whose black and white fangs carved a picture both beautiful and cruel. Eventually, the bitter winds dislodged us from our perch and we clambered down on to a field of large rock slabs which lay strewn like a pack of giant cards in our path. I don't know who started it, but we suddenly found ourselves jumping from one slab to another and before long we were moving headlong downhill racing the Sherpas back to camp, which we achieved at breakneck speed and breathless. It was foolhardy but fun.

It was 5 November and that night the Sherpas built a huge bonfire of juniper to which, to our shame, were added quantities of potentilla, tamarisk and dwarf rhododendrons. Having explained to them the story and tradition of the Gunpowder Plot, we started an exciting if childish game of leaping over the fire through the alternate licking of smoke and flame. The Sherpas joined in with gusto, yelling and catching the brushwood with their feet to send showers of sparks into the night air. To any watching herdsmen or travellers, the scene must have suggested a gathering of demons.

The following day we retreated down the valley as the weather deteriorated. Dense mist was dispersed by a freezing wind which in turn brought a fine hail. By the time we reached our campsite in late afternoon, snow was falling thickly and by the time we were all huddled in the kitchen tent, we were snowed in. Beer told us he had seen a Snow leopard – pale brown with dark head and tail – whilst the only thing of note that I had seen had been a golden-leaved form of *Rhododendron setosum* which had stood out like a beacon in a patch of the normal kind (Colour Plate 142). When we retired to our sleeping bags the snow was still falling but the situation changed during the night for the sun was shining next morning.

The snow had drifted against the stone walls of the yak pen in which we had encamped and we all set about clearing a passage to the track outside. The wind had gone, leaving in its wake a silent white world through which we slowly trudged. For several hours we followed a track which wound its way through birch and rhododendron, their peeling stems lending a warmth to the otherwise wintry scene. The antler-like branches of the Silver firs were lined with snow (Colour Plate 154), whilst at ground level the same snow held tall brown herbs and sedges in an icy grasp.

We reached Thudam at midday, by which time the weather had once again

Colour Plate 151. *Polygonum affine* 'Donald Lowndes' growing in a scree bed in the Sir Harold Hillier Gardens and Arboretum. Collected in Central Nepal by Col. Lowndes in 1950, the same or a similar form grew by the Lhesa Khola north of Thudam. (September)

Colour Plate 150. *Arenaria polytrichoides* at 15,500ft. (4,572mm) in the valley of the Lhesa Khola north of Thudam. It formed hard straw-coloured hummocks 6-10in. (15-25.5cm) across. In summer these would be studded with minute white flowers. (November)

Colour Plate 152. Rock stack above the Lhesa Khola valley north of Thudam. One day we climbed to the rock point beyond the stack to a height of 17,200ft. (5,242m) from whence we were afforded magnificent views in every direction. (November)

Colour Plate 153. The best of pals, Bhotia boys in the village of Thudam. They spent most days in our camp watching our antics

Colour Plate 154. Fresh fallen snow lodged on the branches of a Silver fir, *Abies densa,* in the valley above Thudam. (November)

Colour Plate 155. A young Bhotia in the village of Thudam

Colour Plate 156. A Bhotia with his young son in the village of Thudam. He carries a spindle on which to twine wool whilst his hat is trimmed with fur of the Red panda

deteriorated bringing mist and snow. Four of the Wabak Khola porters turned up for work and we set them to cleaning seed. One of them made great play of a cough and when we enquired as to his condition, he claimed to have developed pains in his chest and left foot. Morris promised him some medicine and left the tent to return five minutes later armed with a box of mixed pills and tablets to cure anything from headaches to dehydration. By this time the wracked porter was putting on a convincing show of suffering emphasised by contorted features and a low persistent moaning. The man's companions were also showing signs of developing pains and when Morris placed a quantity of pills into an outstretched hand, it belonged not to the man with the cough but to another who complained that his throat was on fire. Before we could retrieve them they had been swallowed and a second lot had to be given to the original porter to stop him strangling the usurper.

Dawa returned from the village to announce that there was to be a dance that night and we were all invited. In due course, having first eaten, we trooped along to the river where we spent some time negotiating the log bridges by torchlight. On reaching the far side we were met by a pack of mongrels who snarled and complained in their eagerness to cross the bridges to go scavenging in our camp, which they did just as soon as we had left the area. Picking our way through the rocks we headed for a long wooden building from which singing and shouting could be heard. We bowed our heads to avoid hitting the low doorway and entered the candlelit living space where many people were gathered. Beer, Morris and I were handed tompas of chang and given a place by the fire whilst the Sherpas settled themselves about the room. Four men and four girls were standing in a line, their hands clasping those of a second rank behind. Slowly they shuffled forward and backward occasionally stamping their feet hard on the wooden floor, all the while chanting and wailing. They performed several dances, all basically similar in steps, and Dawa explained that they were old Tibetan dances, some of which he knew well.

It was approaching midnight when Beer and I decided to dance our version of a Highland fling, a suggestion well received by the villagers who settled themselves on the floor. It is certain that no Scot would have recognised the dance that followed. We hopped and skipped, bounced up and down, leapt in the air with arms outstretched, clapped our hands, shouted, screamed and whistled, in fact we did whatever came to our minds. The crowd loved it and encouraged us with shouts and banging of boots on wood. We were just about to stop for a rest when everyone leapt to their feet and joined us in the dance. Even if we had wanted to stop there was now no hope as sundry bodies hemmed us in, preventing us from sliding to the floor. Morris, being the tallest by far, kept banging his head on the ceiling beams and not surprisingly suffered from a headache the next day. I shall never know for how long we danced thus, but much later when the dancing ended and the butter lamps burned dry, we thanked our hosts, stumbled from the darkened room and returned to the river crossing. Our singing and laughing had alerted the dogs and we met them head on in the middle of the log bridge. The lead dog howled, showing a set of white teeth, its eyes glaring in defiance. Any other time we would have retreated but with our fear dulled by the effects of chang and our thoughts focused on our cosy tents we howled back and continued our crossing. The dogs turned tail and ran, one actually falling into the river, and in a matter of minutes we were sound asleep in our bags.

Plate 47. The author at Thudam with the expedition's Sherpa staff and several of the native porters. Dorje squats front row far left with Dawa our sirdar in blue plaid shirt. Right of the author is Pema our cook with Tende by his side. Standing left of the author is Da Norbu while far right is Berma, Dorje's sister. (November)

All the next day the snow fell half-heartedly and we spent the time cleaning seed and writing notes. In mid-afternoon we were called over to the village to witness the slaughter of a yak. When we arrived the animal had already been pinned to the ground and whilst one man held its head another plunged a long bladed knife into its heart. It seemed the yak died slowly with occasional kicks and trembling, and then the knife was withdrawn and the wound plugged with straw. A small bowl of water was then produced and poured down the yak's throat. In the water was a potion prepared by the lama, supporting a superstition which claims that if the yak accepts the drink then the sins of the slaughterers are forgiven. The yak was dead. Several men set about skinning the animal and cutting up the carcass. Every part of the yak was utilised and even the blood which gushed from the severed main artery was caught in a large bowl.

The day of our departure dawned clear and sunny and all morning we busied ourselves with packing and preparations. Some of the villagers came across the river to watch us and to sell or barter goods (Plate 46, Colour Plates 153, 155 and 156). The tail of the slaughtered yak was sold to Beer for R25 and a Singapore nylon shirt. Hats, furs, beads, tompas and rings were produced in turn. Eventually we called a halt to the trading and gathered the Sherpas together for a discussion (Plate 47).

Our next destination lay down-river in the village of Chyamtang. The locals told us that our best route lay over the hills west of Thudam, a journey of about two days. Beer and I, however, agreed that there was much to be gained by following the Bagang Khola which, on our map, appeared to join the river Arun below Chyamtang, Beer arguing that such a route might well reveal new plants including rhododendrons. In the event we split the group; Beer and I and Da Norbu took the river route and Morris and the rest followed the mountain route. It was a decision we almost regretted.

Colour Plate 157. The richly wooded gorge of the Bagang Khola below Thudam. Here grew Silver fir *(Abies densa)* and hemlock *(Tsuga dumosa)* together with birch *(Betula utilis)*, maples *(Acer pectinatum* and *A. caudatum)*, *Prunus rufa* and several *Rhododendron* species. (November)

Colour Plate 158. The Roof of the World! A spectacular panorama from a rock shoulder at 12,800ft. (3,901m) above the valley of the Bagang Khola (left). On the horizon, Makalu (left of centre) dominates. Everest is hidden behind the peak on the right. All the territory to the left of these peaks lies in Nepal, that to the right lies in Tibet. Chyamtang the village to which we were heading lies on the hillside middle left in the Upper Arun valley. (November)

9. DESPERATION VALLEY

It was on spring heels that Beer and I strode down the Bagang Khola valley that day. The river threshed along beside us drowning our shouts as first one plant then another caught our attention (Colour Plate 157). Da Norbu trundled in our wake. Metal pans and containers hung from his pack on bits of string, rattling furiously at every turn, and he reminded me of a travelling hardware man of gypsy origin who used to visit our neighbourhood when I was a child. Da Norbu, however, was no salesman and seemed to gain the greatest pleasure from assisting us in our collecting activities. He caught us up at one point festooned in a glossy leaved vine – *Smilax menispermoides* – whose prickly stems clamber over bushes and into small trees.

We collected seed from a particularly splendid birch by climbing into its crown and shaking its branches. Seed and scales showered down like so much confetti and a plastic sheet spread upon the ground was soon covered with a rich brown booty. *Rhododendron arboreum* and *R. barbatum* now formed trees up to 40ft. (12m) and 25ft. (7.5m) respectively, and the undergrowth consisted mainly of ferns including *Pteris biaurita*, a relative of the so-called finger fern – *P. cretica* – commonly sold as a houseplant in the West.

Around 11,000 (3,353m) we found a 20ft. (6m) specimen of *Hydrangea heteromalla* with large oval leaves and flattened terminal seed heads. Nearby stood a young Silver fir with extra long leaves.

We made camp that night in the dank, dripping darkness of the rhododendron forest, the three of us sharing one tent. The glum atmosphere was relieved next morning by the sun filtering through the layers of leaves and branches and we were quickly on the move following the same track as the day before, collecting all the while. We found a bold bramble *Rubus treutleri* 4-5ft. (1.25-1.5m) high, the arching downy stems carrying downy, vine-shaped leaves 4-5in. (10-13cm) across, turning an attractive reddish-purple. The red fruits were set in large calyces and borne in terminal and axillary clusters.

Daphne bholua became increasingly common and we found an extraordinary specimen with a single stem rising to a height of 20ft. (6m). *Tsuga dumosa* appeared, large trees with tall massive trunks. Beneath these giants *Rhododendron arboreum* formed a dense canopy, their moss-swaddled branches supporting large clumps of *Vaccinium nummularia* and various ferns. Here we found a single specimen of the Sikkim holly – *Ilex sikkimensis* – a small tree to 15ft. (4.5m) with grey bark, shallowly toothed leaves 4-5in. (10-13cm) long with purple stalks and midrib beneath. The axillary clusters of bold red fruits identified this form as the variety *coccinea* of Comber. This holly is occasionally seen in cultivation in Britain, but it is of borderline hardiness and is only successful in the south-west and west. According to Professor H. Hara of Japan, the name *I. hookeri* is a synonym of the above species, but plants I have examined under this name in British cultivation have always proved to be another Himalayan holly – *I. dipyrena*.

The track we had been following suddenly took an abrupt turn and climbed the steep hillside to our right. A suggestion of a track meanwhile continued above the river and this we followed for several hundred yards until faced by a deep ravine across which there appeared to be no discernible crossing. So much for our hope of a riverside route! We turned back and began a long and hard 3,000ft. (914m) climb up the valleyside through bamboo thicket and dense herbage, amongst which we found extensive colonies of a *Strobilanthes* species, already flowered. This is a large genus of the *Acanthus* family but very different in general appearance from the familiar Bear's breeches of western gardens. Like others I have since seen in Kashmir, it was a downy herbaceous perennial 2ft. (60cm) high with sharply toothed, nettle-like leaves. The two-lipped flowers are invariably blue or purple and are produced in clusters over a long period during late summer and autumn. I have seen plants in cultivation, possibly *S. alatus,* which, given a warm border or bed, create a cheerful late splash of colour each year, whilst *S. atropurpureus* reaches 4-5ft. (1.25-1.5m) and its flowers are a rich violet-blue.

After four-and-a-half hours of climbing, we attained the rim of the valley at 12,800ft. (3,901m). On the way we had passed through a scattering of the Himalayan juniper – *J. recurva* – large specimens up to 50ft. (15m) with stems almost rivalling those of the Silver fir in girth. Most of these trees possessed an open-branch system with gracefully drooping branchlets and striking grey or blue-grey foliage.

The bamboo through which we had toiled was almost certainly *Yushania maling,* and looking back into the valley we could see a whole series of dome-shaped hills, their summits capped by the same bright-green bamboo.

A short walk along the ridge track brought us to a suitable place to make camp. Our night was disturbed by yaks crashing and blundering around in their attempts to reach the spring near our tent, but morning saw no damage to our belongings and we began climbing the ridge to where a huge rock outcrop barred our way. Following Da Norbu we scaled the obstacle, to be met with possibly the most breathtaking view of the journey so far. From our perch at approximately 12,800ft. (3,901m) we gazed over the lower Bagang Khola and across the Upper Arun valley to the hillside where lay the village of Chyamtang – our destination. But it was not the intervening valleys and hills which drew our attention, but the magnificent show of mountains on the western horizon. Occupying the centre of the stage was the conical mass of Makalu with Nepal to the south and Tibet to the north. We were looking due west along the very spine of the Greater Himalaya – the roof of the world (Colour Plate 158). For some time we sat on our rock fascinated by the panorama which lay before us, and watching a slender winged lammergeyer gliding far below until I saw the valleys rapidly filling with mist.

The ridge on which we found ourselves was a haven for rhododendrons, which formed dense carpets and thickets. *Rhododendron thomsonii* and *R. hodgsonii* were the two most common, whilst *R. cinnabarinum*, *R. campylocarpum* and *R. campanulatum* were in lesser numbers. Our excitement was complete, however, when we found another species – *R. fulgens* – for the first time. It formed a large shrub 10-12ft. (3-3.70m) high with attractive pink-tinged cinnamon and grey peeling bark (Colour Plate 159). The leaves were 4-5in. (10-13cm) long, elliptic, polished dark green above and covered with a thin woolly fawn pelt below. Nearby, a grassy bank was scattered with the pale-blue trumpets of *Gentiana depressa* (Colour Plate 160) and the fruiting spikes of *Lobelia erectiuscula*, a relative of our native *L. urens*. Plants in cultivation from this seed, however, have proved of little merit.

Descending the hillside we followed a track which took us through a forest of *Rhododendron hodgsonii*, many of which had stems 25-35ft. (7.5-10.5m) high. These were covered with pink-tinted cinnamon bark which peeled away, sometimes in enormous sheets as in the Canoe birch – *Betula papyrifera* – of North America. There was freshly fallen snow on the ground and this, heightened by the slanting shafts of a wakening sun, painted an unforgettable picture.

In the snow we found tracks made by a four-legged animal, probably a Snow leopard. They appeared quite fresh, possibly two or three hours old, and had taken the same line as that which we now followed. In Nepal it is regarded as a sign of great good luck to find the tracks of this rarely seen animal. For several miles we followed both track and leopard until the snow ended abruptly and the track, never clearly marked, now disappeared and left us staring into a deep ravine down which tumbled a white-crested torrent. This we crossed and for the next fifteen minutes toiled up a steep incline to where the snow again covered all. To have lost the track at this stage would have brought us problems so we cast around at the edge of the snow until, to our surprise, we again found the Snow leopard's tracks. They led us up and down the contours for close upon a mile before leaving the snow at exactly the same point as the re-emergent track.

On we trudged through rhododendron and juniper thicket until late afternoon when we found ourselves descending a gully so steep that we slid down on our backsides rather than risk falling head first. It was while negotiating a difficult

Colour Plate 159. *Rhododendron fulgens* growing on a ridge in the valley of the Bagang Khola below Thudam. Note the attractive pink-tinged cinnamon and grey peeling bark and the pale bloomy new bark. (November)

Colour Plate 160. *Gentiana depressa*. The pale blue and white striped trumpets of this lovely species are a common autumn sight in Nepalese mountains. We found it on several occasions spangling the alpine turf. (October)

Colour Plate 161. *Ilex intricata*, a curious evergreen holly of dense twiggy habit, the branchlets clothed with small box-like leaves and studded (on female plants) with bright red fruits. Although we collected a goodly number of fruits, most proved infertile and to the best of my knowledge there are no plants in cultivation from the seed sown. (November)

182

Colour Plate 162. *Vaccinium glauco-album* growing in a steep ravine in the valley of the Bagang Khola. From this seed a free-fruiting form was raised which in 1991 was given an Award of Merit by the Royal Horticultural Society under the cultivar name 'Da Norbu', the name of one of our Sherpas. (November)

Colour Plate 163. The author in a dried stream bed above the Bagang Khola. This area was mainly dominated by bamboo, rhododendrons and *Daphne bholua*. (November)

Colour Plate 164. Len Beer collecting fruits of a small leaved dwarf holly *Ilex intricata*. It was frequent in the valley of the Bagang Khola, here seen beneath birch and *Rhododendron barbatum*. (November)

piece of ground that we came across a large dense colony of the small-leaved holly – *Ilex intricata* – many bushes crowded with red berries (Colour Plates 161 and 164). This was too good a harvest to miss so we spent the next hour filling two cotton bags. The delay, however, gave evening a chance to overtake us and we suddenly had to leave our temporary perch and continue our downward slide. Eventually we found ourselves in the rock-strewn belly of the gully, and there, with darkness upon us, we spent the night wedged between two boulders, spat at by the torrent which passed within a yard of where we lay.

Long before the sun reached us we rose and packed, lingering just long enough to watch dawn fingering the summit of distant Makalu, which we could see through the western mouth of the gully.

Once again we climbed steeply up the hillside through thickets of the common bamboo of the area – *Yushania maling*. Himalayan juniper and Silver fir provided a canopy, beneath which various shrubs and herbs flourished including *Jasminum humile*. This shrub in its typical form is not commonly encountered in cultivation where its nodding clusters of bright yellow tubular flowers are borne profusely and over a long period in summer. This plant was sporting small shining black berries, and judging by the large number of its slender pointed leaflets probably belonged to the variety *wallichianum*.

Our track led us from the trees into an open area over which the mugwort *Artemisia indica (vulgaris)* was rampant. This strong herbaceous perennial is a common weed in Europe, including Britain, where it frequently occupies rail and roadsides, waste places and rubbish dumps. It seemed quite out of place here in the Himalaya, and no doubt, like the nettle, has followed man on his travels. Two small bushy-headed trees now caught our attention, one of which, a cotoneaster, I climbed to retrieve a few dried red berries. This seed has since germinated to produce strong-growing shrubs with powerful stems. These are clothed with dark-green pale-backed leaves which colour richly before falling in autumn, when, at the same time, the red fruits are borne in large drooping clusters. It seems perfectly hardy and to my mind looks to be typical *Cotoneaster frigidus*. The second tree, an evergreen, was very different in appearance from the other. It reached approximately 18ft. (5.5m) with several branches forming a dense spreading head some 25ft. (7.5m) across. The narrow leathery leaves measured 1-1½in. (2.5-3.75cm) long and were prettily veined. No flower or fruit was apparent but I had no hesitation in naming it *Euonymus tingens,* a rare spindle-berry which is represented in cultivation by plants collected as seed by Ludlow and Sherriff from Bhutan. I have since seen this species in Bhutan where I was struck by the slender nature of the leaves. Two of the best specimens I have encountered in gardens in the British Isles are at Knightshayes in Devon, and Glendoick near Perth.

Leaving the trees behind we continued along a track which became progressively vague until eventually it disappeared altogether. Whilst Da Norbu cast around in the undergrowth Beer and I lay in the shade of a large bush which, when our eyes focused on its leaves, proved to be *Viburnum grandiflorum,* a huge specimen which must have measured at least 25ft. x 25ft. (7.5 x 7.5m). This species is uncommon in British cultivation where it is less hardy than the smaller-flowered Chinese *V. farreri*. These two species were crossed at Bodnant Gardens in North Wales and at the Royal Botanic Garden, Edinburgh, to produce the well known hybrid *V.* x *bodnantense* of which the Bodnant selection 'Dawn' is one of the most commonly planted winter flowering shrubs.

After some time Da Norbu returned to tell us he had located a track and we climbed to our feet to follow him into the thicket. The next few hours were spent losing and finding tracks. It was amazing how a track clearly defined one minute could peter out the next and, as always, bamboo thickets proved the most confusing offenders. Casting around on one occasion we broke through the vegetation to find ourselves in a dried up river gully which fell steeply down the hillside (Colour Plate 163).

We agreed to make camp before dark. We were all tired and hungry, covered in sticky seed heads, scratched by rose and bramble and bruised from twanging bamboo. We had had enough for one day so, lacking a flat piece of ground, we found a depression in a large rock slab and there laid out our bedrolls. Da Norbu lit a fire and we located a water supply which at least enabled us to cook our remaining food – a bowl of rice and an Oxo cube! We had placed two stout logs across the base of the depression to prevent us sliding away in the night and it was with some relief that we awoke the next morning to find ourselves intact except for a kitbag which had rolled away.

In the light of morning we were better able to appreciate our situation and, whilst Da Norbu was packing, Beer and I wandered about collecting seed of several interesting plants including two *Hypericum* species – *H. tenuicaule* and *H. uralum*, the latter with frond-like growths and pretty nodding buttercup-like flowers. *H. tenuicaule* was a shrub of some 4-5ft. (1.25-1.45m) with arching stems and narrow elliptic to narrowly ovate, wavy-margined leaves 1-1½in. (2.5-3.75cm) long. The capsules were irregular in surface. This species is now in cultivation but is of little ornamental merit. *Boenninghausenia albiflora, Gaultheria semi-infera, Aster albescens* and several other small shrubs were common, and we discovered a particularly handsome colony of *Vaccinium glauco-album* in fruit (Colour Plate 162). A plant raised from this seed at the Savill Gardens in Berkshire was given an Award of Merit when exhibited before the Royal Horticultural Society in London in November 1991. It has since been given the cultivar name 'Da Norbu' in honour of our Sherpa porter, a reliable, loyal and patient man who not only carried for us in difficult conditions but helped us clean the gaultheria's seed.

From the general thicket *Philadelphus tomentosus* threw its stems 6-8ft. (1.85-2.5m) high and *Elaeagnus parvifolia* reached even higher with its scaly stems flaunting narrow silver-backed leaves. We were excited to find another rhododendron – *R. triflorum*, a straggling shrub to 5ft. (1.5m) with reddish-brown peeling bark. A species of the slightly warmer zones of the eastern Himalaya, it is variable in flower size and colour, pale yellow being typical (Colour Plate 167).

Towering over these shrubs and forming living walls above the gully were several different trees (Colour Plate 165), mainly conifers – Himalayan hemlock, Bhutan pine – *Pinus wallichiana* (Colour Plate 166) and Silver fir. Broad-leaved trees such as *Alnus nepalensis* and *Populus jacquemontiana* variety *glauca* frequented the edges of the gully itself, whilst higher up we spotted the unmistakable presence of the Himalayan larch – *Larix griffithiana*, a single specimen some 40-50ft. (12-15m) tall, its needles already turning a tawny yellow. Uncommon and rather tender in cultivation, this graceful species is

Colour Plate 165. Wooded hillside of the Bagang Khola valley. The pale-leaved trees are *Populus jacquemontiana* variety *glauca* with the darker needled Bhutan pine *Pinus wallichiana* and the pale orange-brown stemmed Himalayan birch *Betula utilis*. Here also we found *Larix griffithiana*, whilst the thicket beneath these trees contained a wealth of shrubs including *Viburnum grandiflorum, Philadelphus tomentosus, Rhododendron triflorum, Jasminum humile, Elaeagnus parvifolia* and *Daphne bholua*. (November)

Colour Plate 166. *Pinus wallichiana* photographed in Bhutan. The Bhutan pine is widespread in the Himalaya and principally found in inner drier valleys. We found it in scattered populations in the Upper Arun valley. The long drooping blue-green needles in clusters of five and the pendant cylindrical cones are characteristic. (May)

Colour Plate 167. *Rhododendron triflorum* photographed in Bhutan. Some forms of this species are most attractive in flower whilst the peeling reddish brown bark is a bonus. We found it growing in the valleys of the Bagang Khola below Thudam. (May)

Colour Plate 168. Len Beer and the author climbing a hillside in the Bagang Khola valley. This proved one of the hottest and most wearying days of the entire expedition. (November)

Colour Plate 169. *Rubus biflorus*, its white bloomy stems standing out in the thicket of secondary growth in the valley of the Bagang Khola. (November)

Colour Plate 170. *Rubus biflorus* demonstrating its whiter than white bloomy stems in the Winter Garden of the University Botanic Garden, Cambridge. (February)

easily distinguished from all others by its large cones with conspicuous exserted bracts.

The rocks in the gully were borne in great slabs, their upper surfaces worn by monsoon torrents into channels and saucer-like depressions. In the crevices, grasses had become established, their bold tufts and plumes waving about in the wind which rushed from the valley below. Three species were mainly present of which the most common was *Calamagrostis emodensis*, its 3-4ft. (.90-1.25m) stems bearing dense drooping plumes of silvery spikelets, most of which had already bleached to a cream or pale straw colour. An attractive contrast was provided by *Erianthus rufipilus*, whose dense, erect plumes of rose-tinted spikelets were just opening. I was particularly pleased to see *Miscanthus nepalensis*, with its silky fulvous spikelets borne in characteristic finger-like arrangements at the tip of a 2-3ft. (60-90cm) stem. The leaves were turning a charming purplish shade contrasting effectively with the pale clear midrib. Whilst less spectacular than its Japanese and Chinese counterparts, this species would be well worth a place in the small garden for its stature and elegance.

Our wanderings were curtailed by the sound of Da Norbu's voice and we descended the gully to where he stood packed and ready to leave. There was no discernible track so we simply swung our parangs (long blades) and cut our way through the undergrowth heading in a westerly direction (Colour Plate 168).

Looking back on this day I believe it to have been the most wearying of the entire expedition. Our progress was slow and laborious, Beer and I taking it in turns to cut a path through the undergrowth which contained such shrubs as *Daphne bholua, Jasminum humile, Elsholtzia fruticosa* and *Philadelphus tomentosus.* I never imagined there would come the day when I would deliberately chop such plants to the ground. The thought almost shames me when I gaze on a *Daphne bholua* in full flower, pampered in cultivation. A jumble of rocks thrust their way through the canopy and for these we headed, guided by a curtain of Himalayan vine – *Parthenocissus himalayana* – whose long growths clad with brilliant crimson leaves gave the impression from a distance of newly spilt blood.

Climbing the rocks we were accompanied by a party of short-billed minivets, the males with scarlet and the females with canary-yellow underparts. On gaining the summit of the largest rock we found ourselves with a clear view into the valley below. The forest continued for perhaps a quarter of a mile giving way to what appeared to be grassland over which were scattered small bamboo huts and shelters. It suggested to us some kind of habitation, so down we climbed from the rocks and once more continued our trail cutting. After an hour we thankfully broke out of the forest to find, to our dismay, that what had appeared as grassland was in fact a sea of head-high secondary vegetation covering land formerly cultivated. Undaunted we plunged onwards in the direction of the huts, our progress now even slower than before. The wretched mugwort was everywhere, its pollen making our eyes and noses smart. A particularly uncompromising trailing vine persistently tripped us and we lost count of the times we fell over. At regular intervals also we ran into large specimens of a white-stemmed bramble – *Rubus biflorus* – which loomed out of the thicket like ghostly octopuses with viciously thorny tentacles (Colour Plates 169 and 170). To think that when I was a student at the University

Botanic Garden, Cambridge, I used to be a fan of this shrub, admiring its winter effect.

Whilst falling to the ground on one occasion I came face to face with *Anemone vitifolia,* an herbaceous species with five-lobed leaves and fluffy cottonwool-like seed heads. The flowers in late summer are white and it makes quite an attractive garden plant although less robust and less hardy than the hybrid Japanese anemones *A.* x *hybrida* of which with *A. hupehensis* variety *japonica* it is a parent (Colour Plate 174). Isolated trees of *Rhus succedanea* carried rich crimson leaves and these we carefully avoided, aware of the poisonous juice they contained. The sun blazed down and the aroma from the bruised mugwort made us feel sick, but still we staggered on until, two hours after leaving the forest, we gained the nearest hut. It was deserted and had been so for some years. From its dilapidated porch we saw several more huts lower down and we foolishly decided to head for them in the hope of finding at least a recently used track. Half-way to the next hut I stumbled and fell, my knee catching a rock hidden in the grass. I ended up on my back gazing at the sun which spun round like a ferris wheel. I managed to sit up and stare at the surrounding hills whose colour alternated between the natural and a curious monochrome. Then nausea took over and I lay back on the hillside until my head cleared. It seemed as though we would be spending another night in the valley, but we were hungry and thirsty and had neither food nor water and this fact determined us to attempt the climb out of the valley before nightfall. It was a long steep haul through solid scrub, painfully slow and several times we sank down to rest and could have slept where we lay. Eventually we made the ridge and peering over the other side we could see the village of Chyamtang on the distant hillside. There was no chance, however, of us making the village before the following day and our attention was then caught by a cluster of houses immediately at the foot of our ridge. There were obvious signs of activity – smoke from a fire and dogs barking – so we made our way down through a forest of Evergreen oak – *Quercus semecarpifolia* – and into the open space between the houses. Here we sank to the ground exhausted and thankful. The dogs, of course, had announced our arrival and two women emerged from the nearest house and approached us carrying a kind of giant cucumber which they sliced into three and offered to us. It was tasteless but thirst quenching and we asked Da Norbu to offer them our thanks. We stayed that night in the larger of the three houses and, after four or five glasses of chang, tucked into a meal of boiled chicken and rice. The chicken which we had seen being chased shortly after our arrival had done a lot of mileage, but we were ravenous and picked the carcass clean, even sucking the bones. Afterwards, considerably satisfied, we laid out our bedrolls and settled down for a good night's rest, at least that was what we intended to do. But our presence in the hamlet was hot news and the single living room which we shared with the family soon filled with noisy neighbours, most of whom brought their food with them to cook on the fire, all the time watching us while chattering.

After a quick breakfast and profuse thanks to our hostess we were on the move again following a well defined track up the hillside. An attractive herbaceous spurge – *Euphorbia sikkimensis* – was plentiful amongst low scrub, its narrow leaves strikingly marked by the almost white midrib (Colour Plate 172). This bold perennial is often seen in cultivation and is particularly

Colour Plate 171. *Lindera neesiana.* A deciduous tree, a member of the Bay family *(Lauraceae)* in flower. (November)

Colour Plate 172. *Euphorbia sikkimensis* flowering with another Nepalese native perennial *Polygonum amplexicaule* in a garden in Devon. In 1971 we found the former growing near a bridge across the Arun river below Chyamtang. (August)

Colour Plate 173. Len Beer crossing the Arun river below Chyamtang. The entire structure wobbled and bounced in a most alarming way. (November)

Colour Plate 174 (right). *Anemone vitifolia* flowering in the author's garden from seed collected in Nepal. Note the lobed but undivided leaves. This species was particularly common on scrub-covered hillsides in the valley of the Bagang Khola. (August)

ornamental in spring when the young growths are suffused coral pink or red. It is one of a number of similar species native to the Himalaya, *E. longifolia* being taller with narrower leaves, and the more recently named *E. schillingii,* discovered by Tony Schilling, probably the most ornamental of them all with broader leaves and bolder brassy yellow flowers.

From the ridge we could look down upon the Arun river and, almost directly across from where we stood, the village of Chyamtang. The Arun is the principal watershed of eastern Nepal. It begins life in Tibet defying all the laws of a normal watershed by carving its way through the world's highest mountains to flow south through the plains of India to join the Ganges and eventually the Bay of Bengal. The Upper Arun valley meanwhile is one of the deepest in the world considering that on its western flank there rises Mt. Everest (29,029ft./8,848m) and eighty miles to the east the 28,208ft. (8,597m) Kangchengjunga. Between these two the river flows at an altitude of 7,600ft. (2,316m).

Our descent to the river was long and steep and we followed a track which in places fell almost vertically. It was an invigorating experience and there was plenty of interest on the way especially in the world of trees. First to catch our attention was a cherry tree 25ft. (7.5m) high in full bloom. It was *Prunus cerasoides,* the species we had last seen above Side Pokhara, where its hard-pruned existence had made little impression on us at the time. Its bark was close and grey and its new leaves, only just emerging, of a bronze-green fringed with hair-tipped teeth. The blush-pink flowers 1in. (2.5cm) across were borne on drooping stalks, singly or in pairs, flooding the branches. It was a lovely sight and yet curious in that it should be flowering now in the middle of November. Later we saw a great number of these cherries scattered across the hillside above the river, many of the apparently planted near villages.

Two *Hydrangea* species were frequent by the track, both shrubs ranging in height from 10-15ft. (3-4.5m). One was a narrow-leaved form of *H. aspera* with large drooping seed heads. In cultivation plants grown from this seed has proved to be of a tender nature. The other, *H. robusta,* had very different broadly oval to orbicular leaves, occasionally as much as 12in. (30.5cm) long and wide. The flowerheads were equally large and flattened with creamy-white, green-tinted ray florets. This species is rarely if ever seen in British gardens due no doubt to its tender nature and its lacking the flower quality of *H. aspera.* of which some authorities regard it a variety. It would be worth its place in a collection, however, if only for its magnificent leaves.

Another plant we found which would grace gardens and arboretums in the milder areas of the British Isles was the Himalayan hornbeam – *Carpinus viminea.* This small- to medium-sized tree of graceful, often pendulous habit, is not even mentioned in Bean's *Trees and Shrubs Hardy in the British Isles* and one must assume that amazingly it has never been introduced or, if it has, that it hasn't survived our colder winters. The lance-shaped leaves, 2½-3½in. (6.5-9cm) long, are slender pointed and doubly toothed and of a delightful copper colour when emerging. Their finest character, however, are the veins which are boldly parallel. In the 1980s, seed of this species was introduced from China and a specimen in my garden has achieved 10ft. (3m) (1993). It is of elegant habit with pendulous branches and reddish purple young leaves and has attracted favourable comment from all who have seen it.

The wealth of broad-leaved trees on the hillside pleased us after having seen endless *Rhododendron arboreum* and conifers and we were especially impressed by the representation of the bay family – *Lauraceae* – with *Cinnamomum glanduliferum, Litsea doshia* and *Lindera neesiana* the most common. The latter was a deciduous tree with oval leaves 2-3in. (5-7.5cm) long and small clusters of yellow flowers (Colour Plate 171). *Lithocarpus elegans* appeared as a small evergreen tree with lance-shaped leathery leaves 6-10in. (15-25.5cm) long, not unlike those of the Chinese *L. henryi* which, in my opinion, is one of the finest hardy evergreen trees in cultivation. I was also pleased to see a 30ft. (9m) *Meliosma*, with coarsely toothed, abruptly pointed leaves. It was later identified as *M. simplicifolia* subspecies *yunnanensis*. Crowding the sides of the track were many shrubs and perennials including *Aster trinervius,* its white daisy flowers 1in. (2.5cm) across borne in large loose heads on 2-3ft. (60-90cm) stems. Far more spectacular, however, was *Senecio cappa (densiflorus)* with stout erect woody stems 4-5ft. (1.25-1.5m) tall clothed with grey-backed coarsely toothed leaves 2½-3½in. (6.5-9cm) long. The yellow flowers were carried in dense bold terminal heads sometimes as much as 1ft. (30cm) long. This would be a much sought after plant for the herbaceous border if only it were hardy. The hillside at this point must have been in the region of 8,000-9,000ft. (2,438-2,743m), and amazing though it may seem to British gardeners this is a little too low in Himalayan terms to expect much in the way of hardy plants, although several might have succeeded out of doors in the mildest areas of the British Isles. It seemed to us at the time a pity that the transition zone between warm and cool temperate should be placed on this richly clad hillside.

We reached the river which, at this point, was young and freshly emerged from Tibet, throwing itself at the rocks with terrific gusto, causing its waters to froth and foam. To cross it we were required to tread a bamboo bridge of the most slender proportions which bounced and swayed under the slightest pressure. Da Norbu would not cross whilst carrying his enormous pack, and I could hardly blame him, so Beer carried half of it, and the sight of him moving gingerly along what was little more than a narrow gangplank is something I shall never forget (Colour Plate 173). Once safely across we climbed the near vertical hillside and trod the stone-paved streets of Chyamtang to where our camp had been pitched in a field of stubble above the village. Having been expected the previous day we received a warm welcome from Morris and Dawa who, aware of our food situation, had been preparing a search party to come to meet us. Beer and I stopped just short of the camp insisting that Da Norbu should arrive first in recognition of his tremendous spirit and physical strength. Without him we would still have been groping about in the undergrowth and hopelessly lost. During the previous days never once had he grumbled or complained, nor had he disagreed with decisions once taken. He was a worthy son of a famous father.

Colour Plate 175. Father and daughter in the village of Chyamtang in the Upper Arun valley

Colour Plate 176. Len Beer photographing a mani wall between Chyamtang and Chepua in the Upper Arun valley. These walls, the stones of which are carved with the Tibetan Buddhist chant 'Om mani padme hum', should be passed on one's right. (November)

10. A DEMON STRIKES

We spent three days in Chyamtang, and for most of this time our activities attracted an audience of villagers (Plate 49). They presented a wild raggle-taggle appearance, sporting a variety of hats of which a trilby seemed the most popular, usually decorated with peacock feathers, badges or flowers, especially orange marigolds and white marguerites. Kukris were carried by most males including quite small boys. They reminded me of a gang of pirates looking for trouble, and the fierce countenance of many lent credence to my theory, which, however, dissolved whenever they smiled. For then their faces split to reveal teeth tarnished and unevenly worn through a lifetime's gnawing and smoking. Cheap Nepalese cigarettes were available in many village stores in the lower valleys and home-made versions could be had wherever certain trees or shrubs such as lyonia grew.

The village lay spread over a large area of hillside, its houses separated by small terraced fields in which many crops were grown. At night villagers moved about with the aid of torches constructed of split bamboo canes, one end lit from the fire. From our elevated position their movements resembled fireflies – now converging, now separating, creating a fascinating pattern of light. On reaching our camp the visitors extinguished their torches, relighting them from our fire on leaving. One night we heard the sound of drums emanating from a house some distance away. We decided to investigate, and on reaching the house entered through a low doorway to find ourselves in a large room lit by a fire in the middle of the earth floor. The place was seething, some people sitting, others standing, all drinking chang which was dispensed by several women who fussed like the witches in *Macbeth* over a large cauldron. In one corner of the room two men sat cross-legged, each holding a long-handled drum which he struck regularly with a curved tong, chanting all the while. Opposite these sat a bearded man also chanting whilst shaking cymbals rigorously. We were told the bearded man was a lama performing some service for the owner of the house, and it seemed to us that everyone had joined the party including our Sherpas and many of the porters who sang and laughed and helped to keep the chang brewers busy. It was a real Irish pub spirit, everyone laughing or singing except the musicians who maintained a serious countenance throughout. Outside the house yet another fire burned around which danced a host of children, whilst nearby around a third fire several men were making sausages out of meat and intestines. Long after we had gone to bed we could hear the sound of the drums throbbing dolefully into the early hours.

Morris continued his morning 'surgeries' which were well attended, some patients travelling several miles for the privilege. Several brought gifts such as eggs, vegetables and even chickens. One man asked for medicine for his sister who had been kicked in the thigh by a bullock, whilst a woman asked for medicine for her husband whose head had been cut by a neighbour's kukri after an argument. Others had festering sores and stomach complaints to whom Morris administered as best he was able. As before in other villages we had passed through, it was depressing to see so many people with misshapen limbs as a result of unattended breakages and fractures.

We discussed village crops with the panchayat leader and learned that, in addition to millet and maize, which were everywhere apparent (Colour Plate 177), wheat, barley, naked barley, potatoes, soya beans, buckwheat and radishes were grown. Several vegetables, including a variety of marrow, were cultivated on a smaller scale.

One morning the Wabak Khola porters chopped down an old stump in a nearby field and brought it to burn on their fire. They were soon followed by an irate women who started shouting at us for taking the log from her field. Her tongue flapped like a flag in the wind and Berma, taking exception to some of the remarks, answered back in like fashion. Very soon the two were going at each other hammer and tongs until Dawa stepped in between and broke them apart, leaving Berma in tears with her tormentor laughing and making fun of her (Plate 48).

Most of the trees in the vicinity of the village had been cut down many years previously but occasional stands of Bhutan pine remained. The Himalayan ivy – *Hedera nepalensis* – was very common hereabouts, climbing over rocks and into shrubs and thickets. Its ovate pointed

Plate 48. This woman of Chyamtang sat belabouring our porters for cutting branches from a tree on her land. Even a cigarette did nothing to calm her

Plate 49. We were never without onlookers in our camp at Chyamtang in the Upper Arun valley. Young and old found much to interest and amuse them

leaves were entire or occasionally with two basal lobes, quite unlike the boldly toothed version of this species in British cultivation, which I suspect originated in Kashmir, at least that is where I once found such a plant, which is quite common in the Dachigam Forest Reserve near Srinagar. The lovely pink flowered cherry – *Prunus cerasoides* – was plentiful and, like the pine, had on the whole been spared the axe due to its religious significance (Colour Plates 178 and 180). *Viburnum erubescens* here made a large shrub of 15ft. (4.5m) or more with leaves polished green above and the occasional small unseasonal cluster of white, pink-tinged flowers. With the last grew a splendid bramble – *Rubus niveus* – with vigorous purple-brown prickly stems up to 8ft. (2.5m) high coated with a white bloom. The leaves consisted of nine to eleven toothed, long-pointed leaflets, white felted beneath. Creeping over rocks and moist banks we found *Parochetus communis*, like a delicate clover with single blue pea flowers, and *Polygonum capitatum,* its red-flushed stems and pill-like pink flowerheads contrasting effectively with the blue of the other.

Spiraea micrantha reappeared, thrusting its strong erect stems 4-5ft. (1.25-1.5m) from the thicket and bearing terminal flattened heads of white flowers. In effect, this shrub resembles a magnificent white-flowered *S. japonica,* and seeds we collected have resulted in vigorous individuals with bold inflorescences, providing a striking contrast with the red and rose flowered kinds.

During this period in camp we checked through the specimens collected by Morris between Thudam and Ritak higher up the Arun. They included *Rhododendron ciliatum* and *Aconitum spicatum,* previously found by us on the Milke Danda. Two red-fruited brambles had been collected as seed – *Rubus thomsonii* and *R. treutleri* – the latter with large palm-shaped downy leaves, its fruits partly enclosed by the large calyces. Another good find was the true

Colour Plate 177. *Eleusine coracana,* the Finger millet, is one of the most commonly planted grain crops in the hills, especially in the Upper Arun valley. It is used for many purposes including the making of tsampa and chang or mountain beer. (November)

Colour Plate 178. *Prunus cerasoides* and *Pinus wallichiana,* both cruelly lopped, still dominate a field below Chyamtang in the Upper Arun valley. (November)

Colour Plate 179. *Sorbus vestita,* a fruiting specimen growing in the Sir Harold Hillier Gardens and Arboretum. We saw this Himalayan Whitebeam on several occasions in east Nepal. (October)

Colour Plate 180. *Prunus cerasoides*, an ancient tree approximately 50ft. (15m) tall with a girth of 8½ft. (2.6m) at breast height, by a track below Chyamtang in the Upper Arun valley. (November)

Sorbus vestita. First Morris had seen a single 40ft. (12m) tree growing between two fields near the village of Ritak, but later found others in mixed woodland. The leaves of these trees were oval and pointed 5-6in. (13-15cm) long on 1-1½in. (2.5-3.75cm) stalks. The leaf undersurface was densely white felted (Colour Plate 179), whilst the fruits were like speckled crab-apples ¾-1in. (2-2.5cm) across, green with a rose-flushed cheek. This species, both in leaf and fruit, differed from the closely related *S. hedlundii* we had seen on the Milke Danda. Young trees from this seed are now well established and growing strongly in several collections including the Hillier Arboretum and Wakehurst Place, Sussex. In the Hillier Arboretum, too, is a *Cotoneaster* species Morris found – a low-growing, spreading evergreen which has only recently (1994) been identified as a new species – *C. zimmermanii*.

The seed of several rhododendrons were in Morris's collection, but two seed lots which particularly pleased us were the red berries of *Viburnum mullaha* a shrub 8-10ft. (2.5-3m) high with toothed leaves 2-3in. (5-7.5cm) long, and the black fruits of a Himalayan dogwood – *Cornus macrophylla* – which he had gathered from a tree of some 30ft. (9m). The former is of borderline hardiness in Britain where it is occasionally encountered in collections. The dogwood, however, which is also found in western China, is generally hardy and somewhat resembles *C. controversa* in its attractive tiered branches. *C. controversa* and the North American *C. alternifolia*, incidentally, are the only species with alternately arranged leaves and are thus easily recognised in cultivation.

On one occasion several young men and women returning from a wood-cutting expedition stopped by our camp to have some fun. A general mêlée developed when a 'young blood' wrestled with the beefy Berma and some village girls chased Dorje through the millet fields. It was all good fun, however, and ended up with everyone laughing their heads off.

Da Norbu soon recovered from his ordeal in the Bagang Khola valley and spent much of his time in camp chopping wood and keeping the fires alive. We called him the 'human bellows' so good was he at starting fires. He would puff at an apparently dead fire from a distance of 2ft. (60cm), his cheeks swollen like a bullfrog, and immediately flames would flicker. He was a natural for camping trips and would be a popular man with scout and guide troops.

That night we had a great sing-song round the camp fire in which everyone joined. Mile meanwhile, busied herself making chang from a huge bowl of millet that Dorje and Tende had brought in the village.

The morning we left Chyamtang dawned bright and sunny. There was an air of excitement as tents were taken down and everything was packed into carryable bundles. Porters milled around and Sherpas shouted instructions, whilst, to judge by the size of the crowd, the entire village had turned up to watch the affair, including a man with a lovely smile who had brought his young daughter to see our departure (Colour Plate 175). Children played games with balloons we had distributed and several boys fired arrows from crudely made bows (Plate 50). Beer and I strolled through the village where the shrubs *Viburnum erubescens* and *Elaeagnus parvifolia* were commonly grown as rough hedges and where a tall shrub *Leucosceptrum canum* sported closely grey-felted leaves and shoots which terminated in conspicuous dense cylindrical flower spikes bristling with long creamy-white stamens. A group of porters were stripping the leaves from a large bush of *Lyonia ovalifolia* for use as cigarettes in the days to come. Returning to camp we found that all was ready and, to a rousing chorus from villagers and porters, we set off along a track down the valley towards Chepua.

On leaving the village we passed beneath a huge specimen of the pink cherry – *Prunus cerasoides*. It was at least 50ft. (15m) high with a girth of 8½ft. (2.6m) at breast height (Colour Plate 180). *Edgeworthia gardneri* occurred frequently as a shrub up to 6-7ft. (1.85-2m) with an 8ft. (2.5m) spread. The pale-brown shoots bore elliptic pointed leaves 2-2½in. (5-6.5cm) long and terminated in tight nodding heads of greenish flower buds surrounded by narrow bracts. This is an attractive shrub, the yellow flowers imparting a delicious fragrance. It is, however, more frost tender in cultivation than the Chinese *E. chrysantha*, from which it differs in its smaller evergreen leaves. *Edgeworthia gardneri* commemorates both Michael Pakenham Edgeworth (1812-1881) of the East India Company who collected many Indian native plants, and George Gardner botanist and one time Superintendent of the Botanic Gardens, Peradeniya, Sri Lanka who in 1849 at the age of thirty-seven died suddenly from apoplexy.

Plate 50. A small boy on our campsite at Chyamtang about to demonstrate his prowess with a home-made bow and arrow

Sharing the same gullies as the *Edgeworthia* was a small spreading tree to 15ft. (4.5m) whose large pinnate leaves, 12-18in. (30.5-45cm) long, had turned a brilliant orange and red. These trees, which we recognised as sumachs, fairly smouldered across the hillside and we could even see them on the opposite side of the valley. It was later identified by the British Museum (Natural History) as *Rhus semialata* which enjoys a tremendous distribution from the Himalaya eastwards to Japan and south to Sumatra. Not surprisingly it has received several names over the years and in the *Enumeration of the Flowering Plants of Nepal* the above name is placed as a synonym of *R. javanica* L., whilst in Bean's *Trees and Shrubs Hardy in the British Isles,* and the more recent *Flora of Bhutan,* the name *R. chinensis* is preferred. The wide distribution of this tree obviously produces forms varying in hardiness, and hardy specimens in the Hillier Arboretum are admired for their handsome foliage and later flowering, without however producing the brilliant autumn colours described above.

At one point on the track we encountered a mani wall, its stones inscribed with the Tibetan Buddhist chant 'Om mani padme hum'. In accordance with custom, we passed this on our right (Colour Plate 176). Shortly after we met a woman resplendent in an emerald green dress adorned with jewellery and carrying a baby in a cradle on her back (Colour Plate 181).

In the thicket above the track occurred a large evergreen shrub or occasionally a small tree to 20ft. (6m). It resembled at first glance *Camellia sasanqua,* but on examination proved to be *Eurya acuminata*. The young shoots were greyish-brown, pubescent and the leaves oblong-elliptic 2-2½in. (5-6.5cm) long, toothed and abruptly pointed. They were of a dark glossy-green above, paler below. The flowers were quite small, ⅛in. (.33cm) long, bell-shaped, creamy-white and crowded beneath the shoots of the second year. Our pleasure increased however on finding another *Rhododendron* species – *R. virgatum* – by the track at a height of approximately 8,300ft. (2,530m). It formed an erect shrub 3-4ft. (.90-1.25m) high with slender straight brown scaly stems and oblong to narrowly lance-shaped leaves 2in. (5cm) long, slightly longer on

Colour Plate 181. A Bhotia woman of Chepua in her best clothes taking her baby in its basket to visit family or friends in a nearby village. She carries a tompa filled with chang and wears a necklace probably handed down from mother to daughter. It comprises a Tibetan silver box studded with turquoises and hangs on a string of large amber beads interspersed with turquoises and cornelians

Colour Plate 182. A pygmy form of a juniper *(Juniperus recurva)* flat headed and neglected in the village of Chepua. It was probably originally planted outside a house when a seedling and has since, through circumstances, assumed the appearance of a bonsai specimen. It was approximately 12in. (30cm) high. (November)

Colour Plate 183. *Vaccinium dunalianum*, an evergreen shrub growing by the track between Chyamtang and Chepua in the Upper Arun valley. The fruits eventually ripen to black. The only places I have seen this species growing in Britain is at Caerhays Castle in Cornwall and the Royal Botanic Garden, Edinburgh (from our seed). (November)

Colour Plate 184. A small hamlet on a plateau of ground in the Upper Arun valley. Almost the entire plateau is under cultivation. (November)

Colour Plate 185. Dog and hog in the village of Chepua in the Upper Arun valley. When we first approached them early in the morning the dog was asleep with its head on the hog. Another second and its eyes were open and its ears alert. Not so the hog's

strong shoots. All leaves were of a distinct bronze-green in colour and densely glandular scaly below. The seed capsules ⅓in. (.85cm) long were borne singly in the leaf axils, appearing racemose once the leaves had fallen. Several clumps of this rhododendron grew on a dry stony bank along with *R. triflorum*, *R. arboreum*, *Lyonia ovalifolia* and several of the shrubs just previously mentioned. On looking across the valley at one point we spied a vast steep hillside, in the middle of which was a small shelf-like area occupied by a tiny hamlet surrounded by fields of cultivation. As far as we could tell, it was completely isolated nor could be see the tracks which undoubtedly were there connecting this hamlet with the outside world (Colour Plates 184 and 185).

On arrival at Chepua we found ourselves in the compound of the police post and checkpoint where we were welcomed by the inspector, a likeable man called Baradhur, a Gurong. He was about sixty and had served with the British Army in the Second World War. We were invited to stay the night and, although we would have preferred to move on as it was still early in the afternoon, it seemed churlish to refuse so we accepted. The inspector proved a great story-teller and in the comfort of his office he described to us many of his wartime exploits. During a lull in the conversation, a large bearskin on the floor caught our attention and elicited another story from the inspector who, when his English failed him, spoke urgently in Nepali with Dawa translating. The bear had been shot by the inspector close to the village and he then told us how, when the millet and maize are being harvested, the bears descend the hillside at night in search of food. Every year several villagers, mostly children, are mauled.

Having spent the night in the inspector's quarters, we headed down the track to Hongoan and Hatia, but not before we had admired a remarkable miniature juniper tree – *Juniperus recurva* – growing in the dust outside a house. It had a flattened head and was the perfect bonsai specimen (Colour Plate 182). It was our intention to reach Hatia before nightfall. The sun blazed down upon us and much of the vegetation around bore a withered appearance except for the ubiquitous bamboo and a handful of interesting shrubs, chief amongst which was a large *Buddleja* – *B. paniculata* – 6-8ft. (1.85-2.5m) tall, whose 5-7in. (13-18cm) long leaves were covered below, like the shoots, with a dense grey pelt of hairs. The flower spikes were still developing, but when open are perhaps amongst the least ornamental of the genus, being small and lilac or lavender. It is, however, too tender for general cultivation in the British Isles except in a cool greenhouse. Amongst the rhododendrons we found several plants of *Deutzia staminea,* a shrub of 4-5ft. (1.25-1.5m) with roughly hairy shoots and leaves. The clusters of white flowers were long since spent but, like the buddleja, are rarely seen in British cultivation owing to this species' tender nature. Indeed most, if not all the plants in this area would be of borderline hardiness in Britain, and although 8,000ft. (2,438m) may seem a good altitude by European standards, it is low by Himalayan standards and we were constantly reminded of this during the following days.

Vaccinium dunalianum was another shrub of the borderline zone. It was an evergreen, 2-3ft. (60-90cm) high with arching reddish-brown branches clothed with elliptic leathery leaves 2-3in. (5/7.5cm) long, each ending in a slender tail-like point and of a shining dark green above. We had missed the flowers but the resultant fruits were globular, ¼in. (.65cm) across and red in colour, turning to black (Colour Plate 183). They were carried in slender spikes 1½-2 in. (3.75-5cm) long from the leaf axils. From seed we collected I planted this handsome shrub in the Hillier Arboretum but it perished and as far as I am aware it is now only grown from our seed at the Royal Botanic Garden, Edinburgh. *Anaphalis triplinervis* was scattered across the hillside, its grey herbaceous clumps up to 1½ft. (45cm), the elliptic leaves with three to five main veins and white felted.

After lunch we hurried on until we reached an area of large rocks and cliffs where we decided to wait for the Sherpas and porters to catch us up. It was a fascinating place covered in dense vegetation, amongst which we found several interesting and unusual plants. First of all we spied a banana – *Musa balbisiana* perhaps – growing above the track, its conspicuous paddle-shaped leaves rising above the low herbage. *Hydrangea anomala* climbed its way up the trunks of many trees to heights of 50-60ft. (15-18m). Unfortunately this too is rather tender in the British Isles where its place is taken by the hardier and more ornamental Japanese subspecies *petiolaris* commonly sold as *H. petiolaris*. Other climbers here included *Jasminum dispermum*, a twining jasmine with pinnate leaves and, in season, sweetly scented white flowers pink in bud, and *Embelia floribunda*, a member of a large, mainly tropical genus *(Myrsinaceae)*, with green glabrous stems and oblong, slender pointed leaves 3-3½in. (7.5-9cm) long. The most conspicuous aspect of this powerful climber however was the small scarlet berry-like fruits which hung in large, dense, conical clusters often 2-3ft. (60-90cm) long (Colour Plate 186). Seeds of this magnificent plant have produced an abundant supply of plants, but it can only be recommended for a conservatory or, if outside, in a warm sheltered corner in the mildest areas of the British Isles or in the Mediterranean regions.

Two *Clematis* species grew amongst the boulders, where their stems tumbled down the rockface. *C. buchananiana* bore pinnate leaves with three to five rounded, coarsely toothed leaflets, the whole plant covered with short soft hairs. The second species *C. grewiiflora*, unlike the other, was in full flower, the bell-shaped blooms 1-1¼in. (2.5-3cm) long, pale yellow in colour with tepals slightly recurved at the tips. These were carried in three to five flowered drooping clusters and looked most ornamental. The entire plant was clothed in a thick velvety pad of golden-brown hairs (Colour Plate 187). Both species are related to the hardier and therefore better known Chinese *C. rehderiana* grown as much for its cowslip fragrance as for its late flowering.

Debregeasia longifolia was a common shrub, a member of the nettle family, *Urticaceae*, but very different in general appearance from that well-known stinging herb. It attained 10-15ft. (3-4.5m) in height with numerous long downy branches and lance-shaped, roughly hairy leaves 3½-4½in. (9-11.5cm) long, silvery-white beneath. Both male and female plants were present and the latter bore clusters of small bright orange fruits all along the second-year shoots (Colour Plate 189). By far the most productive area, however, was a group of tall boulders covered in debris from the overhanging trees. Growing in the debris were three plants which caused a great deal of excitement. The first and most noticeable was *Vaccinium gaultheriifolium*, an evergreen shrub rather like a taller version of *V. glauco-album*. Its reddish-brown arching stems reached fully 9ft. (2.75m) and carried bold leathery leaves 4-5 in. (10-13cm) long of a polished dark green above, vivid blue-white bloomy beneath. The shining black berries too were covered by a blue-white bloom and were gathered into dense bunches in the leaf axils and beneath the branches (Colour Plate 190). It really was a striking species and I recognised it from having seen a specimen in a cool

Colour Plate 186 (above). *Embelia floribunda*, an impressive climber in fruit which we found between Chepua and Hatia in the Upper Arun valley. (November)

Colour Plate 187 (above right). *Clematis grewiiflora:* the whole plant was clothed in a thick velvety pad of golden-brown hairs. It is related to the Chinese *C. rehderiana* but is not nearly so winter hardy in British cultivation. This plant we found growing in a ravine between Chepua and Hatia in the Upper Arun valley. (November)

Colour Plate 188 (right). The village of Hatia in the Upper Arun valley. From here we set off for the Barun Khola. (November)

Colour Plate 189. *Debregeasia longifolia* growing between Chepua and Hatia in the Upper Arun valley. It is a large spreading shrub of the nettle family *Urticaceae*. Male and female flowers are borne on separate plants, the females bearing an abundance of tiny colourful fruits. It requires a dry, warm and sunny situation in cultivation. (November)

Colour Plate 190. *Vaccinium gaultheriifolium*, a bold, vigorous evergreen with leaves chalky white beneath. We found it growing in a shady ravine between Chepua and Hatia in the Upper Arun valley where it reached 9ft. (2.75m). For a time a plant grew in a teak-framed greenhouse in the Hillier Arboretum but it is not winter hardy out of doors there. (November)

Colour Plate 191. *Acer sikkimense* growing as an epiphyte on a rock above Hatia in the Upper Arun valley. This is one of the most striking maples in leaf and is here in the early stages of autumn colour. (November)

greenhouse in the Hillier Arboretum. That plant had also been collected in east Nepal in the early 1960s by Tom Spring-Smyth. It is worth trying outside in the milder parts of the British Isles, but is hopeless in the face of frost.

The other two plants were rhododendrons – *R. dalhousiae* and *R. vaccinioides*. The first of these we later saw on several occasions as an epiphyte on rocks and in trees. The leathery leaves, 4-5in. (10-13cm) long, were generally concentrated in the upper third of each stem, whilst the stem itself terminated in a large fat bud. The straggly habit of this species, which is also a feature in cultivation, can be forgiven when the clusters of two to six tubular flowers are borne in spring. Each flower is approximately 4in. (10cm) long and can vary in colour between forms, usually cream or white or occasionally lemon-yellow. Fragrance too varies and can be powerful and heady. It was first introduced into cultivation from Sikkim by Sir Joseph Hooker in 1849 and is named after Christine Ramsay, Countess of Dalhousie (1786-1839) who collected plants in India and elsewhere. It is usually seen in cultivation as a cool greenhouse subject, but is occasionally grown outside in the milder areas of the west and south-west of the British Isles. I have often wondered how it would fare, grown as an epiphyte, in some of the damp woodland gardens of Cornwall and south-west Ireland.

When we found *R. vaccinioides,* both Beer and I first mistook it to be a *Vaccinium* species with its slender, flexible, grey-brown stems and small box-like leaves. The stems reached 12-18in. (30.5-45cm) in length and were produced from a thickened tuber-like base which lay embedded in moss. The wiry young shoots were rust coloured and warty, whilst the leaves, which were clustered towards the ends of the shoots, measured ½-⅔in. (1.25-1.70cm) long, broadening towards the tip which was shallowly notched and possessed a small point. The leaf upper surface was dark green and shining, whilst the underside was paler and bore scattered glands. We found several clumps of this rhododendron on these damp moss-covered rocks and later found it growing from the crotch of a tree. Although distinct and fascinating botanically, it is of little ornamental merit, the flowers being rather small and insignificant.

Having exhausted the immediate area we decided to explore the hillside below the track, but before we could do so we were interrupted by the arrival of one of the porters to say that the rest of the party were still in the village of Hongoan and preparing to stay the night. Annoyed by this we turned the porter round with instructions to go and tell Dawa that we intended moving on and that he must bring the porters down as quickly as possible. It was obvious to us that the Sherpas had been tempted to stay the night in Hongoan with promise of a party or some such celebration, but time was short – it was 20 November and although this area was interesting botanically, it was nevertheless warm temperate and no hardy plants would ensue. We were anxious to reach the valley of the Iswa Khola before winter set in and every delay meant lost time and less seed collected. Just as night was falling, Dawa and the other Sherpas arrived sullen faced and Da Norbu and Namgyal were sent back with the tilley lamps to guide the straggling porters in.

The next morning we set off down the track which here was well frequented by travellers and villagers. A small tree with stout shoots and large boldly-veined magnolia-like leathery leaves 12in. (30.5cm) long occurred in some quantity by the track. It was indeed a handsome tree for foliage effect and reminded me of a loquat – *Eriobotrya* species – but proved to be *Saurauia napaulensis,* a magnificent evergreen which I have since seen in fine fettle growing in the

Colour Plate 192. *Prunus cerasoides* branches drooping and filled with pale pink cherry blossom.
It was everywhere to be seen above the village of Hatia. Unfortunately this species is not winter
hardy in British cultivation. (November)

famous Quinta do Palheiro of the Blandy family in Madeira.

We had not seen a maple for some time and so we were pleased to find *Acer oblongum*, several trees of 30-40ft. (9-12m) scattered along a gully below the track. The evergreen lance-shaped leaves 3-4in. (7.5-10cm) long were entirely without lobes or teeth and were dark glossy-green above, blue-white beneath. Emerging leaves were reddish-green or coppery, whilst those of strong sucker shoots were even more colourful and reached 6in. (15cm) in length. Although this maple was first introduced to cultivation from the Himalaya as long ago as 1824, it was not truly hardy and was eventually replaced in gardens by a hardier form collected by E.H. Wilson in western China in 1901. Several trees of the latter source may be found in collections in the south and west of the British Isles and it has proved a most handsome addition to the garden.

The only other tree to draw our attention that morning was *Alangium alpinum* which I mistook for a *Styrax* species. It reached a height of 40ft. (12m) and had large rounded leaves 5-6in. (13-15cm) long, pointed, heart-shaped at base and covered with soft short hairs beneath.

Hatia lay basking in the sun when we arrived (Colour Plate 188). It was surrounded by paddy fields which were now dry and only the stubble gave any hint of their recent use. Here we spent the rest of the day sorting out supplies, seed and notes whilst Morris and Dawa engaged new porters to replace those from the Wabak Khola and Thudam who now wished to return to their homes.

After a sleepless night during which Beer's yak tail had been snatched from his tent and carried off by a dog, we marched up a stony track out of the village. We were surprised to find two familiar British native plants growing amongst the stones. These were *Plantago major*, the broad-leaved plantain, and *Polygonum hydropiper*, the water pepper. The pink cherry – *Prunus cerasoides* – was still everywhere apparent and looked decidedly out of place amongst the surrounding 'sub-tropical' vegetation (Colour Plate 192). Around the village, which lies at approximately 5,800ft. (1,768m) had been planted several clumps of a giant bamboo *Dendrocalamus hamiltonii,* whose massive canes are commonly used for construction purposes.

All day we toiled in the heat up the steep hillside until at approximately 7,000ft. (2,133m) we stopped to rest beneath a huge rock. Beer and I climbed up the obstacle to examine the vegetation growing in the moss on its summit and were delighted to discover several epiphytic shrubs. *Rhododendron dalhousiae, Agapetes serpens* and *Vaccinium dunalianum* were present but were dwarfed by five small trees of *Acer sikkimense*, a most unusual and attractive maple. Their stems reached 15-18ft. (4.5-5.5m), strong, stout and green. The magnificent leaves 4-6in. (10-15cm) long – larger on sucker shoots – were ovate with a heart-

Plate 52. Young man pulling a bundle of freshly cut canes from above the village of Hatia in the Upper Arun valley. These bundles averaged 10-12ft. (3-3.70m) in length and contained eighty to one hundred canes. (November)

shaped base and an abrupt point. In colour they were glossy dark-green above, paler and matt beneath, their margins shallowly and distantly toothed. Both surfaces were smooth except for minute tufts of chocolate-coloured hairs in the axils of the veins beneath. Young leaves were a delightful coppery-red when unfolding, whilst the leaves of two trees had already turned to orange and red prior to falling (Colour Plates 191 and 193). *A. sikkimensis* is occasionally grown under glass in the British Isles and less commonly outside in the mildest most sheltered gardens. *A. hookeri*, once regarded as a closely related species, is now considered by leading authorities on the subject to be the same, and from what I known of this maple in cultivation I would agree. Close by the rock we passed a row of stone chortens looking out on to a spectacular view of the Upper Arun valley and the mountains of the Lumbasumba Himal to the east (Plate 51). Not long after we again found *Rhus succedanea*, several isolated shrubs on field margins, their shining leaves a brilliant scarlet and red (Colour Plate 194).

Late in the afternoon we entered virgin forest and forsook the sun-drenched world outside for one of darkness and gloom. Huge trees soared towards the sky including *Acer campbellii* and *Quercus lamellosa*, and beneath them grew several species of *Araliaceae* of which a *Schefflera* was the most common. The stems of the maple and oak were clothed with a variety of creepers, amongst which *Hedera nepalensis*, *Hydrangea anomala*, *Euonymus echinatus* and *Celastrus stylosus* were prominent. *Daphne bholua*, an evergreen form, was plentiful in the undergrowth, its white flowers already well open and scenting the air around. We also spotted another *Acer sikkimense* approximately 35ft. (10.5m) tall growing in the crotch of a tree some 30ft. (9m) above the ground, its leaves turning to yellow.

We slept around the fire that night, and I lay in my sleeping bag watching the forest trees in the glow of the fire, their stems tall and stout like columns in a cathedral nave. Their dense canopies formed a roof above our heads except for one gaping hole through which I could see the stars in the night sky. Early in the morning while still dark we heard a loud shriek and on investigating, Dawa told us that a porter had been bitten by a demon. We had to wait until light to check out the incident and when the porter was brought to us for treatment he dropped his shorts and showed us an angry red mark on his behind. The demon, he explained, had struck him as he was about to relieve himself, upon which he had panicked and rushed back to camp fearful of his life. We asked him to take us to the scene of the attack and he led us out of camp through the vegetation to a point some 10-15 yards (9-13.5m) away and there was the demon – or rather demons – because there were lots of them – nettles! But these were no ordinary nettles; they were 10-15ft. (3-4.5m) high with stout stems and large lobed leaves clothed with stinging hairs. It was *Girardinia diversifola* – or Giant nettle – and I remembered an

Colour Plate 193. The large handsome leaves of *Acer sikkimense*; coppery-red when young, they turn orange and red before falling. (November)

incident in my student days at the University Botanic Garden, Cambridge, when a colleague of mine was watering a batch of plants in pots, one of which was a young girardinia. He accidentally brushed against this plant and let out a yell at the same time dropping his can. For at least a week the hand was swollen and painful and although he may have been especially allergic to stings the incident left me with a healthy respect for the girardinia's reputation. The porter suffered considerable discomfort for several days after and always stood at mealtimes.

Halfway through the morning and still in the dark forest, we heard a noise somewhere along the track ahead of us. Birds were fleeing the disturbance, and as the noise was getting louder and was heading in our direction we stopped, slightly apprehensive, wondering if some animal was the cause. The crashing and clattering of bamboo was unmistakable and we braced ourselves for a surprise, taking the precaution of stepping off the track into the undergrowth. Suddenly from out of the thicket ahead burst several men trotting in single file each hauling a bundle of green bamboo. The canes measured 10-12ft. (3-3.70m) in length and ¾-1in. (2-2.5cm) thick and were packed eighty to one hundred a bundle. The weight of the smallest bundle was as much as I could lift let alone carry and I could only stare in amazement. The men had cut the canes from thickets on the ridge and were taking them down to Hatia where they would be used to repair roofs and fences. The bundles were tightly bound with rope fastened to a headband also of rope (Plate 52). After a brief exchange of news the bamboo men continued on their way, yodelling as they ran, the bamboos clattering against the trees and over roots and stones in their wake. Later we heard another group somewhere in the forest, their calls echoing through the trees.

We reached the bamboo thickets and I wandered alone for some way along the ridge before settling down amongst them and closing my eyes so that I might better hear the gentle clicking of the canes and the soft urgent whispering of their myriad leaves. A new porter had arrived from Hatia to guide us along a track which, to his knowledge, had not been used for several years. As one would expect, the track was, in parts at least, long overgrown and without our guide would have been invisible to our eyes. As it was, Beer and I twice took the wrong direction thinking that we knew the way.

The thicket produced several shrubs which kept up our interest. A beautiful bramble – *Rubus lineatus* – was particularly plentiful, its arching, silvery-silky shoots, 6-8ft. (1.85-2.5m) high, carrying leaves 4-6in. (10-15cm) long made up of

Colour Plate 194. *Rhus succedanea,* with its foliage already ablaze. Several isolated specimens of this sumach grew on field margins above Hatia in the Upper Arun valley. (November)

several slender leaflets, green and parallel-veined above, silvery-silky below. This is a desirable shrub but unfortunately of borderline hardiness in the British Isles where it is generally represented in collections in the milder areas. A well-established plant suckers freely, or once used to, in a sheltered border in the Hillier Arboretum but was cut to the ground in a hard winter. In the same thicket as the last we found a single tree of *Ilex sikkimensis,* a handsome holly 15ft. (4.5m) high with smooth pale greyish-brown stems and bold evergreen leaves 4-5in. (10-13cm) long, sharply toothed along the margin. Later on, the silver-backed *Rhododendron arboreum* appeared and beneath its canopy our track descended between clumps of *Viburnum grandiflorum* and *Berberis insignis* to the bottom of a narrow valley. Here in the shelter of the steep hills, oaks and maples flourished, and I was particularly impressed with an *Acer campbellii* which must have been all of 100ft. (30.5m) with a huge trunk straight as a gun-barrel supporting a beautiful autumn canopy of golden leaves. Both *Hydrangea anomala* and *Euonymus echinatus* climbed the stems of many of these trees and nearby rocks. The latter, a charming evergreen spindle, resembled somewhat the Japanese *E. fortunei* variety *radicans* which is so common in cultivation, but the two are easily separated when in fruit, those of the Japanese plant having smooth capsules, whilst those of the present species had capsules covered with tiny points or prickles, hence the name *echinatus* (with prickles, like a hedgehog). *E. echinatus* is rarely seen in cultivation, possibly because of its somewhat tender nature, although it grows in my garden and in a border in the Hillier Aboretum without, however, showing any inclination to flower and fruit.

Pushing through the undergrowth at one point we met a fellow traveller heading in the opposite direction. He was a wild unkempt-looking individual, a Tibetan who, on beholding us, kissed our hands before placing them on his head. He chattered away, obviously excited, and when we made to leave he wailed loudly and seemed loath to let us go. Dawa said he was mad, whilst Pema claimed he was probably drunk.

Our camp that night was surrounded by bamboo mainly, although a few trees came to the water's edge including *Lindera assamica,* a small tree of 15-18ft. (4.5-5.5m) bearing glaucous-backed deep-green leaves 4-6in. (10-15cm) long and small axillary clusters of greenish-white flowers. It is a member of a large family, most members of which are unfortunately too tender for cultivation out of doors in the British Isles.

11. THE MAKALU TRAIL

Next morning we crossed the torrent by way of a hastily constructed bundle of branches which moved about beneath our weight. Once across we began the long haul up the thickly wooded side of the ravine which in places was vertical, entailing ropes, persistence and a fair amount of sweating and swearing. The most difficult stretches occurred in bamboo thickets where projecting spikes of broken canes made our passage doubly hazardous. So dense was the undergrowth and so engrossed were we in the climb that we had ascended 1,000ft. (305m) before we thought of examining the trees around, and then only because we found ourselves in a small clearing on a gentle slope. Here grew several trees 60ft. (18m) high of *Magnolia campbellii* (Colour Plate 195) whose fruiting spikes we collected from the leaves at our feet, though most of the bright red seeds had already been damaged by weevil larvae. Here too we found the sycamore-like *Acer sterculiaceum* which we had first encountered on the Milke Danda. It reached heights of 50-60ft. (15-18m) here, its branches carrying large drooping bunches of shortly hairy fruits with parallel wings 1½in. (3.75cm) long. Large bushes of the evergreen *Mahonia napaulensis* (*M. acanthifolia*) now appeared, standing 6-8ft. (1.85-2.6m) tall with ruffs of bold pinnate leaves 12-18in. (30.5-45cm) long, each composed of seventeen to nineteen spine-toothed oblong leaves 1-2in. (2.5-5cm) long and glossy-green above. Authorities at the British Museum (Natural History) have since suggested that this plant is related more to *M. borealis* than to *M. napaulensis,* but I am not convinced.

Eventually we attained the ridge at a height of 9,500ft. (2,895m), having climbed 2,000ft. (609m) above the torrent. A track now led along the crest of the ridge climbing gently through the trees, several of which we had encountered before, including *Sorbus vestita, Populus jacquemontiana* variety *glauca, Acer pectinatum* and *Betula utilis. Pieris formosa* appeared, some bushes up to 25ft. (7.5m) in height, creating what must be a wonderful spectacle in spring when the white flower clusters drape the branches. Both *Rhododendron barbatum* and the buff-backed *R. arboreum* now formed thickets, and in the leaf mould beneath them crept a dwarf evergreen spindleberry – *Euonymus frigidus* variety *elongatus.* Here it reached 12in. (30.5cm) in height though we found it again later up to 4ft. (1.25m). The slender green four-angled stems bore pairs of narrow, long-pointed leaves 2½-3½in. (6.5-9cm) long by ¾in. (2cm) across, the margins shallowly toothed and wavy. They were a dark glossy-green above, paler beneath and quite smooth. They carried a few fruits singly on slender drooping stalks, the pink capsules opening to reveal orange-coated seeds. The conspicuous buds were purple and up to ½in. (1.25cm) long. This struck me as being a delightful creeping shrub, quite different in looks to others I have seen of a similar nature and yet, as far as I was aware at the time, it was not in cultivation, and unfortunately of those seeds we managed to collect I have heard no more. However, years later this plant was introduced by Tony Schilling, and I now have it in my own garden in a cool shady corner.

The track soon left the ridge and continued along the slope at just below the

Plate 53. Walking through a sea of *Gaultheria semi-infera* and dwarf rhododendrons – *R. ciliatum* and *R. glaucophyllum* – at 10,500ft. (3,200m) in the valley of the Barun Khola. The Makalu Trail enters this valley from the left higher up and continues up river towards the famous mountain of that name. (November)

10,000ft. (3,048m) contour. We passed a large rock-face down which water trickled and were delighted to see here the Himalayan Maidenhair fern – *Adiantum venustum* – with its delicate fronds flowing in green waves over the wet rock surface. Here too were *Primula glomerata* and *P. bracteosa*, the latter with pale mauve greenish-yellow-eyed flowers protruding from tufts of slightly powdered, toothed leaves. This species in Nepal is restricted to the far east, its distribution stretching from there east to Assam. It is most common in central Bhutan where I encountered it quite frequently in the Bumthang valley area in 1991. Later on, the scape develops carrying the flowers up to 10in. (25.5cm) high. In the crotch of a tree 6ft. (1.85m) above the ground we found a plant which I am convinced was *Dianella ensifolia* although, according to the Nepal Enumeration, this plant has not been recorded from Nepal. In his *Flora of British India,* Hooker gives its distribution as Nepal eastwards. Our plant had tufts of grass-like dark-green leaves 9-12in. (23-30.5cm) long from out of which arose an 18in. (45cm) arching stem bearing towards its summit a cluster of deep blue berries. The fruits and a specimen were collected but neither have been heard of since.

Following close on the heels of the last, we discovered another plant which I have since had cause to ponder upon. It was a tree of some 60ft. (18m) with slightly downswept branches, the slender branchlets bearing what appeared to be ranks of long slender drooping catkins of seed. Most of the leaves had already fallen and we were able to retrieve a good number for examination. These were ovate to elliptic, 4-5in. (10-13cm) long and rather leathery in texture. They were pointed and possessed an obliquely rounded or straight base with sharply toothed margins, the main veins emanating fan-like from the base. I have reason to believe this tree to have been the monotypic *Tetracentron sinense,* with which

Colour Plate 195. *Magnolia campbellii* photographed with *Abies densa* on the Dochu La in Bhutan. We saw this tree several times on the Milke Danda and in the valley of the Barun Khola but seed was scarce. This photograph well illustrates the pure white flowers of the wild tree, those in western cultivation being commonly pink flowered. (May)

Colour Plate 196. *Inula hookeri* flowering in the author's garden in Hampshire. This plant originated from seed collected in the valley of the Barun Khola. The whole plant is downy whilst the curious woolly flower buds are almost as attractive as the expanded heads. (August)

Colour Plate 197. *Cornus macrophylla* flowering in the Hillier Arboretum in Hampshire. Native to the eastern Himalaya and south-west China, this attractive tree dogwood is not commonly seen in British cultivation where it makes a small tree of tabulated growth. We found it growing in a wood in the valley of the Barun Khola. (August)

Colour Plate 198. *Rhododendron ciliatum* in the valley of the Barun Khola where it sometimes forms continuous ground cover among the rocks. (November)

Colour Plate 199. *Rhododendron ciliatum* flowering in the author's garden in Hampshire from seed collected in the valley of the Barun Khola. It has proved a most satisfactory species here, reliable in its flowering and rarely spoiled by frost. (April)

Plate 54. Unfinished bamboo basket in Sedua. These strong containers are commonly used by hill people in Nepal to carry virtually everything including the 'kitchen sink'

I am quite familiar from cultivated specimens in the Hillier Arboretum and also in the wood at Caerhayes, Cornwall. All those in cultivation, however, are of Chinese origin, having been introduced by E.H. Wilson when collecting for the nurseryman Veitch in 1901. In his book *A Naturalist in Western China* Wilson makes several references to this tree where he remarks on its often large size, trees of 60-70ft. (18-21m) being not uncommon, and to its thin and characteristic leafage. I have since seen this tree twice in Sichuan province, west China: on Emei Shan in 1980, and again in Leibo county, south Sichuan, in 1993. The first record of *Tetracentron* from east Nepal was made by the Japanese in the early l960s and later by L.H.J. Williams in 1969. According to Professor Hara of the University of Tokyo, the Nepal tree belongs to a western race, differing in the generally larger leaves, abruptly pointed and with smaller more pointed teeth.

Our track continued along the slope for most of the day before veering rapidly downwards to the Barun Khola. Here we found the Sherpas had made camp in a bamboo thicket. Bamboos are ornamental and most acceptable in a garden, where they can be looked at and admired at leisure, but after several days of toiling through vast bamboo thickets in the wild, I was beginning to change my mind about their helpful attributes. Where a track has been cut through bamboo, the severed canes can gash legs and arms, and pointing, as they do, in all directions, they are a constant danger to one's face, especially the eyes, whilst pieces of bamboo lying on the ground, particularly when covered by dead leaves, cause one to slip or trip. Bamboo thickets are hot and dusty on sunny days causing prickly heat, and a track, unless it is broad and straight, soon becomes obscured causing delay and frustration. On the other side of the coin the catalogue of useful attributes of the bamboo is endless. During our travels in Nepal we had seen it used for bridges, supports of many kinds, houses, shelters and other structures, baskets, trays, containers, head bands for carrying, ropes, fences, tree guards, whistles, flutes, mats, cow muzzles, flag-poles, utensil handles, water carriers, drain-pipes, churns, stakes, packing material, wrappers, cigarette holders, swings, pea-shooters, bows and arrows, baskets and many other things (Plates 54 and 55). Nevertheless, I found myself cursing the bamboo all night as I was bitten all over by Crab lice, one in particular on the inside of my arm caused me a lot of pain. We were thankful, therefore, the next morning to be up and away from this cursed place, our trail following the river over boulders and rocks, occasionally climbing the steep bank whenever waterfalls made direct progress impossible. The day gave us sunshine all morning deteriorating to mist and drizzle in the afternoon, by which time we had cleared the forest.

A last search amongst the trees revealed a wealth of interesting plants including large clumps of *Vaccinium nummularia* hanging from mossy trunks and boulders. Two trees in particular caught our eyes, one of which we recognised as a hazel. There were several specimens, similar to our native species *Corylus avellana* in habit, with several grey-barked main stems 30-35ft. (9-10.5m) tall carrying parallel-veined, elliptic to obovate leaves 4-5in. (10-13cm) long which were smooth above, downy beneath. Several trees had their branches draped with bunches of pretty pink catkins 3-3½in. (7.5-9cm) long adding a warm tinge to the now decidedly wintry scene above. It proved to be *Corylus ferox*. Scratching about in the fallen leaves we found a few old fruiting clusters covered in short branched spines, hence the name *ferox* (ferocious, spiny). This unusual species is rare in British cultivation but has been reintroduced recently by Tony Schilling, amongst others.

Near the hazel we found a small multi-stemmed tree with stout pithy branches up to 15-20ft. (4.5-6m). These carried large alternately arranged leaves over 12in. (30.5cm) across, borne on 10-15in. (25.5-38cm) stalks. The leaf blade varied from entire to three lobed, each lobe rounded, slender-pointed and finely downy all over, more so on the underside where it was more or less mealy. Some leaves had turned an attractive bronze-purple. The tree, which has since been identified as *Toricellia tiliifolia,* was in fruit with large drooping terminal clusters of black berries, rather like elderberries, the juice of which left dark stains on our hands. It was a handsome if unusual tree related to *Cornus,* and as far as I am aware is not in cultivation in the British Isles. Sadly, our seed was inexplicably lost in transit.

Plate 55. Bamboo strips being plaited into a rope by a Tamang porter in Sedua

At one point during the morning we walked through a grove of a Himalayan whitebeam which, with its broad, almost rounded leaves 6-10in. (15-25.5cm) long, put me in mind of the tree in cultivation commonly known by the name *Sorbus* 'Mitchellii', correctly 'John Mitchell'. This handsome tree originated at the Westonbirt Arboretum in Gloucestershire and is now considered to be a clone of *S. thibetica*. Strangely enough, a specimen collected by Beer above Sedua on a later trip in 1975 has since been assigned to this species by the *Sorbus* authority Eleonora Gabrielian, and I am tempted to believe that the specimens in the Barun Khola valley also belonged here. It was certainly an invigorating experience walking beneath these trees which reached 40-50ft. (12-15m) in height and had littered the ground with their bold leaves, brown or occasionally still green above, greyish-white beneath, creating a bi-coloured carpet of exceptional beauty.

On returning to the river, we found our way blocked by a sheer-sided gorge through which there was no possible access. We turned about face to climb the hillside again but before doing so stopped to examine two more trees which spread their branches above the water. The first of these, *Litsea confertiflora*, had all but dropped its leathery leaves and our attempts to climb it only succeeded in dislodging the remainder which fell to the river and were carried away like miniature rafts. A few however settled on the bank and we were able to retrieve them for examination. They were quite handsome, measuring 4-5in. (10-13cm) long with three to five main veins arising from the base. The upper surface was dark-green and glossy, the lower surface pale or blue-green and softly hairy. The tree itself had an attractive grey-brown flaking bark and stout hairy twigs with conspicuous chestnut-brown buds. More intriguing still was a neighbouring tree some 15-20ft. (4.5-6m) in height with a spreading head of branches. The young shoots were a deep red, whilst the leaves, mostly fallen, were elliptic to oblong-elliptic, 5-6in. (13-15cm) long, slender-pointed with a rounded base. They were green and smooth above, greyish-green below and had a bold curving venation. Small dark-blue fruits were carried in flattened heads. For many years the dark red-twigged plants we grew from this seed in

Colour Plate 200. *Rhododendron glaucophyllum*, showing the silvery white scaly undersurface of the leaves. Below it are the leaves and flower buds of *R. ciliatum*. Both were plentiful in the valley of the Barun Khola at 10,500ft. (3,200m). (November)

Colour Plate 201. *Gaultheria semi-infera*, the bloomy deep blue fruits are the chief ornament of this dwarf evergreen shrub. (November)

Colour Plate 202. *Coriaria teminalis* forma *xanthocarpa* fruiting in a Shropshire garden. The orange fleshy surrounds to the tiny black seeds are the swollen persistent petals. We found this species growing in the valley of the Barun Khola at approximately 10,500ft. (3,200m). (August)

Colour Plate 203. *Gaultheria pyroloides* and *G. trichophylla* growing together on a mossy bank in the valley of the Barun Khola. Note the impressed venation and the bloomy fruits of the former and the tiny narrow leaves and deep blue fruits (partially hidden) of the latter. (October)

Colour Plate 204. *Vaccinium sikkimense* growing at Wakehurst Place in Sussex from seed collected by Tony Schilling in Nepal. We found this attractive species growing in the valley of the Barun Khola. (May)

Colour Plate 205. *Rhododendron pumilum* covering a mound by the track at 14,400ft. (4,389m) above the Barun Khola. Picture taken by Len Beer during his recce. (July)

the Hillier Arboretum I imagined to be an osier dogwood related perhaps to the Chinese *Cornus hemsleyi*. Subsequently, collections of *C. macrophylla* from west China, however, have convinced me that this was the tree we found in the Barun Khola valley that day (Colour Plate 197).

At approximately 10,500ft. (3,200m) there was hoar frost in a gully and the air became colder as the sun was swallowed up by cloud. *Rhododendron hodgsonii* appeared, the intervening spaces being occupied by large bold clumps of the bamboo *Thamnocalamus spathiflorus*. The dwarf, box-leaved holly *Ilex intricata* formed an understorey, sharing the debris beneath the rhododendrons with *Euonymus frigidus* variety *elongatus*. We were surprised to renew our acquaintance with *Rhododendron camelliiflorum*, a small bush of which we found growing 10ft. (3m) up in the crotch of a hemlock – *Tsuga dumosa*.

On rounding a corner of the hillside we saw groups of a large yellow daisy-flowered perennial growing by a stream. It was *Inula hookeri*, its erect downy stems 3-4ft. (.90-1.25m) tall clothed with narrow leaves 5-6in. (13-15cm) long. The flowerheads measured 2-3in. (5-7.5cm) across and bore conspicuous narrow strap-shaped marginal florets which in turn were surrounded by dense, crowded and recurved downy bracts. A later introduction of this species by Beer is now growing in my garden where it has formed a substantial clump, its flowers annually attracting late flying insects (Colour Plate 196). With the *Inula* grew a shrubby honeysuckle – *Lonicera purpurascens*, a bush 5-6ft. (1.5-1.85m) high with ovate, hairy leaves 1-2in. (2.5-5cm) long and ovoid berries ¼in. (.65cm) long, black with a blue-white bloom. Growing on the slope above the track Beer came upon a small plant of *Daphne bholua* whose leaves were splashed with yellow and pale-green, rather like those of the popular cultivated holly *Ilex* x *altaclerensis* 'Lawsoniana'. We could only imagine what a winner this might have been in cultivation, but there is no way scions of this plant would have survived the journey home.

The porters had all this time followed in our wake and were still behind us when we descended to the river to take a closer look at a low evergreen shrub which covered a wide area, crowding its way between boulders on both sides of the river. It was *Gaultheria semi-infera*, and as most plants were fruiting we called up the porters to help us gather in the harvest. Morris, Beer and I produced cotton bags in which to collect the fruits which were of a striking China-blue colour. In no time at all we had filled our bags and eager for a large haul we turned to check how the porters were progressing. To our consternation we found that they were picking the fruits faster than we and popping them straight into their mouths. We called Dawa over asking him to explain what it was we wanted, and on being told they looked mystified, retorting that they thought we were collecting the fruits to eat later. Continuing our harvest we filled four more bags before calling it a day and moving on. We headed for a gully down which a stream flowed and found the whole area covered with a mixture of two dwarf rhododendrons – *R. ciliatum* and *R. glaucophyllum*. Both species we had already seen on the Milke Danda but those had been isolated individuals, whilst before us in the gully stretched a continuous low cover of the two intermixed. *R. ciliatum* formed dense spreading bushes up to 3ft. (90cm) high, the stems and branches with peeling bark. The elliptic leaves 2-3½in. (5-9cm) long were glossy-green and hairy above, the margins fringed with long hairs, hence the name.

Some bushes had occasional early flowers which were bell-shaped 1½-2 in. (3.75-5cm) long and white with a faint pink flush (Colour Plates 198 and 199). *R. glaucophyllum* on the other hand, although of similar height, was a more leggy, open bush with wiry stems covered in a thin, flaking, chestnut-brown bark. The leaves were mainly clustered towards the ends of the shoots, being elliptic to narrowly so, 1-2in. (2.5-5cm) long, pointed, dark glossy-green above, white beneath and speckled with glands which were aromatic when rubbed (Colour Plate 200). Even the young shoots and fruit clusters were glandular scaly. Both species were first discovered and introduced to British cultivation by Joseph Hooker in 1850. Of the thirty species he introduced at this time *R. ciliatum* was the first to flower at Kew while still only 7in. (18cm) high.

During the rest of that day we encountered both rhododendrons often growing in large colonies together with *Gaultheria semi-infera,* either by the river or in lateral gullies. Nearly always they grew in wet places either in shade or on north-facing slopes. Seed of both was introduced and *R. ciliatum* is represented in several collections including the Hillier Arboretum, where, however, its early flowering is usually frustrated by frosts. *R. glaucophyllum* was also well distributed and in 1977 a plant with pure white flowers was exhibited at the Chelsea Flower Show under the clonal name 'Len Beer'.

The whole stretch of riverside for a mile or more beyond the forest was a paradise for plants which, being late in the year, were mainly shrubs in fruit. I recognised a number of familiar 'faces' including *Deutzia compacta* with its attractive flaking brown bark and the low growing *Coriaria terminalis* variety *xanthocarpa* bearing its terminal cylindrical spikes of amber-yellow fruits enclosing black seeds (Colour Plate 202). Eventually the mist, which had been gathering strength for several hours, made plant collecting impossible and we were pleased therefore to find that camp had been established on a flat piece of ground above the river.

Although Makalu (27,790ft./8,470m) was some way up the valley, out of sight of our camp, it was not our intention to continue in its direction. Snow had already fallen on the higher slopes above the valley and if we were to attempt to gain access to the Iswa Khola then we would need to leave the Barun Khola valley as quickly as possible.

The way out of the valley lay via the so-called Makalu Trail, a track by which climbers reached the mountain from the Arun valley by way of Sedua and the valley of the Kasuwa Khola. This track ran along the opposite flank of the river and for the best part of the afternoon Dawa and the others had been looking for a way across by a bridge which our Hatia guide had assured us we would find. It was to locate the bridge that we sent Da Norbu and Namgyal next morning and in their absence we searched the hillside above our camp. The sun was out early and conditions were pleasant if a little cold. There were many *Rhododendron* species present forming thickets and bold groups. *R. campanulatum,* *R. campylocarpum* and *R. hodgsonii* often growing together, with *R. lepidotum* and *R. anthopogon* forming dense low ground cover. By far the most dominant species, however, was *R. barbatum,* including an unusual form with leaves a distinct sea-green above. Specimens of this plant were later considered by one authority to be nearer *R. imberbe,* now considered a hybrid between *R. barbatum* and *R. arboreum. R. ciliatum* continued to inhabit the damp hollows which, in some instances, were little more than bogs, and it suggested to me that

Colour Plate 206. *Rhododendron vaccinioides* showing its small polished leaves and curved red seed capsules. This small epiphytic species we found several times on mossy tree stems and branches. Here it grows in the forest above the valley of the Kasua Khola above Sedua. (November)

moisture must be an important factor in the successful cultivation of this species. Curious then that a plant in my own garden flourishes in a dry sandy loam. In another area *R. cinnabarinum* and *R. thomsonii* occurred, the latter forming mixed stands with *R. barbatum*. We even found a lone bush of *R. lepidotum* bearing clusters of purple flowers ⅜in. (2cm) across.

We returned to camp along the river, a route which proved lucky because on one area of stony bank we found three species of *Gaultheria* and a *Vaccinium*. *G. trichophylla* we had seen previously at Topke Gola and elsewhere, and *G. pyroloides* we had also seen below Topke Gola (Colour Plate 203), whilst *G. semi-infera* was everywhere around (Colour Plate 201 and Plate 53), but *Vacciniuim sikkimense* was quite new to us. This shrub here formed a low mound 6-9in. (15-23cm) in height with roughly hairy shoots bearing several extra large, conspicuous, red-pointed buds in the upper leaf axils. The leaves themselves were obovate to elliptic-obovate 1½-2 in. (2.5-3.75cm) long, rounded and with a short sharp point, narrowing gradually to the base. The margins were sharply toothed especially towards the apex and there were hairs on the midrib beneath, otherwise quite smooth and green (Colour Plate 204).

Having crossed the river by way of a hastily assembled clutch of logs, we followed the Makalu Trail as it wound its way up the hillside away from the threshing and noisome waters of the Barun. Soon we were walking through a dense forest of hemlock and Silver fir where birch and maple made tentative intrusions. Rhododendrons again formed thickets between the trees, whilst creeping gaultherias and the rosettes of primulas coated the banks by the track. Walking through the giant trees was a dream-like experience after the bamboo nightmare of Hatia and the cold damp valley of the Barun Khola. The sun dominated the sky sending great arms of light and warmth down through the canopy, illuminating the numerous clearings like stages in a darkened theatre.

Two Himalayan tree creepers appeared on several occasions, playing hide-and-seek amongst the trees, moving jerkily over the bark like slender brown and white mice. The higher we climbed the colder it became and the first stray patches of snow gradually united until the slopes above were completely white.

Colour Plate 207. *Acer campbellii*, its yellow autumn leaves contrasting with a blue sky above the valley of the Barun Khola. These magnificent trees were in the region of 70ft. (21m) tall and stopped us in our tracks. Their branches were clothed with epiphytes including ferns and orchids. (November)

Where the track passed through rhododendron thicket it was easy to follow. At 13,000ft. (3,962m) the dominant rhododendrons were *R. wightii* and *R. fulgens,* and through many fine stands of these a broad passageway had been cleared. Once the track left these areas, however, conditions became more difficult and, although we knew roughly where the pass lay, the snow on the track and the sleet in our eyes made progress slow and separated the party several times, each occasion necessitating a halt and roll-call.

We tramped upwards, our feet catching in the dense tangled growth of *Rhododendron anthopogon* hidden beneath the snow. The slope steepened appreciably and soon, every few steps were followed by a slide, and to cap it all the mist descended, making further progress virtually impossible. The track appeared barely discernible but we followed its erratic course all the way to the pass where a chorten (a Tibetan Budhist cairn) marked the summit at 14,600ft. (4,450m). On crossing the pass we were relieved to see the track continuing down the other side clear of snow, and a few hundred feet below we reached our camp by a frozen lake. The porters trailed in for some time, carrying loads of dry wood on their packs and set to making their fires. That night was the coldest we had experienced and for the first and only time I wore my sweater in my sleeping-bag.

After supper we sat round the fire discussing what to do. It was obvious that we would not now be able to enter the Iswa valley. The delaying tactics of the porters in the Arun valley were borne of a natural reluctance on their part to enter a high valley which, at the best of times, was difficult to get into and would now be fraught with problems. Those Sherpas who had accompanied Beer on his reconnaissance were even more aware of the risks and their response to the plan was, not surprisingly, lukewarm. We were all three bitterly disappointed, especially Beer, who had been to the Iswa, but all agreed that, time and weather being against us, the most sensible plan was for Beer to push on to Sedua and there begin the final seed cleaning and drying, whilst Morris and I followed at a more leisurely pace collecting whatever seed we could. While we discussed our plans someone noticed a satellite moving across the starlit sky. Our porters stared at it incomprehending except for one, an ex-lama, who firmly believed it to be the eye of the exiled Dalai Lama watching and encouraging his followers.

Next morning, after Beer and Namgyal had left, Morris and I climbed back to the pass and continued up the hillside to the ridge, where we were presented with a magnificent view of the Iswa valley. Most of its length was bathed in sunshine, but this did little to detract from the menace of the place. In parts it was a steep-sided gorge and innumerable hanging glaciers stood seemingly poised to fall. Beer had described to us the awful desolation he had found in the upper reaches where ice, snow and rock combined to form the most bizarre effects. Progress had been painfully slow, and having reached the terminal glacier, he had then to make a hurried exit when one of his porters fell seriously ill. Yet, despite the difficulties he had encountered, Beer had discovered many rare plants, several of which are as yet unnamed and probably new to science including two yellow-flowered species of *Saxifraga.* Amongst the more exciting plants collected as specimens by Beer in the Iswa valley, the following give an idea of the floral riches to be found there.

Gentiana elwesii, a desirable species up to 6in. (15cm) high with trumpet-shaped blue flowers, white at the base and borne several to a stem; *Meconopsis bella,* a delicate plant with large blue flowers, growing in crevices, sometimes from the roofs of overhanging rocks; *Aconitum orochryseum,* with creamy-

yellow helmeted flowers; *Androsace lehmanii* and *A. globifera,* both forming large hummocks of tightly packed rosettes.

Our party left the campsite around mid-morning and, having skirted the frozen lake, began the long haul up the opposite slope. We took a different route from the one used by Beer and Namgyal, whose footprints we could trace very clearly in the snow. We reached the summit of the col at 14,400ft. (4,389m) where our lama added a piece of white cloth to the prayer flags fluttering from canes on the summit chorten (Plate 56). We dropped down the south slope to a ridge track, but with mist gathering the conditions were fast deteriorating. We moved along the ridge at a brisk rate, stopping only once to examine a small plant growing in tufts by the side of the track. It reminded me of a narrow-leaved stonecrop – *Sedum* species – with wiry woody stems 3-5in. (3.5-13cm) high. In the event it proved to be *Diplarche multiflora,* a member of the heather family – *Ericaceae.* The small pink flowers in summer are born in terminal clusters. It is a charming little shrublet rarely if ever seen in cultivation. Another member of the *Ericaceae* grew with it and it was only when we crouched to look at the *Diplarche* that we noticed the miniature *Rhododendron pumilum,* a gem of a species with slender branches prostrate or ascending to 3in. (7.5cm) carrying elliptic, pointed leaves ½-1in. (1.25-2.5cm) long. These were a shining bronze-green above, pale green and speckled with brown scales below. Indeed the whole plant was speckled with scales including the slender seed capsules borne singly or up to three in a cluster from the shoot tips. This is a charming shrublet with usually single pink or rose bell-shaped flowers (Colour Plate 205), but it is rarely met with in cultivation where it demands a high degree of skill and not a little bit of luck. Its growths are repeatedly damaged by frosts which, of course, would not normally happen in the wild where they are protected by the snow.

Whilst we were examining these plants, our porters had gone on ahead and on resuming our walk we discovered two sets of tracks in the snow. We followed what appeared to be the most popular route, to find after half-an-hour that it veered steeply downhill and on the wrong side of the ridge. Then we found tracks going straight up the hill back towards the ridge and we guessed rightly that some of our porters had missed their way. For two miles we plodded through snow, occasionally floundering, climbing to our feet and plodding on until at last we broke through to the crest of the ridge again and refound the Makalu Trail. Shortly afterwards, the track left the ridge and plunged steeply down the southern slope,

Colour Plate 208. *Daphniphyllum himalense* fruits on a female tree. Sadly, plants grown from these fruits proved tender in Hampshire although they just might have survived in the milder areas of south-west England and in Ireland. (November)

Colour Plate 209. *Dichroa febrifuga*, a common shrub in the forest above Sedua. A relative of the hydrangea, this tender species is important in Nepal as a medicinal plant helping to reduce fevers, especially in cases of malaria. (November)

Colour Plate 210. *Daphniphyllum himalense*, a magnificent and stately evergreen frequent on the slopes above Sedua, this individual approximately 70ft. (21m) tall. All species of this genus are dioecious – male and female flowers borne on separate trees. (November)

cutting its way through dense thickets of rhododendron in similar mixture to those we had seen in the Barun valley. Gradually we left the mist and snow behind and progress became easier and more leisurely. The dwarf box-leaved holly – *Ilex intricata* – was very common here as a ground cover but gave way lower down the slope to another evergreen shrub 3-5ft. (.90-1.5m) high with spreading or shortly ascending branches crowded with obovate to oblanceolate, sharply toothed and abruptly pointed leaves 3½-4½in. (9-11.5cm) long, polished dark-green above, paler beneath. Small flower buds were present, borne singly or in pairs in the leaf axils. Specimens of this shrub have been identified at the British Museum as *Eurya cavinervis,* a new record for Nepal although it has long been known in neighbouring Sikkim.

The site of our evening camp was still some way off and as the light was beginning to fade we broke into a jog. It is amazing that one of us did not at least sprain an ankle as we descended the steep track through thicket and boulders. We entered the forest at a run, catching up with the tail-end of our porters as they entered camp, which was situated within a large natural cave at the base of a gigantic rock wall.

Our arrival was the signal for Pema to start cooking, and whilst waiting for supper we entered our notes by the light of the fire, darkness having already descended. Later, fully satisfied, we lay back in our sleeping bags listening to the Sherpas singing and watching the fire's glow. At one point we saw a sizeable creature gliding across the mouth of the cave to land with a crash in the hanging branches of a nearby tree. It then scrambled up into the dense heart of the tree. We saw no more of it and concluded that it must have been a Giant Flying squirrel – *Petaurista petaurista.*

Next morning, the mouth of the cave was alive with people moving about in all directions, calling and chattering, to which was added the gurgle of water boiling in pots and the spiralling smoke of several rekindled fires. Outside in the forest, shafts of sunlight pierced the branches of a giant magnolia tree and somewhere close to hand a bird made wolf-whistles until it changed to an equally monotonous single note version. The rock was higher than I had imagined, its damp face masked by green and brown moss and partially concealed by the long roots of trees and creepers which hung like a veil of dark string.

I wandered down through the forest on my own, enjoying the changing vegetation and what the plant hunter Reginald Farrer once called 'the sweet rotting smell of autumn', except that autumn here was later – it was the end of November. We were about to enter the cool temperate zone, and with my eyes I drank in the plants which would, all too soon, be replaced by others from the warmer valleys. Many of the trees and shrubs we had seen before appeared including *Helwingia himalaica, Taxus wallichiana, Ilex dipyrena* and *Hydrangea robusta* with its rounded leaves big as frying pans. *Lyonia ovalifolia* was common, its leaves apparently varying in size depending on altitude. The lower the altitude the larger the leaf. Indeed I had several times mistaken these latter trees for magnolias.

Campbell's maple – *Acer campbellii* – reached a great size, resembling an English elm in its branching and autumn colour (Colour Plate 207). It is a pity that this tree is too tender for the majority of gardens in the British Isles. Into several of these trees two by now familiar plants climbed – *Hydrangea anomala* and *Euonymus echinatus,* both of which ascended to heights of 50-

60ft. (15-18m). *Rhododendron vaccinioides* appeared 7ft. (2m) up on the moss covered branch of a maple. Any doubts we may have had as to its identity were now cleared by the evidence of small curved seed capsules 1-1¼in. (2.5-3cm) long borne singly on a slender stalk from the tip of each shoot (Colour Plate 206).

Several large whitebeams came into the picture, one specimen at least 70ft. (21m) high with a correspondingly large girth. As far as I could tell by the fallen leaves, it was similar to those we had seen in the Barun valley and in retrospect this may well have been the *Sorbus thibetica* collected 'above Sedua' by Beer when he again visited this region in 1975.

Gradually the vegetation began to change and the *Viburnum grandiflorum* which had accompanied me downhill most of the morning now handed over to *V. erubescens*. Clearings appeared where large trees had been drastically pollarded for firewood and fodder. These included *Actinodaphne reticulata*, a member of the bay family.

Walking through open grassy areas between groves of trees I encountered a magnificent evergreen with tall straight stems occasionally up to 70ft. (21m) in height. It was *Daphniphyllum himalense*, a member of the spurge family – *Euphorbiaceae* – and its stout green shoots carried large elliptic leaves 10-12in. (25.5-30.5cm) long, even longer on vigorous shoots (Colour Plates 208 and 210). These were a dark glossy-green above, blue-green beneath with reddish veins and stalk. The flowers of this tree are dioecious, i.e. male and female on separate trees, and I saw a good number of female trees carrying their drooping clusters of purplish-black, small damson-like fruits ⅔in. (1.70cm) long each containing a single stone-like seed ½in. (1.25cm) long. Seedlings raised and planted out of doors in the Hillier Arboretum sadly perished in their first cold winter.

I saw *Rhododendron dalhousiae* again several times, either on boulders or sprouting from the tops of dead tree stumps, whilst in the undergrowth an unusual shrub – *Dichroa febrifuga* – became dominant. Its erect stems to 5-6ft. (1.5-1.85m) carried pairs of elliptic, sharply toothed leaves 5-6in. (13-15cm) long and terminal as well as axillary heads of small metallic blue berries (Colour Plate 209). It is related to the hydrangea, differing in its inflorescences lacking ray florets and most distinctly in its berried fruits. It is a very important medicinal plant particularly useful in reducing fevers especially in malaria. Indeed, according to Dobremez, it is the most ancient remedy known for this disease. It enjoys a tremendous distribution in the wild, ranging from Nepal to Taiwan and Malaysia.

At approximately 7,000ft. (2,133m) the track skirted a gully crowded with trees supporting an abundance of epiphytes, mainly ferns and orchids. Amongst the latter I was delighted to find *Pleione praecox*, a single clump in full flower, its fig-shaped green mottled-purple pseudobulbs embedded in deep moss on a branch. The flowers, each 2in. (5cm) long, were pale-purple except for the base of the tube which was white. The inner surface of the lacerated lip was yellow, with five raised toothed ribs. The 1in. (2.5cm) long ovary curved like a swan's neck and each flower was borne on a 2in. (5cm) long stalk which was green mottled-purple. A green capsule with six prominent ribs was also present.

I emerged from the gully feeling elated and as I rejoined the track met Da Norbu and together we strode down the hill into the village of Sedua.

Colour Plate 211. The Arun river snaking its way through the hills of east Nepal below Num. Our trail led us down the shoulder in the foreground across the river and up the far side to the village of Num. (December)

Colour Plate 212 (left). Dorje clutching a cane of the giant bamboo *Dendrocalamus hamiltonii* whose canes (known botanically as culms) can reach as much as 80ft. (24m) tall and are valuable for construction purposes. (November)

12. THE BRIDGE AT NUM

For two of the Sherpas – Dorje and Tende – Sedua was home and both their families turned out to greet us, leading us excitedly through the village to Tende's house where, sitting outside in the sun surrounded by an ocean of seed, we found Beer. That night we had a party in the open space between several houses, to which the families and friends of Tende and Dorje were invited, but which, in the event, proved a free-for-all with most of the village turning up.

The activities increased as the night wore on and I lost count of the dances I took part in and the glasses of chang I drank. I cannot even remember at what time I staggered to my tent, but I do know that the village throng continued to make merry, singing and dancing into the early hours of the morning, and when they finally drifted home they were replaced by dogs whose incessant howling and barking prevented sleep.

In a gully above the village, I made some last minute collections, including a climbing rose with powerful prickle-clad stems and leaves composed of five to seven elliptic, abruptly pointed leaflets of a dark polished green. On the fruiting branches leaves were trifoliolate. The hips were ellipsoid, just over ½in. (1.25cm) long, and russet red in colour, carried in loose clusters along the arching older stems. Plants germinated from this seed have proved vigorous in cultivation, but in Hampshire at least, unfortunately subject to frost damage. However, such is its habit and leaf characters that I strongly suspect it to be *Rosa longicuspis* with which I am familiar in cultivation and have since seen many times in western China where it is common. I found a plant of *Agapetes serpens* with green-washed white flowers, a pleasant contrast to the normally red veined ones growing as an epiphyte in a moss-covered tree. I did not collect this plant but two years later a similar form was collected by Harry van de Laar of Boskoop during a spring trek I led to the Milke Danda. This plant has been distributed in cultivation, rooting easily from cuttings, and is to be found in the temperate houses of Kew and Wisley and other places under the cultivar name 'Nepal Cream' (Colour Plate 214).

A common tree in the gullies was *Alnus nepalensis*, the Nepalese alder. It followed rivers and streams for several thousand feet into the hills, in places forming a tall tree 60-70ft. (18-21m) high with grey bark and greyish-green, downy, angled shoots with stalked buds. The leaves were elliptic to ovate-elliptic, 5-7in. (13-18cm) long with a short slender point and a rounded base. They were obscurely toothed and in colour glossy-green and smooth above, pale greyish-green and downy beneath, borne on downy stalks ½-¾in. (1.25-2cm) long. The young leaves were a pretty bronze or coppery-green. Although this is an autumn-flowering species, the long drooping male catkins had long since fallen. This is a tender tree in cultivation in the British Isles where it is rarely seen.

Back in Chepua, one of our Thudam porters had sold Morris, Beer and me each a pair of home-made yak hair boots, or rather the colourful woven uppers. On reaching Sedua, Da Norbu arranged to have the bottoms made and sewn on and, on completion, filled the boots with earth and proceeded to bury them in the ground outside our tents, an operation designed to keep the hide bottoms soft and pliable as they dried. At night Da Norbu placed rocks over the buried boots to prevent them being dug up and chewed by dogs.

That night we visited Dorje's home where his parents squatted either side of a fire (Colour Plate 213). Others present included a young harelipped brother, an older brother wearing a cap and boots from a French Makalu Expedition, for which he had been a porter, and a deaf mute brother-in-law, husband of Dorje's bossy sister Berma. We sat on goatskins on the earth floor and were given tompas of chang and bowls of roasted maize, both of which were refilled as soon as they were emptied. After a couple of hours Dorje's father undressed and retired beneath a large blanket in the corner of the room, and although this gesture was by no means meant as a hint that we should leave, we welcomed the opportunity to thank our hostess and claim an early night's sleep. Outside, the air was cold and crisp and the sky clear and sprinkled with stars. In the distance we could see the whole length of the Jaljale Himal along which we had trekked on our way to Topke Gola.

The next morning was the first day of December and we awoke again to a brilliantly sunny day. There was much to be done and we quickly set to, sorting and packing, throwing in a heap those items we would not be requiring any more and distributing our unwanted gear and clothing to Dorje's and Tende's parents and to some of our favourite porters. All those who have employed porters in Nepal know that there are good and bad porters and until one is well into the march it is difficult to know how lucky or otherwise one has been in his choice. Some porters did all and often more than one asked of them without expecting any extra remuneration. These porters put up with the worst conditions and accepted the characteristics and surprises of a route without complaint and could always be relied upon (Plate 57). Others, however, could be idle, disobedient or even dishonest. They might complain incessantly about

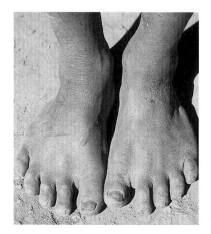

Plate 57. Have feet, will travel. A typical Nepalese porter's main asset. (December)

234

food, pay, conditions and everything else and rarely showed appreciation when luck or compassion brought them a reward or a change of fortune. Some porters drank themselves silly whilst others changed their minds somewhere along the way and would drop out to return home. The unreliable porter could be a danger to his colleagues and, at the very least, cause despondency or dissension. Happily, such porters were a minority.

Several of our porters who had been with us for some time were remaining in Sedua including, reluctantly, Berma. She was desperate to continue and Dawa tried several times to persuade us to take her with us, but we had no further need of her services. She had become a source of argument and resentment among the other porters and we felt it was best that she stayed with her husband.

At last we were on the move and struck off through cultivated fields on our descent to the Kasuwa Khola where we intended spending the night. On the outskirts of the village we passed several clumps of the giant bamboo – *Dendrocalamus hamiltonii* – we had seen in Hatia with canes 40-60ft. (12-18m) tall. Canes of 80ft (24m) and 4-7in. (10-18cm) in diameter are recorded (Colour Plate 212). This commonly planted bamboo is a native of north-east Himalaya and in these regions is universally employed for building and basket and mat work. Most villages in the warm valleys are marked by their bamboo clumps and it is referred to as Tama in Nepalese. The young shoots are sometimes eaten as a vegetable whilst, according to Gamble in his *Bambusae of British India*, the inner layer of the culm sheaths was once used for covering Burmese cigarettes.

Gradually the vegetation assumed a more tropical appearance and I was delighted to see one of the so-called Screw pines – *Pandanus furcatus*. This peculiar tree is not unlike a loose leaved cordyline or a yucca in appearance, its main stem branching in the upper half, each branch supporting a great cluster of bold, flexible, sword-shaped leaves edged with sharp teeth (Colour Plate 216). The Nepalese tree is one of a group of 600 species native of the Old World tropics and sub-tropics. Despite the common name, these trees are no relation to the pine, being more closely, though distantly, related to the palms. The male and female flowers are borne on separate trees, the females, when fertilised, producing rounded pineapple-like fruits. The stems often twist spirally like a screw. In India the fragrant flowers of the most common species – *P. odoratissimus* – are used in making Kewda Attar, whilst its leaves are used for thatching. According to at least one authority the Nepalese tree is a distinct species – *P. nepalensis*, but following Henry Noltie (*Flora of Bhutan* vol. 3 pt. 1) I am staying with the old name.

We arrived at the river and there made camp at a height of approximately 4,200ft. (1,280m). Here we found a colourful spider – *Argiope amoena* – its large abdomen strikingly banded yellow and brown. It resembled a humbug with legs and we took several photographs before it tired of basking and moved into the shade of a deep crevice (Colour Plate 217). The Sherpas sang round the fire that night and I lay in my sleeping-bag watching fireflies amongst the trees. In the light of the moon I could see the vast blanket-like webs of the giant wood spider (*Nephila maculata*) stretching between branches and occasionally connecting the canopies of separate trees. This species is just as striking as the 'humbug' spider, differing in its long narrow grey and black

Colour Plate 213. Dorje's father who welcomed us to his home in the village of Sedua. (November)

Colour Plate 214. *Agapetes serpens*, a greenish-white flowered form of this epiphytic shrub which we found on a tree above Sedua. Two years later, a similar form was collected on the Milke Danda by a Dutch friend Harry van de Laar. It was subsequently named 'Nepal Cream'. (November)

Colour Plate 215. Terraced paddy fields above Num. Note the banana clumps in the village. (December)

Colour Plate 216. *Pandanus furcatus,* a Screw pine growing in the forest of the Kasua Khola below Sedua. Not unlike a *Cordyline* at a glance, these remarkable plants have saw-toothed leaves and often produce stilt-like aerial roots whilst the fruits are large and heavy. They are not hardy in Britain being plants of the warm temperate zones and the tropics. (December)

Colour Plate 217. A colourful 'humbug' spider, *Argiope amoena,* on a boulder by the Kasua Khola below Sedua. (December)

abdomen 1-1½in. (2.5-3.75cm) long marked with two yellow stripes.

The next day we climbed out of the gorge of the Kasuwa Khola. The whole area was a maze of fields, in many of which wheat was being harvested, while others which had produced rice now lay fallow (Colour Plate 215). Bananas were grown in every village and we were delighted to be approached at one point by an old woman offering bananas for sale. They were the fattest bananas I had ever seen, huge by western standards, though lacking the characteristic shape.

Our track led us through villages where the flowers of tall poinsettias glowed scarlet against whitewashed walls, and babies swung gently in cradles suspended from the eaves. We reached a point where the track ran downhill towards the Arun river (Colour Plate 211), and there, connecting the high banks at its narrowest point, we saw that remarkable structure, the Bridge at Num. It was constructed entirely of bamboo, U-shaped in section and approximately

235ft. (71m) long. The bridge sank towards the middle and the whole structure bounced and swayed as we crossed one at a time (Plate 58). The river, though powerful enough, was almost at its lowest and we could imagine the perils involved in crossing at the height of the monsoon or after the spring thaw in the mountains. We had been told of the porters who had been lost whilst crossing the bridge and it required no imagination to believe such stories. On this occasion, however, there were no problems and after an hour the whole party was safely assembled on the other side where we made camp.

At the bridge we met a government official, an engineer charged with constructing a new bridge with steel instead of bamboo. It was his first field assignment and he was excited at the thought of the task ahead. The bridge he told us was being assembled in Khambari and brought to the site by porters. Each steel cable needed 100 porters to carry it, which, in this terrain, was quite some feat. He seemed confident that the bridge would be constructed within six months.

The climb from the bridge up to the village of Num was long and steep and it took us the whole of the next morning. In the village the autumn-flowering cherry was again common, but our interest was mainly centred around a large evergreen shrub of 8-10ft. (2.5-3m) with erect branches, brown hairy when young, and elliptic to obovate-elliptic leaves 2½-3in. (6.5-7.5cm) long. These were polished dark-green above, with a slender point and small teeth. The flowers, borne singly in the leaf axils, measured 1in. (2.5cm) across with creamy-white, obovate petals and a central bundle of yellow-anthered stamens. They possessed a slight musky fragrance and were quite obviously those of a camellia, an opinion which was later confirmed by the Botany Department of the British Museum (Natural History) who named our specimen *C. kissi,* a species rarely seen in British cultivation because of its tender nature and small flowers (Colour Plate 219).

After taking lunch at Num we continued along the track which climbed the ridge, rising in one place to 7,000ft. (2,133m). Here many interesting plants appeared including *Gleichenia volubilis,* a large fern which scrambled into small trees displaying its magnificent paired fronds in impressive feathery green walls (Colour Plate 221). The yellow-flowered *Clematis grewiiflora* occurred again and *Viburnum grandiflorum,* one specimen with leaves to 8in. (20cm) long. It was another viburnum, however, which next occupied our attention. *V. cylindricum* is a large shrub, occasionally a small tree up to 20ft. (6m), producing large flattened clusters of tubular white flowers with conspicuous protruding lilac anthers. Its main interest, however, certainly to the botanically inclined, lies in its large grey-green leaves, the upper surfaces of which are coated with a thin wax which cracks and turns white when handled (Colour Plate 220). It is sometimes seen in cultivation especially in southern and western areas of the British Isles. We had previously seen it on Phulchoki in the Kathmandu valley and I have since seen it further east in Bhutan and in south-west China in Yunnan province.

The track continued through a narrow defile with thickly mossy banks where *Rhododendron ciliatum* occurred as a few scattered mounds. It then ran downhill into a dark dank area beneath the silver-backed form of *Rhododendron arboreum,* their branches and stems heavily encrusted with epiphytes including several specimens of the maple – *Acer sikkimense* – 30-35ft.

Plate 58. The bridge across the Arun at Num, 235ft. (71m) of swaying bouncing bamboo. Several native travellers have been lost here over the years. (December)

(9-10.5m) tall, their leaves turning orange and yellow. Several plants first seen in similar woods on the Milke Danda now reappeared and we were pleased to renew our acquaintance with the red-fruited *Daiswa polyphylla* (Colour Plate 222) and the delicate scrambling *Dicentra scandens* with its purple, bullet-shaped fruits.

It was a great relief to us not to have Berma in camp and we realised more than ever just how may hours of sleep we had lost because of her incessant chatter. The nights were now comparatively quiet but it wasn't to last. Early next morning before light we were woken by the unmistakable sound of her voice somewhere out there in the dark. At breakfast we were told by a triumphant Dawa that she had decided to join some village friends on a trip to Dharan Bazaar and that although they had left Sedua a day after us they had conveniently caught us up. He knew we were angry, she knew we were angry, but there was little we could do about it whilst she kept her distance, and this she thankfully did.

All that day our track followed a sun-drenched ridge with tremendous views on either side. The little spindle bush – *Euonymus frigidus* variety *elongatus* – which we had seen above the Barun Khola valley we found again bearing pale greenish-white, hanging capsules containing two to four orange-coated seeds. A huge climbing shrub also attracted our attention. It looked to me like an *Elaeagnus* species and indeed so it proved. *E. infundibularis* is a powerful species with long scandent, brown scaly stems and elliptic evergreen leaves 2½-3½in. (6.5-9cm) long, glossy-green above covered with silvery scales beneath. The scented flowers, too, are silvery scaly on the outside and are carried in dense axillary clusters. Close by another climber, this time a honeysuckle – *Lonicera glabrata* – twined its slender brown shoots 15ft. (4.5m) into surrounding trees and shrubs. Its shining black berries ¼in. (.65cm) across were borne in clusters in the axils of the long pointed elliptic leaves 1½-2½in. (3.75-6.5cm) long. These were smooth and glossy above but minutely downy beneath. Plants grown from a seedling of this species collected by Harry van de Laar in 1973 have proved hardy in the Hillier Arboretum, but it is not the most ornamental of the group and I doubt if it will be widely grown in cultivation. *Smilax ferox,* a thorny scrambler, was common here and displaying bold clusters of rounded red fruits (Colour Plate 223).

Growing on a grassy bank by the track, in full sun, we found a large group of

Colour Plate 218. A delightfully abstract study of paddy fields near Chiplagong in the Arun valley. (December)

Colour Plate 219. *Camellia kissi,* a small flowered species growing on the hillside near the village of Num in the Arun valley. (December)

Colour Plate 220. *Viburnum cylindricum* flowering at Jenkyn Place in Hampshire. We saw this large shrub several times in the drier valleys of east Nepal. It is just about hardy in British cultivation, in the south certainly, and is easily recognised by its late appearing cylindrical flowers in dense heads and by a thin layer of grey wax on the leaf upper surface. (August)

240

low perennial plants sporting large yellow salver-shaped flowers. This really was a spectacular flowering display and we were pleased to have specimens later identified as *Reinwardtia cicanoba,* a tender relative of *Linum,* the flax, and not unlike a large-flowered flax in general appearance.

Our lunch break that day was taken on a hillside scattered with large plants of the angel's trumpet – *Brugmansia suaveolens* – its huge pendent white trumpets creating a scene more reminiscent of its native Peruvian Andes (Colour Plate 224). Several travellers shared our hillside and one of these produced from his pocket a bamboo flute on which he proceeded to play (Plate 59). It was a plaintive tune yet at home in this place of giant hills and deep valleys and we all listened attentively, each in his own private world shaped by the experience of the last three months.

Our camp for the night was in a dried-up paddy field in the village of Chiplagong (Colour Plate 218). Most of the field margins in these parts were pink and purple-splashed with the flowers of various *Osbeckia* species. Members of the large family *Melastomataceae,* they are characterised by their beautiful leaf venation as well as by the curious 'elbowed' stamens. The genus *Osbeckia* commemorates Pehr Osbeck (1723-1805), a Swedish clergyman and a student of Linnaeus who travelled in India and China. From the same family we also found *Oxyspora paniculata,* a shrub of some 6ft. (2m) with the most attractive leaves coppery when young (Colour Plate 226).

Bananas and tangerines were now available in every village and we purchased enough of each to fill our packs and spare pockets. We walked along the ridge all morning, stopping for lunch in Khambari, main bazaar town of the upper Arun with a stone-paved main street and white-walled two storey houses. On 5 December, my birthday, a porter picked a rose for me to wear in my buttonhole and then kept pace with me pointing out all those plants which were known for their medicinal value. Early in the afternoon we again sighted the Arun river and could see the air strip at Tumlingtar (Plate 60).

At breakfast that morning I had opened a parcel I had been keeping, a birthday present from Sue Lloyd which contained a card, a poem by Goethe and a small book of Lancashire jokes. The joke book was particularly welcome as we were in need of some new ones and their Lancashire flavour filled me with nostalgia for my native county. At the end of the day, of course, we had a birthday party and at the height of preparations the campsite looked like the beginning of a medieval feast with chickens arriving from every direction together with baskets of fruit and vegetables all of which were the subject of much haggling between Dawa, Pema and the villagers. Eventually, all was ready and we sat down on the ground with our Sherpas, porters and what seemed an army of onlookers. We began with mugs of steaming tea followed by soup, and then came a huge metal dish piled high with boiled rice, chicken, green vegetables, yams, pumpkin, sweet corn, soya beans and gravy. This was consumed and allowed to settle before Pema produced bowls of fresh bananas with chocolate sauce. After the meal chang was prepared and the porters were invited to join us for a birthday drink. They converged on the camp fire armed with a mixture of pots, bowls and other containers and soon everyone was merry and singing their favourite songs. The night wore on and when all the chang had been drunk we decided to open our last tinned Dundee cake which we washed down with what was left of our precious whisky ration purchased

Plate 59. Music on the trail as a porter plays on a home-made bamboo flute near Chiplagong in the Arun valley. (November)

Colour Plate 221. *Gleichenia volubilis*, a large bold scrambling fern with creeping rootstock like a giant bracken. (December)

Colour Plate 222. *Daiswa polyphylla* in a wooded defile on the ridge above Num in the Arun valley. (December)

Colour Plate 223. *Smilax ferox*, a thorny scrambling shrub not uncommon in thickets and on forest margins in the Arun valley. (December)

Colour Plate 224. A porter holding the flowers of *Brugmansia sauveolens*, a native of Central America long naturalised in the Nepalese foothills. Note the porter's T-shaped stick on which he supports himself or his load when resting. (November)

Colour Plate 225. A last look at the high Himalaya from a hilltop above the Arun valley. The snow covered mountains to the north seem to hang apparently without support in the blue sky. (December)

Colour Plate 226 (far left). *Oxyspora paniculata*, a member of the large family *Melastomataceae*. The beautifully veined leaves, coppery when young, are characteristic. (December)

Colour Plate 227 (left). A spider's web in the mist above Tumlingtar. (December)

243

Plate 60. The Arun river at Tumlingtar. (December)

in the duty free shop in Singapore. We stayed up just long enough to drink steaming mugs of sweet coffee prepared by Pema before crawling into our tents feeling sleepy and satisfied. It had been a birthday I shall always remember.

Next morning we beheld the Arun valley filled with mist like some ghostly river and shortly afterwards we entered this strange wonderland where spiders hung their intricate webs from grasses and herbs (Colour Plate 227). We left the mist behind in Tumlingtar, however, emerging to brilliant sunshine, and saw the flash of a flock of green pigeons alighting in a nearby field. Soon after, we encountered a flock of Rose-ringed parakeets, screeching their way through the trees. Before midday we had reached our previous crossing point on the Sabhaya Khola, thus completing a circle which had lasted almost three months and had taken us through some of the most fantastic terrain on earth. As the waters were not so deep, this time we waded across the river, and so hot was the sun, that within ten minutes we were completely dry again.

Our route now lay along the valley bottom and all day we sweated in the sun thankful for the occasional stops to replenish our water bottles. The track was now broad and well travelled. This was the main route from the Terai to the hills and a great deal of trade passed along it. The porters who used it regularly were the long distance 'truck drivers' of Nepal. They knew every inch of the route: the best stops, the best tea houses, the best river crossings and the best places to spend the night. Essentially, things could hardly have changed along these routes for hundreds of years and one wondered for how much longer this state of affairs would remain.

For the best part of two days we followed the river, fording several tributaries on the way, the water sometimes waist deep. Crossing one such, we met a line of ten women holding hands to prevent them being carried away by the current. For most of these people what was a bit of an adventure and a hard slog to us was all in a day's work, something they did probably many times in a year. Some of the time we walked along sandy shores covered in river debris and we regularly met water buffalo being brought down from the hills to drink and bathe at the water's margin. The sun beat down and the dusty red earth reflected its heat which was almost unbearable at times. Eventually, we left the river to follow a track which climbed steeply up a hillside (Colour Plate 225) and after several hours brought us to a tea house surrounded by brilliant scarlet poinsettias. Here we spent the night, sleeping on the wooden balcony from which the following morning at dawn we were afforded a superb view of the Makalu range white and pristine against a blue sky.

We continued our climb and later that morning reached the village of Hile where we sampled our last chang, unfortunately of inferior quality to that which we had drunk in the mountains. Moving on from there we walked along an open ridge before descending the hill to the village of Dhankuta where we spent the night in a woodland consisting almost entirely of Chir pine – *Pinus roxburghii* – its fallen needles forming a soft thick carpet over the ground.

On our way through the village we called in at the British Medical Trust to have breakfast with Dr. Don Patterson and his wife. They had been in Dhankuta for twelve months and seemed settled and happy. Like the Trust in Chainpur, this was financed mainly by Oxfam and dealt primarily with the treatment of tuberculosis, the patients staying in the vicinity, many of them living in temples. We crossed the Tamur river at Mogart by way of a narrow suspension bridge constructed of steel and wood by the Gurkhas. Shortly afterwards we began the long haul up to the Sanguri Ridge – 3,500ft. (1,067m) above the river. On the trail we met many porters carrying baskets of tangerines covered with banana leaves. These they were happy to sell us at 1 rupee for fifteen. Bananas were the same price. At the summit of the trail was a small tea house dispensing hot tea, and after several glasses we were ready for the descent. Tired as we were, we felt rejuvenated when we met an old man toiling up the trail carrying a stout metal girder on his back. Between gasps, he told us that it was intended for the new bridge planned to replace the bamboo one at Num (Plate 61).

The walk down to Dharan Bazaar was excruciating in the heat, but we were intent on reaching Gopa Camp before nightfall. Here in a large tent specially set up on a lawn we were reunited with Witcombe who, after he had left us on the Milke Danda, together with Mortimer had journeyed to Sedua and then moved westwards eventually to arrive in Namche Bazaar. They had made large collections of seed of cereal crops as well as samples of other food crops and a smattering of seed of ornamental plants including Silver fir and several junipers. Finally they had returned to Kathmandu where both of them had become ill; Mortimer was still unwell and Witcombe, although feeling groggy himself, had had to leave him in order to come to meet us.

It was at this time that we heard about the India-Pakistan confrontation and we wondered whether we would be able to leave Kathmandu. No one seemed to know which Indian airports were open to civilian traffic and someone told us that Calcutta airport (where we would have to change planes) had been closed for some time. As always in such situations, rumours were rife and varied in content so we decided to ignore them and concentrate on repacking our gear and our precious seed which arrived with the porters the next day. All our unwanted gear and clothing we gave to our Sherpas and porters together with other remuneration according to their seniority. Then there was time at last to relax and we particularly enjoyed having tea one afternoon with the camp commandant Brigadier Smith. We sat on his patio in the sun, afterwards walking round his garden, admiring fine specimens of gardenias, frangipanis, hibiscus, ixias and the inevitable bougainvilleas in purple, crimson, orange and creamy-white. Because of the border conflict there were no film shows and at night we made do with the sounds of jackals howling and scavenging outside our tent.

Colour Plate 228. *Polygonum amplexicaule* 'Arun Gem' in the author's garden. A selection from the variety *pendulum* collected as seed from the riverside at Thudam. (August)

Colour Plate 229. *Polygonum runciforme* in the Sir Harold Hillier Gardens and Arboretum, collected on the Milke Danda. (October)

Colour Plate 232. *Inula hookeri* in the author's garden raised from seed collected in the valley of the Barun Khola. A hardy, easy, free-flowering perennial. (September)

13. HOME AGAIN

On our last day in Gopa camp Morris and I cleared up all the odds and ends and rubbish as well as preparing two large boxes of supplies for the British Medical Trust in Biratnagar. Beer and Witcombe had left that morning for Kathmandu with our seed and essential equipment. In the afternoon we wandered round camp visiting the kukri makers who make the most impressive and efficient kukris from the merest scraps of steel. We selected and paid for two apiece. That evening after supper we received a cable from Singapore via the British Embassy in Kathmandu. It was from R.A.F. Changi offering the expedition members indulgence flights to Britain leaving on 21st December. This was great news, but could we get ourselves to Singapore in time? The waiting room at Biratnagar airport was crowded and we found ourselves standing next to a Bhutanese lama and his two attendants in full regalia. An hour later we were at 11,500ft. (3,505m) heading west with clear views of Kanchengjunga, Makalu, Everest and many other peaks and ranges. Forty minutes later we were in Kathmandu where Mortimer, looking much fitter than we had dared hope, welcomed us at the Panorama Hotel. We then met up with

Colour Plate 230 (opposite far left). *Hypericum uralum* in the Sir Harold Hillier Gardens and Arboretum grown from seed collected in the Bagang Khola valley below Thudam. (August)

Colour Plate 231 (opposite left). *Hypericum choisianum*: our collection of this lovely shrub was probably the first ever introduction of the species into cultivation. (July)

Beer and Witcombe before heading for lunch at Aunt Jane's Place, a café run by the American Peace Corps and popular with hippies and travellers. The food tasted smashing after three months of mainly rice and eggs, but even this paled by comparison with the lunch I had next day with Tom and Jenny Spring-Smyth at their home which resembled a little bit of England inside and I was reminded of my family and friends back home and the tales I had to tell them. One can write all the letters one likes, but nothing can replace the spoken word and the telling of a story with facial expressions and the wave of a hand to emphasise a point. I had much to tell the Spring-Smyths that day, and they were genuinely thrilled and happy to hear of our experiences.

The plane situation was quite complicated by now and we were exploring the possibility of flying by Air India to Singapore via Delhi and Bombay. We heard Calcutta airport had been closed and the rumour was that Bombay would be next. On my return to the hotel I met Witcombe just back from the airport with news that we had bookings from Delhi onwards but not out of Kathmandu.

Next day Beer managed to fly out, but because of the border troubles he left minus the freight which included our precious seed and herbarium specimens. We were told that it would be sent on as soon as conditions allowed, and although this wasn't very reassuring we had no choice but to agree. Around 4p.m. we all went to the Spring-Smyths for tea and to say our goodbyes and then we had a race back to the hotel in trishaws for an early night.

At the airport the next day we learnt that Witcombe alone was assured of a seat on the plane, whilst the rest of us just had to sit tight and hope. Eventually the plane, a Viscount arrived and thankfully we were all four called to board.

We arrived in England on Christmas Eve. The freight did not arrive until February when Beer drove in a newly acquired car to Heathrow to extract the herbarium specimens, for the Natural History Museum, and the seed. The successful outcome of our expedition seemed about to take place. Beer decided to stay the night in London in order to visit the Botany Department at the Museum when it opened the next morning. Having booked into a hotel he drove into the West End, parked his car in a side street and went to see a show. When he returned to where he had parked the car, he found to his horror that it was gone. He called at the local police station to report the theft and was informed that so may cars were stolen in London each night that they held out very little hope for its return. Beer told them of the car's contents, to which the officer shrugged his shoulders, saying that more than likely the car was in some back street workshop being resprayed and that the seed and dried plants would probably be burned as rubbish. Beer then told them of the British and American Ambassadors' efforts in having the cargo flown out of Kathmandu and the suggestion of a diplomatic involvement seemed to lend a sudden urgency to the enquiries. He was told to return to his hotel whilst the police pursued their investigations. Of course he could not sleep at all and almost panicked at breakfast next morning when told he had a telephone call. It was the police and to Beer's joy he was told that his car had been returned to the place where he had parked it the previous night. It was with some trepidation that Beer approached the car, trepidation which turned into ecstasy when he discovered that both seed and specimens were intact and even his camera, which he had left unthinkingly under the driver's seat, was still there. Beer asked no further questions and having first delivered the specimens to the Museum headed for home.

The packeting of seed and distribution of shares lasted several weeks and involved the help of several others in addition to expedition members. A total of 396 seed collections had been made by the Horticultural Project, to which the Agricultural Project, which had made collections of cereal crops from 110 different sites, had added a further twenty-one making 417 collections in all. The seed shares were distributed to over 100 individuals and organisations who had together finally contributed approximately £3,000 to the expedition's total budget of £7,200.

Holders of general shares (£25 each) received eighty packets of seed, whilst special shareholders (£50) received the same plus a special collection of sixty packets, making 140 packets in all. Seed lots in excess of 8,000 were eventually distributed to shareholders in Britain, Europe, North America and Australia. A set of field notes accompanied each batch of seeds. In a comparatively short time the experts at the British Museum had furnished us with a number of identifications to add to those which we had made in the field.

Writing in 1995, almost twenty five years since our seed was distributed, it is an interesting and sobering exercise to assess the impact of our introductions. As expected and despite our written request for details of germination and cultivation results, the majority of those individuals and institutions in receipt of seed failed to keep us informed. Such information that we did collect was based mainly on the results of shareholders known to us. But many shareholders shared their seed amongst friends. This was a commendable action and served to spread the results over an even greater area. On the whole the fate of our seed has come to me by accident. Years later quite by chance I have come across our introductions in gardens, often in the most isolated places. Very often the garden's owner had no personal knowledge as to its origin and only occasionally have I found a plant we introduced labelled with its name and more importantly its number. Still more uncommon are those instances where records have been kept as to our introductions despite the number of field notes we distributed. As one might have expected, it is mainly in the botanical institutions and specialist collections that our plants are not only grown but correctly labelled and their details included in a record system. The Sir Harold Hillier Gardens and Arboretum, the University Botanic Garden, Cambridge, the Royal Botanic Gardens at Edinburgh and Kew and Wakehurst Place in Sussex are such institutions, whilst in Vancouver, Canada, the Asian Garden of the University of British Columbia Botanic Garden is likewise exemplary.

Given this situation it is impossible to assess exactly which of our introductions are presently in cultivation. I suspect that many if not most of the alpines have been lost and of the perennials only a handful remain. They include *Inula hookeri* which, thanks to a gift from Sheila Hargreaves, flourishes in my garden (Colour Plate 232). I also have *Polygonum amplexicaule* 'Arun Gem' which is available from a number of nurseries (Colour Plate 228). *Polygonum capitatum* from our introduction was for many years maintained on the rock garden at Kew when Brian Halliwell was in charge, but since his retirement this may no longer be the case. It may well have been superseded by other introductions. *Polygonum runciforme* which we collected on the Milke Danda quickly settled into cultivation where, in some places at least, it has proved rampant, its pale pink globular heads and beautifully marked leaves

Colour Plate 233. *Rubus nepalensis* growing in the Sir Harold Hillier Gardens and Arboretum. This plant was raised from seed collected in the valley of the Bagang Khola below Thudam. It forms a useful ground cover in shade, flowering and fruiting more prolifically, however, in a sunny situation. (August)

Colour Plate 234. *Cotoneaster frigidus* in a Hampshire garden grown from seed collected in the Upper Arun valley. (November)

Colour Plate 235. *Spiraea micrantha,* a free-flowering, erect-stemmed shrub collected from scrub on a steep hillside in the Upper Arun valley, here flowering in the Sir Harold Hillier Gardens and Arboretum. (September)

Colour Plate 236. *Rhododendron ciliatum* in the author's garden raised from seed collected in the valley of the Barun Khola. (August)

making it a valuable if seasonal ground cover (Colour Plate 229).

Many of our *Primula* and *Meconopsis* introductions may still be around, though the original seedlings no doubt have passed away. Among our more spectacular introductions *Rheum nobile* failed at Hilliers but grew for some years with Jack Drake's Inshriach Nursery in Scotland who offered plants of it for a while. I also saw *Saussurea gossypiphora* germinating at Hilliers only to wither away, whilst *S. obvallata* fared no better. The same goes for *Leontopodium monocephalum*, the Golden Edelweiss. Most of these high alpines are notoriously difficult if not impossible in cultivation and require exceptional skill as well as patience.

Only recently I heard from a specialist nurseryman growing *Bergenia purpurascens* from one of our collections. Its exact collection details had long since been lost but because of its unusual character, small leaves, slow spread and more importantly, white flower with pinkish calyx, the nurseryman has named it *Bergenia purpurascens* 'Len Beer'. I have never heard of a white form of this species before and I look forward to seeing it being distributed. Our collection of *Cautleya cathcartii* proved new to cultivation and is still grown in a few specialist collections.

Of the woody plants we introduced several of our rhododendrons are well represented in specialist collections both in Britain and north-west North America. In October 1985 for instance, I enjoyed seeing unseasonal flowers on a group of our *Rhododendron thomsonii* in the Asian Garden of the University of British Columbia Botanic Garden in Vancouver. *Rhododendron ciliatum* from seed collected in the Barun Khola valley flourishes in several gardens and has proved an attractive addition to the dwarf species in cultivation, although other collections of this species are well represented too. A fine plant in my own garden has formed a low mound covered in white, pink-flushed funnel-shaped flowers in March or April (Colour Plate 236). *R. glaucophyllum* meanwhile produced a lovely white-flowered seedling which Mrs. Kathleen Dryden has named 'Len Beer'. Several of our *Hypericum* collections are about still, especially *H. uralum*, *H. choisianum* and *H. tenuicaule* (Colour Plates 230 and 231). The last two named were new to cultivation whilst one of our *H. hookerianum* seedlings proved to have larger flowers than normal attracting a good deal of attention amongst shrub enthusiasts.

Other of our shrub collections to have established themselves in at least some gardens include *Spiraea micrantha* a strong growing, erect-stemmed species with bold flattened heads of white flowers (Colour Plate 235), *Berberis erythroclada* a dwarf deciduous species with often rich autumn colour and *Rubus nepalensis*, a delightful carpeting plant not unlike an alpine strawberry in effect which is now available from a number of nurseries and has even been used as a parent to produce at least one hybrid (Colour Plate 233).

Our introductions of *Sorbus vestita* and *S. hedlundii* are still grown in the Sir Harold Hillier Gardens and Arboretum, as are several specimens of *Betula utilis* and *Cotoneaster frigidus* that we collected. The last named, an impressive sight when in red fruit, was originally wrongly identified as *C. gamblei* (Colour Plate 234).

One of our most notable introductions was *Vaccinium glauco-album* a smaller-leaved, hardier form than previously grown, and free-fruiting too. A plant of this collection growing in the Savill Gardens, Windsor, received an

Award of Merit from the Royal Horticultural Society in 1992 under the cultivar name 'Da Norbu'. *Prunus rufa* looked like being a remarkable introduction but the few seedlings produced from our limited collection have not lived up to their early promise and a much better introduction with more ornamental bark has been made by Tony Schilling.

My biggest disappointment, however, was the failure of the *Juniperus recurva* collections to produce anything other than ordinary seedlings. Considering the wide and exciting range of forms we saw in the wild, particularly above Topke Gola, I had expected better. One reason for this I believe lies in the fact that several juniper seed lots went missing and I fear these included the Topke Gola collections. We did however, produce a few seedlings of the dwarf green *J. indica*, one at least of which grows in the Sir Harold Hillier Gardens and Arboretum.

Seed of *Aster albescens* produced seedlings with somewhat darker lavender-blue flowers than those previously grown. Tony Schilling grew our collection of this sub-shrub in the Sir Henry Price Garden at Wakehurst Place and expressed his admiration for it.

We had high hopes for *Potentilla arbuscula*, which we saw in the Lumbasumba Himal, and having spent some considerable time filling bags with its seed I was dismayed to hear on our return that this collection had gone missing along with a promising collection of *Toricellia tiliifolia* from the Barun Khola valley. What became of them I never did discover. Of course, every plant hunter has his or her stories of the ones that got away and if I could choose just one plant which we saw but did not collect seed of or if we did it didn't germinate it would be *Myricaria rosea* which to the best of my knowledge is not in cultivation in the West. Also rans would certainly include *Hippophae thibetana*.

One of several disappointments concerning seed successfully introduced and germinated was the number of plants which, swans in the wild became ugly ducklings in the garden. *Delphinium viscosum* and *Cicerbita macrantha* were two for which we had such high hopes in the field.

14. RETURN TO THE MILKE DANDA

In 1972, on the strength of our successful expedition to Nepal I was approached by a specialist interest travel firm to lead a botanical trek back to the Milke Danda. Like all such treks it would comprise a group of keen, mostly amateur horticulturists intent on enjoying the adventure of their lives. I agreed and the following year I was off to Nepal again with twenty-one companions.

Instead of three months the trek would last three weeks and as a consequence our journey would take us no further than the Milke Banjgang, the saddle on the Milke Danda ridge over which a major hill route crosses. To compensate for this, however, we would be travelling in April which for me certainly would allow comparisons to be made between the flowers of spring and autumn. Our route was to follow the main track from Dharan Bazaar north to Dhankuta and thence along the ridge to Hile and up the Taplejung trail via Basanteur and Lam Pokri to the Milke Danda ridge. We were then to return via Pokhari and Chainpur to Tumlingtar from whence we would fly to Kathmandu.

Much of the vegetation encountered on this trek I had seen two years before but there were more plants in flower than in 1971, including the magnificent tree rhododendrons – *Rhododendron arboreum* – which alone were worth journeying from Britain to see. Naturally, I took many photographs and as this

Colour Plate 237 (opposite). A fruit bat hanging from a branch high in the crown of a Silky oak *(Grevillea robusta)* stretches a wing in the late afternoon sun. It will not leave its perch, however, until dusk. (April)

Colour Plate 238 (far left). *Jacaranda mimosifolia* flowering its heart out on a Kathmandu street. Few flowering trees can match this Brazilian native in the colour and elegance of its flower panicles. (April)

Colour Plate 239 (left). In the streets and gardens of Kathmandu the Australian tree *Grevillea robusta* reaches an impressive size and is spectacular when in flower. Here it is seen with a bougainvillea clambering into its branches. (April)

255

Plate 62. Carrots freshly grown in the Kathmandu valley being sold on the streets of the capital. (April)

new edition seemed an ideal opportunity to publish some of these I am also providing the following brief account of the more important plants seen together with a few of the interesting events experienced.

As before Kathmandu was our first contact with Nepal, our short stay at the Annapurna Hotel best remembered for our early evening vigils outside the entrance waiting for the awakening of the fruit bats or flying foxes in the branches of the same dead Bunya-Bunya pines (*Araucaria bidwillii*) across the road. Something else we noticed in the roads and gardens were the flowers on trees we had first seen flowerless in 1971. Most spectacular were the heliotrope-blue panicles of the jacarandas – *Jacaranda mimosifolia* – from Brazil which is a favourite here as in many other cities, enjoying warm summers and mild winters (Colour Plate 238).

It was the same with *Grevillea robusta,* the Australian Silky oak, a native of the rainforests of New South Wales and Queensland. The branches of these tall stately trees were crowded with conspicuous comb-like racemes of rich golden-yellow or orange-yellow tubular flowers (Colour Plate 239). In its native land this tree is prized for its attractively patterned yellow-brown timber which is used in furniture making. It has been commonly planted in towns and cities in Australia as well as in the south-western U.S.A. and southern China. The flowers are packed with nectar providing a valuable food source for insects, birds and fruit bats! (Colour Plate 237).

Other flowering plants which caught our attention were the Coral tree – *Erythrina crista-galli* – and the Crimson Bottle-brush *Callistemon citrinus.* The former is native to South America east of the Andes and is not uncommon in Kathmandu gardens where it makes a large, spreading shrub or occasionally a small tree with trifoliolate leaves, thorny stems and large elongated racemes of scarlet-red waxy flowers, a real eye catcher (Colour Plate 240). The Bottle-brush on the other hand develops here into a large tree with graceful weeping branches crowded with evergreen needle-like leaves and crimson, long-stamened flowers in dense cylindrical clusters towards the ends of the branches. A native of south-east Australia, these tree specimens in Kathmandu are spectacular especially when the wind blows through them. They look for all the world like exotic flowering Weeping willows (Colour Plate 241).

Weeping too are the cypress trees – *Cupressus corneyana* – native to Bhutan but commonly planted here and elsewhere in Nepal where it makes a superb and graceful specimen or screen. One day, on a visit to a fruit and vegetable market (Plate 62), we found the fruits of a wild bramble being offered for sale wrapped in sal – *Shorea robusta* – leaves. These were orange-yellow in colour and undoubtedly belonged to *Rubus ellipticus* which grows commonly around the villages. They are claimed to be the best flavoured of all the Himalayan brambles (Colour Plate 242). Bamboo trays filled with a dark red berry – another *Rubus* species – were also displayed (Colour Plate 243), whilst the largest crowd of onlookers we found clustered around a man with an owl nestling for sale.

We flew to Biratnagar on 15 April and proceeded by bus to a campsite at

Colour Plate 240. *Erythrina crista-galli,* the Coral tree from South America east of the Andes, is frequently planted in Kathmandu gardens where its long racemes of waxy scarlet-red flowers are attractive over a long period. (April)

Colour Plate 241 (right). *Callistemon citrinus*, a native of south-east Australia but commonly planted in Kathmandu gardens, this spectacular Bottle-brush reaches a large size. With its long, gracefully weeping stems it looks for all the world like an exotic flowering version of the Weeping willow. (April)

Colour Plate 242 (top). The orange fruits of a wild bramble *Rubus ellipticus* being sold in a packet made from a folded leaf of the Sal tree *Shorea robusta*. These fruits are claimed to be the best flavoured of all Himalayan brambles. (April)

Colour Plate 243 (above). A tempting tray of wild raspberries – *Rubus* species – on sale in a Kathmandu market. (April)

Plate 63. A Limbu girl at Dharan Bazaar. She was one of fifty porters who helped carry baggage into the hills. Her earrings can be worn in several positions

Dharan Bazaar where we were to spend our first night. We were told that the weather had been hotter than was usual for the time of the year and we decided to leave camp as early as was reasonable the next morning in order to clear our first obstacle, the Sanguri Ridge, before the sun got too high. We left before dawn, our party of twenty-two accompanied by nine Sherpas including a Sirdar, a cook and two assistants, whilst to carry the tentage and stores a total of fifty porters, mostly Limbus, had been hired (Plate 63). It was an impressive sight to be sure, especially when we began the climb and people formed a long snaking column on the trail.

We barely made the ridge summit and its tea house before the sun shone bright and fierce on our backs and already two of our number were experiencing difficulties. By comparison our descent on the other side was more leisurely and comfortable and we made camp by a stream where shallow pools provided an opportunity to cool off. The next day another early start saw us crossing the Tamur by the suspension bridge at Mugar Ghat and starting the long climb up the hillside towards Dhankuta where our next night would be spent. The track was steep and stony and we hardly seemed to have got started before the sun was gazing at us over the Sanguri Ridge. By midday the sun was riding high and the temperature as on the previous day had soared to 110°F (43.5°C). To cut a long story short, we all made it to Dhankuta that evening suffering only four casualties. Two of my party had collapsed from heat exhaustion and needed ponies to bring them in, whilst the wife of one of these had been attacked by some debilitating bug a complaint shared by the fourth casualty, me!

Our tents had been pitched on terraced ground beyond the town and beneath the huge spreading crowns of several Pipal trees – *Ficus religiosa* (Plate 64). Each morning around dawn we were subjected to a continuous barrage of figs dislodged from the branches of these trees by a troop of macaque (rhesus) monkeys.

Having been seen by a doctor, it was decided that three of our casualties were in no fit state to continue and a radio request the next day brought a helicopter which evacuated them to Kathmandu. Our 'leader' meanwhile soldiered on although he suffered the indignity of being carried all the next day on the back of a porter! I shall never forget him, Ramdos was his name, a Limbu whose slight build belied a toughness and tenacity characteristic of these hill people (Plate 65). He adapted a bamboo basket so that he could carry it on his back with me sitting in it and by this means he somehow transported me to the next camp which, because of the unexpected scarcity of water, was situated in a dried paddy field well beyond our intended stop at Hile. Ramdos, with his severely jolted but thankful cargo arrived after dark. More tired than hungry I crawled into my sleeping bag while Ramdos tucked into a well earned supper.

Up to this point I had noted few plants of interest other than an extraordinary yellow dodder – *Cuscuta reflexa* – which covered hedges and bushes above Dhankuta (Colour Plate 246). I told my colleagues that it was none other than the Himalayan spaghetti plant and so closely did its stems resemble that well known pasta that I think one of them – a trusting soul – actually believed me.

Plate 64. The campsite at Dhankuta lay on a dry terrace beneath a huge Pipal tree – *Ficus religiosa* – from the branches of which each morning we were subjected to a regular bombardment of figs dropped by monkeys. (April)

Since then I have seen what I believe to be this same or a similar parasite growing in similar situations in Bhutan and in south-west China.

Our route from the Hile camp to the Milke Banjgang on the Milke Danda led us by way of Basantpur, Chowki and Sida Pokhari on the Taplejung track through some very interesting terrain where cultivated terraces gave way to fragments of forest in which interesting plants clung to an increasingly precarious existence. *Mahonia napaulensis* (this particular form regarded by some authorities as *M. acanthifolia*) occurred several times as a large multi-stemmed shrub or small tree often loaded with large dense bunches of small bloomy blue berries (Colour Plate 244). These are used by some hill people to produce a dark blue dye. Into one of these clumps a specimen of the Himalayan ivy – *Hedera nepalensis* – climbed and we later met with it on trees, boulders and cliffs, some plants bearing their ochre yellow fruits (Colour Plate 245).

Plate 65. Ramdos, a Limbu porter with umbrella, collecting equipment and basket decorated with the flowers of *Piptanthus nepalensis*. (April)

259

Colour Plate 244. Two of the Sherpas collecting the fruits of a large *Mahonia napaulensis* by the track above Hile. This particular form is regarded by some authorities as a distinct species – *M. acanthifolia*. (April)

Colour Plate 245 (right). *Hedera nepalensis*, the Himalayan ivy, scrambling into a much pruned specimen of *Mahonia napaulensis* by the Hile-Basantpur track. (April)

Colour Plate 246. *Cuscuta reflexa*, a giant yellow Himalayan dodder swamping shrubs and small trees in a thicket above Dhankuta. This parasitic plant looks for all the world like yellow spaghetti. (April)

Colour Plate 247 (right). Dutch horticulturalist Harry van de Laar photographing an orchid *Coelogyne corymbosa* growing in an old *Mahonia napaulensis* by the track above Hile. (April)

Colour Plate 248. *Coelogyne corymbosa* growing on a bank by the trail above Basantpur. (April)

Plate 66. Limbu women dressed in their finery on the trail between Hile and Basantpur. (April)

This general area was also rich in orchids which grew epiphytically on the stems and in the crotches of trees and large shrubs. One of these, *Coelogyne corymbosa* with pendulous white inflorescences actually grew in a mahonia (Colour Plate 247), and another plant of this species we found on a shady bank above the trail (Colour Plate 248), meanwhile *Vanda cristata* (Colour Plate 249), *Dendrobium aphyllum* and *D. fimbriatum* (Colour Plate 250), peered down at us from branches above our heads.

As the track wound upwards towards the outskirts of the forest we encountered *Rhododendron arboreum*, the low-altitude form tender in most areas of Britain but impressive here with its leathery foliage, glossy-topped and silver-backed and its tight rounded trusses of glowing crimson blooms. Many once fine specimens had been hacked about and flowering sprigs were commonly seen decorating porters' baskets and bullock carts. Some village girls wore the rhododendron blooms as decorations in their hair whilst others preferred to wear beads and sometimes ear and nose rings. Limbu women we passed on the trail were especially fond of such adornments and the amount of gold we saw was a constant source of amazement to us. Typical of these were two girls dressed to the nines in rich and colourful costumes and wearing outsize gold earrings and smiles to match. They looked fabulous and they knew it! (Plate 66). In stark contrast to them was a young Limbu woman we saw busily thatching an extension to the family home. Her dress was plain and workaday and her only adornment, small gold earrings and a green cotton wristband (Plate 67).

The forests now became larger and denser and at around 8,500ft. (2,590m) above the hamlet of Chowki we were excited to find both *Rhododendron dalhousiae* and *R. lindleyi* in flower. The former species I had previously seen in the Upper Arun valley in 1971 and here as then it occurred as an epiphyte on mossy branched trees, mostly mahonias and lyonias but preferring, however, to perch on the top of dead tree stumps above one's head (Colour Plate 251). The cream-coloured or pale sulphur-yellow trumpeted blooms gave off a delicate perfume matched only by that of the related *R. lindleyi*, a similarly lax-habited shrub, we found only once growing 10ft. (3m) up in the crotch of a *Lyonia* species. The 4-5ft. (1.25-1.5m) long, rather bare stems leaned out over the track flaunting bold terminal clusters of large trumpet-shaped white blooms (Colour Plate 252). A specimen was taken and dried in a press, later to be deposited in the Botany Department of the Natural History Museum in London.

Like *R. dalhousiae*, *R. lindleyi* belongs to a subsection of *Rhododendron* known as the Maddenia, most members of which are too tender for cultivation out of doors in Britain and are generally grown here in tubs or pots in the conservatory. *R. lindleyi* is named after John Lindley (1799-1865), Professor of Botany at the University of London and a famous Secretary of the Horticultural Society of London, now the Royal Horticultural Society. *R. lindleyi*, along with *R. dalhousie* and many other fine species, was among the rhododendrons discovered and introduced by Joseph Hooker in the middle of the nineteenth century.

The further we climbed above Chowki the better the flora became. We were now between 9,000 and 10,000ft. (2,743 and 3,048m) and our track led us

Plate 67. A young Limbu woman busy thatching an extension to the family home in the hills above Hile. (April)

through forests dominated by *Rhododendron arboreum*. This tree, as we had expected, provided the greatest flowering spectacle of the entire trek. For the next six days it was never out of our sight and we never tired of it. Its flowers stared us in the face when we emerged from our tents each morning, while its lengthening shadows on the track signalled the approach of evening. Sometimes we emerged from its dark dense canopy into wide open grassy spaces where we could stand well back and view the waves of rhododendrons like tapestries at an exhibition. It seemed the finest specimens occurred on the periphery of the forest, dense, compact, conical or columnar trees up to 50ft. (15m) high bedecked with flower trusses from head to foot. The flowers varied in colour from carmine through various shades of pink to an occasional white. The dominant colour, though, began rose-red in bud, opened to rose and faded to flesh pink, the indumentum beneath the leaves, unlike the silver of those seen at lower altitudes, was buff-coloured. This form occurred up to an altitude of 11,500ft. (3,505m) on the Milke Danda Ridge above Lam Pokhari 2. According to the classification devised by Chamberlain and Cullen at the Royal Botanic Garden, Edinburgh it would answer to *R. arboreum* subspecies *cinnamomeum* variety *roseum* (Colour Plates 253-255).

Rhododendron arboreum was the first Himalayan species to be named. It was first discovered by Captain, later Major General, Thomas Hardwicke (1755-1835), an all round amateur naturalist but with a preference for zoology. He found it in the Siwalik Hills of Kumaon in north-west India in 1796 and very soon its seeds were being distributed in Britain, bolstered in 1805 by a further introduction from Nathaniel Wallich. Many people vied to grow it and the first flowering is said to have occurred at The Grange, in the Hampshire village of Alresford in 1826. This would almost certainly have been the low altitude

Colour Plate 249. *Vanda cristata*, a curious epiphytic orchid found in trees on the forest edge near Basantpur. (May)

Colour Plate 250 (above right). *Dendrobium fimbriatum* growing epiphytically on a tree on the forest margin near Basantpur. Note the fimbriate (fringed) margin of the lip. (April)

Colour Plate 251 (right). *Rhododendron dalhousiae*, a wild collected specimen from east Nepal flowering in the conservatory of Major Tom Spring-Smyth in Hampshire. We saw this species on several occasions growing epiphytically on mossy stems and branches in the forests of the Milke Danda ridge. As in the related *R. lindleyi* the flowers are fragrant. Unfortunately neither is fully hardy out of doors in Britain. (June)

Colour Plate 252. *Rhododendron lindleyi* flowering in the conservatory of Major Tom Spring-Smyth in Hampshire. This specimen was collected in the wild in east Nepal and we saw the same species growing epiphytically on mossy branched trees above Chowki on the Milke Danda. The trumpet-shaped flowers are richly fragrant. (June)

Colour Plate 253. Trekking on the Milke Danda above Chowki. *Rhododendron arboreum* subspecies *cinnamomeum* variety *roseum* forms a tapestry in the background. (April)

Colour Plate 254. *Rhododendron arboreum* flowers. (April)

Colour Plate 255. *Rhododendron arboreum* subspecies *cinnamomeum* variety *roseum*: a magnificent specimen above Chowki on the Milke Danda (altitude 9,500ft./2,895m). This 50ft. (15m) tree would cause a sensation at the Chelsea Flower Show. One of the Limbu porters, Ramdos, stands beneath. (April)

crimson flowered form which, because of its tender nature, was probably being grown in a greenhouse or conservatory.

One of our camps was situated in a series of glades in the rhododendron forest. Here grew a cherry *Prunus rufa* with small single white flowers and a dark polished and peeling bark. *Piptanthus nepalensis (laburnifolius)* formed large spreading bushes 10-15ft. (3-4.5m) across, their clusters of yellow pea-flowers lining the branches creating a bright splash from a distance (Colour Plate 256). *Rosa sericea* and *Berberis hookeri* accompanied it, the former with characteristic four-petalled cream-coloured flowers, the berberis scrubby to 6ft. (1.8m) with evergreen silver-backed spine-toothed leaves and clusters of small rich yellow bell-shaped flowers. I first met with this berberis in Bolton's Moss Bank Park when I was an apprentice gardener. It used to be fairly common in northern gardens in the 1950s but it now seems to have become scarce, its place taken by sundry hybrids, whilst in the south of England it is mainly represented by the variety *viridis* with leaves green beneath.

The most common shrub in these grazed areas however was *Daphne bholua* which formed colonies of erect suckering stems around large individuals. Drifts of this shrub occurred on the edge of the rhododendron forest often forming substantial stands in glades and pastures and must have presented a fine sight earlier in the year when plastered with clusters of white, rose or purple stained flowers. The fragrance from these has to be smelt to be believed and it is without doubt one of the most exquisite scents I know. Indeed, if the smell of frangipani (*Plumeria*) flowers is redolent of the tropics then that of *Daphne bholua* for me certainly recalls the rhododendron and evergreen oak forests of the eastern Himalaya (Plate 68). Most if not all the daphnes we saw above Chowki seemed to be evergreen and not the deciduous variety *glacialis* from higher altitudes. It was one of three seedlings of the last named collected by Tom Spring-Smyth on the Milke Danda in February 1961 that we eventually named 'Gurkha'. All three seedlings had been wrapped in moss and packed in a bamboo basket on the back of a porter. When he returned to the British Gurkha headquarters at Dharan, Spring-Smyth sent the seedlings by jeep to Calcutta where they travelled by air in a diplomatic bag to London and six months' quarantine at Kew Gardens (Colour Plate 257).

Two of the seedlings were eventually planted in the New Milton, Hampshire, garden of Spring-Smyth's parents where they grew strongly for several years before one, for no obvious reason, turned up its toes and died. Spring-Smyth had served for a number of years as an officer in a Gurkha regiment, and it was the remaining plant that we named 'Gurkha' in honour of those brave, tough and hardy Nepalese mountain people. *Daphne bholua* 'Gurkha' is now well established in British cultivation although it remains expensive to buy as plants are normally grafted. There are other named clones in cultivation, one of which, 'Jacqueline Postill', was raised by Hilliers' propagator Alan Postill and named after his wife. Unlike 'Gurkha', of which it is a seedling, 'Jacqueline Postill' is evergreen. It is also more robust in growth with larger rose-purple stained flowers in larger clusters (Colour Plate 258). All forms enjoy a sheltered position in the garden preferring a lime-free, moist but well-drained soil. A large plant of 'Jacqueline Postill' by my front door flowers each year from Christmas into late March or early April depending on the weather, its fragrance attracting regular comment from visitors. Planted in 1983 as a 1ft. (30cm) grafted plant from a pot

Plate 68. *Daphne bholua* flowering in a forest glade at Puiyan in Nepal. When in flower it fills the forest around with its fragrance. It is plentiful on the Milke Danda. (November)

it had reached a height of 10ft. (3m) in 1991. One of the most impressive plantings of *Daphne bholua* in cultivation was made by Tony Schilling at Wakehurst Place in Sussex, where he sited a whole drift of seedlings in a valley above a stream. This is regularly an experience to be remembered when the flowers scent the air in late winter and early spring.

So much of the April flower power in the Nepalese forests is produced by woody plants that it is easy to overlook the contribution made by perennials. It was still too early for many things but we did find *Daiswa polyphylla*, previously known as *Paris polyphylla*. Its curious green flowers above ruffs of slender-pointed leaves were not uncommon in the dappled dead leafage of the forest floor. And then there were the arisaemas. These curious, some would say bizarre, members of the Arum family are widely distributed in the Himalaya eastwards into China and Japan. Although all possess the same basic parts, a tuber, fleshy false stem comprising long erect sheathing bracts, leaves with several leaflets and a flower spathe consisting of a funnel-shaped wrap-around base expanding into a limb or sail with a central column (spadix), they vary enormously in colour and form. We found three species over several days either growing in the forest's shade or in rough pasture amongst scrub and rocks. The most plentiful was *Arisaema nepenthoides*, a tall elegant plant with slender green and brown mottled or reticulated stem and similarly coloured striped spathe which curved over and forward, looking for all the world like a snake about to strike, hence the common name Cobra plant. The green spadix meanwhile is relatively short and club shaped. The leaves which develop after the flowers emerge have five rather thick and glossy leaflets. Certain individuals were greener than others whilst some had a pink suffusion (Colour Plate 259).

The most remarkable thing about *Arisaema tortuosum* was its spadix which continued as a thickened appendage which curved out from under the green spathe and then straight up like a slender green or purple rat's tail. The leaves meanwhile had dark stalks bearing five to seven abruptly pointed leaflets (Colour Plate 260). Different again and the strangest of all was *A. griffithii*, a striking plant with a broad short tubed spathe curved back at the top and coloured a dark lurid purple with a fine green netting or reticulation. The spadix of this plant had a long tail-like appendage whilst the leaves consisted of three large coarse often yellow-margined leaflets borne on stout mottled stalks (Colour Plate 261).

Colour Plate 256. *Piptanthus nepalensis*, the so-called evergreen laburnum, is common in the east Himalaya. A large, spreading shrub, we found it in open glades in the forest and on exposed hillsides on the Milke Danda. (April)

Colour Plate 259. *Arisaema nepenthoides*, a fine plant of this curious aroid with slender-tubed flowers handsomely marbled and striped. We found it on the edge of a glade on the Milke Danda. (April)

Colour Plate 257. Major Tom Spring-Smyth with the original *Daphne bholua* 'Gurkha' of the deciduous variety *glacialis*, collected on the Milke Danda, which he sent home to his parent's Hampshire garden as a tiny seedling wrapped in moss. It is available as a grafted plant from specialist nurserymen. (January)

Colour Plate 258. *Daphne bholua* 'Jacqueline Postill'. This is one of the most satisfactory forms of the species in cultivation and can be obtained as a grafted plant from specialist nurserymen. (January)

Colour Plate 260. *Arisaema tortuosum*: we saw this species several times on the Milke Danda above Chowki. The long tail-like spadix is characteristic. (April)

Colour Plate 261 (opposite). *Arisaema griffithii*, one of the most striking members of a bizarre family, the large squat blooms with a broad, flared, reticulated limb. The leaves have three coarse, yellow-margined leaflets on darkly mottled stalks. It was frequent on the Milke Danda above Chowki. (April)

In case the reader is wondering how I managed to see and write notes on all these plants within days of being incapacitated, suffice to say that plants to enthusiasts like me are the perfect tonic. When they are growing wild in one of the world's most exciting landscapes they will cure all but the most serious afflictions!

Our climb through the woods of the Milke Danda provided me with one of the most memorable experiences of my life. The skies were clear, the temperature on the comfortable side of cool and the flora totally absorbing. Several more species of *Rhododendron* began to appear among which *R. barbatum* was outstanding with its beautiful peeling bark and its jewel-like compact trusses of brilliant red blooms. It reached 20-30ft. (6-9m) in height and continued to occur up to 11,500ft. (3,505m) (Colour Plate 264). Other species included *R. triflorum*, non-flowering, loose-habited bushes dwarfed by columns of *R. barbatum*, as well as *R. glaucophyllum* clothing a steep bank by the track, its flowers white flushed with pink especially noticeable in bud. There was also a single 6ft. (1.75m) bush of *R. thomsonii* with trusses of dark wine-red lightly bloomy bellflowers.

Our highest camp was at a place called Lam Pokhari 2, altitude 10,500ft. (3,200m). It was situated on a windy ridge surrounded by yak pasture and with magnificent views of snow-capped mountains to the north and Kangchengjunga (28,208ft./8,598m) to the east. A few minutes walk, however, found us in the comparative shelter of the forest which here was dominated by *Abies densa* and *Rhododendron hodgsonii*. The latter I had got to know well during the 1971 expedition and I was pleased to make its acquaintance again. In really sheltered areas there were trees of this rhododendron 25-30ft. (6-9m) tall with creamy stems, pink flaking bark, large leaves and large loose terminal trusses of pink flowers. Above our camp, however, on the east facing slope it formed dense thickets huddled against the wind which stunted growth and damaged flowers. The flowers of these higher populations were of a deeper colour than those previously described, more magenta or reddish-purple and borne in more congested heads. We found that the larger pink flowered plant occurred between the 10,500ft. and 11,500ft. (3,200 and 3,505m) contours (Plate 69) while the tighter magenta flowered plant took over at the other's upper limit and continued to 12,000ft. (3,657m) or more.

Also growing in the forest around this camp was *Rhododendron camelliiflorum*, a straggly-stemmed species we found several times as an epiphyte in old specimens of a Himalayan whitebeam *Sorbus vestita* and a large leaved maple *A. sterculiaceum*, better known by the name *A. villosum*. We even found one of the rhododendrons several feet up in the crotch of a *Rhododendron arboreum*. Some of these specimens were quite old and large with stems several feet in length and bore small white-petalled camellia-like flowers quite unlike the layman's idea of a rhododendron flower.

In the forest too, where the canopy was mixed evergreen and deciduous and the shade dappled, we came across large colonies of one of my favourite hardy ferns *Dryopteris wallichiana*. Its big bold shuttlecocks of pale or yellowish-green fronds on stout golden scaled stipes (stalks) were stunning and it is a fern I would never be without in my garden (page 10).

Moss and lichens were everywhere coating branches and stumps and it came as no surprise to me to find well established colonies of those small leaved

Plate 69. *Rhododendron hodgsonii* at 10,500ft. (3,200m) on the Milke Danda. Slightly past its best when we saw it, the bold leaves and peeling bark are a wonderful bonus. (April)

evergreens *Vaccinium retusum* and *V. nummularia* thriving in this often misty, moisture laden world. One of us, Nan Thompson, found a colony of *Primula listeri* growing on a damp mossy bank and called excitedly for me to come. It belongs to the same section as the well known *P. obconica* and although smaller and more modest, had similar long-stalked, rounded and lobed leaves and loose umbels of pale rose flowers with a yellow eye (page 14).

Growing with the primula and plentiful throughout these forests was an alpine strawberry with neatly veined and glossy-topped leaflets and charming white flowers 1in. (2.5cm) across. It was *Fragaria nubicola,* the name meaning 'dweller among the clouds' which seemed appropriate. It is one of two wild strawberries commonly found in the Himalayas the other being the smaller flowered though larger fruited *F. daltoniana,* named after Joseph Dalton Hooker who first discovered it. Both have been introduced to British cultivation a number of times, the former being the more ornamental. They spread quickly and make a useful ground cover in woodland or beneath shrubs.

We had intended climbing higher to camp on the Milke Danda ridge but our Sirdar changed our minds after meeting a group of shepherds who came through our camp one day having travelled along the ridge. They told us that no water was to be found due, presumably, to the springs having dried up. We did, however, spend a day climbing to the ridge and back. It was a brisk ascent of some 1,500ft. (4,572m) and to me was worth doing if only to see which other rhododendrons might be in flower. In the event we found the ridge dominated by the three Cs – *Rhododendron campanulatum, R. campylocarpum* and *R. cinnabarinum.* Flowers of the first of these were just opening and in some places had already imparted a bluish haze to distant hillsides (Colour Plate 262). *R. campylocarpum* whilst well budded was not yet open and the same went for *R. cinnabarinum* bar a few early blooms which were apricot in bud opening yellow, a far cry from the red and salmon-pink flowered forms one sees in cultivation (Colour Plate 263). It was rather disappointing for us being by my reckoning two to three weeks too early. We wandered around for an hour or so with no great surprises before retracing our steps to our camp where that night we had a grand feast to celebrate the turning point of our trek. From here it would be all downhill as we made for Poklavan, Chainpur and ultimately the airstrip at Tumlingtar.

On our descent the next morning one of my party, Harry van de Laar, found a queer looking parasitic plant growing on the branch of a *Lyonia villosa*. It was shrubby in growth with slender greyish stems pale green leaves and red spiked

Colour Plate 262 (top). *Rhododendron campanulatum* flowering in the Sir Harold Hillier Gardens and Arboretum in Hampshire. One of the commonest species in Nepal, it was plentiful on the Milke Danda ridge where it grew with several other species. (April)

Colour Plate 263 (above left). *Rhododendron cinnabarinum,* collected in east Nepal and flowering in a Hampshire garden. This lovely species we found commonly mixed with *R. campanulatum* and *R. campylocarpum* on the ridge of the Milke Danda. (May)

Colour Plate 264 (above centre). *Rhododendron barbatum,* a stunning species with its relatively small but compact rounded trusses of brilliant red blooms. It was frequent on the Milke Danda above Chowki and continued to a height of 11,500ft. (3,505m). (April)

Colour Plate 265 (above right). *Loranthus odoratus,* a parasitic shrub of the mistletoe family, we found growing on *Lyonia villosa* on the Milke Danda. (April)

Colour Plate 266 (left). *Kaempferia rotunda* we found below Chainpur. A member of the ginger family *Zingiberaceae,* this tuberous perennial is native to tropical south-east Asia, though commonly cultivated in the lower hills of Nepal. It makes a handsome flower and foliage subject for the greenhouse. (April)

Plate 70. Limbu porters relax between marches in a bamboo grove above Chainpur in the Arun valley. (April)

inflorescenses. It proved to be *Loranthus odoratus*, a member of *Loranthaceae* – the mistletoe family (Colour Plate 265).

All that day we followed a track which ran steadily downhill through mixed scrub and forest where bamboo, oak and a host of deciduous trees and shrubs crowded in. We saw the Himalayan hornbeam – *Carpinus viminea*, one of my favourite small trees, as well as *Hypericum hookerianum* and *H. uralum*, *Viburnum grandiflorum*, *Cotoneaster cavei* and several maples including *Acer campbellii* and *A. pectinatum*. From out of one of these hung a long, lush swag of *Holboellia latifolia*, a woody climber with elegant leaves divided into three to nine long-stalked leaflets. It was in flower, long-stalked, bell-shaped purplish or pinkish flowers hanging in clusters from the leaf axils. When I had last seen this climber in October 1971 it was in fruit, its large purple squelchy pods weighing down the stems.

Harry van de Laar collected sporing fronds from a host of ferns: *Cheilanthes farinosa* variety *chrysophylla* on rocks, *Polypodium subfalcatum*, *Asplenium unilaterale* and a *Drynaria* species on a tree being just a few. He also found on a tree an *Agapetes serpens* with greenish-white flowers, a cutting of which he later established in cultivation under the name 'Nepal Cream'.

The track meanwhile was getting busier and we met many villagers and others homing in from all directions. When we camped near the village of Poklavan a crowd of people, many of them children, came to our morning surgery seeking treatment. Most of the problems – knife wounds, sores, rashes and headaches – our doctor (Nan Thompson) could deal with, but there were a few more serious problems to which our medicine box had no answer. Whilst helping our doctor one evening we were entertained by a Limbu boy playing a Jew's harp watched by some of our porters who sat smoking beneath a line of tall bamboo (Plate 70).

The next day we walked into Chainpur, camping just beyond the town in a dried out paddy field. It was great to see the place again and I was delighted that evening when after supper we were visited by a doctor and his wife from the British-Nepal Medical Trust. Sitting round a crackling fire we swapped stories and discussed the problems and the highlights of life in the hills. The doctor's wife told us how she had once been bitten by a rabid dog and how, with her husband away for several days attending to patients, she had to inject herself in her stomach with an anti-rabies vaccine. That she was alive to tell the tale was testimony to her prompt action and her common sense.

Plate 71. A Rai fisherman with net and catch in the Sabhaya Khola, a tributary of the Arun river. The net which is weighted with stones is flung over a fish while the stick dispatches it. (April)

From Chainpur, it was another steep descent into the Arun valley and Tumlingtar. We found two beautiful flowering perennials along the way, neither of which are native to Nepal. The first of these *Zephyranthes carinata* (Plate 72) is a native of Mexico and yet is commonly found in cultivated areas of the Himalaya. Here it was growing on banks between fields, each solitary pink funnel-shaped flower on a smooth 8in. (20cm) stem above the flat glossy green grass-like leaves. It is a bulbous perennial and was presumably introduced originally for some medicinal purpose although its flowers are ornamental enough. Similarly with *Kaempferia rotunda* a member of the ginger family – *Zingiberaceae*. It is a native of tropical south-east Asia and is found in these hills only as a cultivated plant, its aromatic tubers being used, we were assured by a villager, as a cure for stomach complaints. Here it was growing in a vegetable plot on the outskirts of a village and was in full flower, the white and lilac orchid-like flowers produced in short spikes direct from the rootstock. The oblong leaves to 8in. (20cm) long appear after flowering and are equally ornamental being variegated dark and silvery-green above and a rich purple beneath (Colour Plate 266). It does in fact make a handsome pot plant for a warm greenhouse or conservatory. The man after whom this plant is named, Engelbert Kaempfer (1651-1716) was, according to W.T. Stearn, a learned and adventurous German physician who travelled widely throughout the East, lived for two years in Japan and who wrote books on its history and its plants.

Our path now wound it way through a grove of evergreen trees – *Schima wallichii,* a member of the Camellia family *Theaceae.* The small white golden stamened flowers were not unlike those of a camellia. A stately tree when mature this species is sadly too tender for all but the mildest gardens of Britain and Europe.

On our arrival at the river, the Sabhaya Khola, which two years ago we had crossed in a dugout boat, we were told that there was no boat and we would have to wade across. The river was high, the result of an overnight deluge, so there was nothing else for it but to take a long rope and form a chain with the Sherpas and stronger porters. By this means with the water above our waists our party safely reached the other side. On making it across we were surprised to see a Rai fisherman in the shallows proudly holding a pair of fine fish he had caught with his net which is weighted at the margins with stones. This he throws with remarkable dexterity and accuracy (Plate 71). The villagers knew we were coming, for when we arrived at the airstrip it seemed the entire population of Tumlingtar had turned out to watch us setting up camp on the periphery. It was then mid-afternoon and the plane was not expected until the next morning.

Night fell and after supper we retired to our sleeping bags excited and exhausted by the day's activities. The quiet was broken however by the screams of jackals (*Canis laureus*) in the bush. Not long after, Kancha our Sherpa Sirdar shouted for everyone to zip up their tents as these fox-sized wolf relatives were

Plate 72. *Zephyranthes carinata,* a native of Mexico, is commonly cultivated and naturalised in the Himalaya as here near the village of Chainpur in the Arun valley. It is in the same family – *Amaryllidaceae* – as the Autumn crocus *(Colchicum)*. (April)

Plate 73. Specimens of *Prunus rufa* (lower) and *Rhododendron lindleyi* being dried in a plant press loaned to the author by the Natural History Museum, London. The thin white paper folders (flimsies) are placed between sheets of drying paper which require changing at least once a day

scavenging in the camp area.

The following morning we climbed aboard a Twin Otter having said our goodbyes to Tumlingtar and a group of children who ran down the airstrip in the plane's wake. For a time I could still see them standing waving on the edge of the plateau, then we headed into cloud. It was strange returning to the comparative order of Kathmandu after our sojourn in the hills. We met up with our three sick colleagues again who were now recovered having spent most of their time on excursions in the surrounding hills and had even managed a flight to the Everest region. There were stories to be swapped, diaries to be completed, plants to be pressed (Plate 73) and a last minute hunt for gifts and souvenirs in the bazaar. The next day we were off again, and as we cleared the cloud above the valley heading west for Delhi, I settled deeply into my seat whilst my mind focused once again on the rhododendron forests of the Milke Danda.

APPENDIX: NUMBERS AND NAMES OF SEED COLLECTED BY BEER, LANCASTER AND MORRIS (B.L.&M.) IN NEPAL, 1971

01 Rubus paniculatus
02 Sambucus adnata
03 Zanthoxylum acanthopodium
04 Zanthoxylum oxyphyllum
05 Dicentra scandens
06 Tripterospermum volubile
07 Cautleya cathcartii
08 Arisaema sp.
09 Holboellia latifolia
10 Cautleya spicata
11 Lilium nepalense
12 Lilium nepalense
13 Daiswa polyphylla
14 Clematis tongluensis
15 Clematis tongluensis
16 Rubus calycinus
17 Helwingia himalaica
18 Acer pectinatum
19 Magnolia campbellii
20 Sorbus hedlundii
21 Vaccinium retusum
22 Symplocos theifolia
23 Sorbus kurzii
24 Sorbus microphylla
25 Sorbus insignis
26 Rhododendron ciliatum
27 Sorbus microphylla
28 Aconitum spicatum
29 Geranium polyanthes
30 Sorbus microphylla
31 Rosa sericea
32 Codonopsis dicentrifolia
33 Betula utilis
34 Senecio alatus
35 Acer pectinatum
36 Polygonum emodi
37 Meconopsis napaulensis
38 Gentiana prolata
39 Lomatogonium sikkimense
40 Piptanthus nepalensis
41 Berberis erythroclada
42 Codonopsis dicentrifolia
43 Polygonum milletii
44 Euphorbia himalayensis
45 Jurinea macrocephala
46 Saxifraga sp.
47 Gaultheria pyroloides
48 Saussurea taraxicifolia
49 Prunus cornuta

50 Sorbus kurzii
51 Ribes laciniatum
52 Cyananthus inflatus
53 Rheum acuminatum
54 Juniperus squamata
55 Primula dickieana
56 Primula obliqua
57 Vaccinium nummularia
58 Cicerbita macrantha
59 Aster himalaicus
60 Saussurea gossypiphora
61 Cremanthodium ellisii
62 Salix sp.
63 Saussurea uniflora
64 Cremanthodium reniforme
65 Aconitum spicatum
66 Bergenia purpurascens
67 Iris kumaonensis
68 Morina nepalensis
69 Megacodon stylophorus
70 Rheum nobile
71 Salix sp.
72 Juniperus squamata
73 Juniperus indica
74 Geum elatum
75 Anemone polyanthes
76 Ligularia sp.
77 Swertia multicaulis
78 Salix lindleyana var. microphylla
79 Primula capitata ssp. crispata
80 Cremanthodium pinnatifidum
81 Cremanthodium oblongatum
82 Juniperus recurva
83 Gaultheria trichophylla
84 Cotoneaster glacialis
85 Abies densa
86 Aconitum spicatum
87 Spiraea arcuata
88 Berberis sp.
89 Cyananthus sp.
90 Sorbus foliolosa
91 Sorbus microphylla
92 Rhododendron wightii
93 Pleurospermopsis sikkimensis
94 Megacodon stylophorus
95 Potentilla cuneata
96 Myricaria rosea
97 Primula hopeana
98 Primula megalocarpa

99 Meconopsis grandis
100 Betula utilis
101 Clematis montana
102 Lonicera myrtillus
103 Stellaria sp.
104 Parnassia nubicola
105 Cremanthodium reniforme
106 Rubus nepalensis
107 Prunus rufa
108 Ribes luridum
109 Acer caudatum
110 Meconopsis paniculata
111 Saussurea obvallata
112 Meconopsis sinuata
113 Saussurea taraxicifolia
114 Mandragora caulescens
115 Soroseris pumila
116 Silene setisperma
117 Draba sp.
118 Silene sp.
119 Polygonum sp.
120 Fritillaria cirrhosa
121 Aster himalaicus
122 Rheum sp.
123 Morina nepalensis
124 Potentilla peduncularis
125 Anemone polyanthes
126 Thalictrum elegans
127 Daiswa polyphylla
128 Delphinium viscosum
129 Salix disperma
130 Salix calyculata
131 Salix lindleyana var. microphylla
132 Aster stracheyi
133 Leontopodium himalayanum
134 Primula buryana
135 Silene sp.
136 Saxifraga moorcroftiana
137 Juniperus recurva
138 Rosa sericea
139 Gueldenstaedtia himalaica
140 Stachyurus himalaicus
141 Gaultheria semi-infera
142 Neillia thyrsiflora
143 Rubus splendidissimus
144 Gaultheria griffithiana
145 Berberis insignis
146 Sarcococca hookeriana
147 Hypericum choisianum
148 Clematis connata
149 Ribes himalense
150 Ilex intricata
151 Viburnum nervosum
152 Rubus nepalensis
153 Rhododendron camelliiflorum
154 Vaccinium glaucoalbum

155 Rubus thomsonii
156 Berberis sp.
157 Berberis hookeri
158 Cimicifuga foetida
159 Primula geraniifolia
160 Cardiocrinum giganteum
161 Tsuga dumosa
162 Euphorbia pseudosikkimensis
163 Cotoneaster staintonii
164 Ligularia amplexicaulis
165 Compositae
166 Umbelliferae
167 Cotoneaster glacialis
168 Meconopsis discigera
169 Hemiphragma heterophyllum
170 Juniperus indica
171 Meconopsis horridula
172 Cortiella hookeri
173 Potentilla argyrophylla var. leucochroa
174 Leontopodiom monocephalum
175 Potentilla microphylla var. depressa
176 Potentilla eriocarpa
177 Potentilla sp.
178 Saxifraga pseudopallida
179 Potentilla arbuscula
180 Anaphalis cavei
181 Waldheimia glabra
182 Aconitum hookeri
183 Cremanthodium ellisii
184 Anemone polyanthes
185 Aster albescens
186 Juniperus recurva
187 Spiraea bella
188 Senecio alatus
189 Allium sp.
190 Potentilla fruticosa
191 Pedicularis sp.
192 Scopolia stramonifolia
193 Aconitum spicatum
194 Saxifraga brunonis
195 Unnamed
196 Sorbus microphylla
197 Thalictrum virgatum
198 Aruncus dioicus ssp. triternatus
199 Androsace hookeriana
200 Polygonum amplexicaule var. pendulum
201 Acer pectinatum
202 Polygonum polystachyum
203 Oryzopsis munroi
204 Sorbus microphylla
205 Lyonia villosa
206 Fritillaria cirrhosa
207 Saussurea hieracioides
208 Lomatogonium sikkimense
209 Juniperus indica
210 Polygonum affine

211 Saxifraga sp.
212 Clematis sp.
213 Primula macrophylla
214 Deyeuxia pulchella
215 Rosa sericea
216 Eriophytum wallichii
217 Rhododendron setosum
218 Delphinium sp.
219 Betula utilis
220 Rhododendron cinnabarinum
221 Betula utilis
222 Hydrangea heteromalla
223 Berberis sp.
224 Rubus nepalensis
225 Pieris formosa
226 Senecio wallichii
227 Allium sp.
228 Rhododendron thomsonii
229 Lobelia erectiuscula
230 Lyonia sp.
231 Rhododendron anthopogon
232 Ilex intricata
233 Rhododendron hodgsonii
234 Rhododendron cinnabarinum
235 Polygonum vacciniifolium
236 Polygonum amplexicaule var. pendulum
237 Hypericum uralum
238 Hypericum tenuicaule
239 Rhododendron triflorum
240 Hypericum hookerianum
241 Jasminum humile f. wallichianum
242 Miscanthus nepalensis
243 Erianthus rufipilus
244 Iris decora
245 Boenninghausenia albiflora
246 Anemone vitifolia
247 Hydrangea aspera
248 Calamagrostis emodensis
249 Gaultheria semi-infera
250 Cotoneaster frigidus
251 Vaccinium glaucoalbum
252 Vaccinium nummularia
253 Hypericum hookerianum
254 Gaultheria nummularioides
255 Senecio tetranthus
256 Rubus treutleri
257 Rubus thomsonii
258 Polygonum sp.
259 Aconitium spicatum
260 Rhododendron thomsonii
261 (Number omitted in the field)
262 Sorbus microphylla
263 Cotoneaster staintonii
264 Umbelliferae
265 Circium involucratum
266 Cotoneaster zimmermanii

267 Potentilla cuneata
268 Gaultheria trichophylla
269 Sorbus cuspidata
270 Ilex dipyrena
271 Viburnum mullaha
272 Ficus sp.
273 Sambucus adnata
274 Rubia manjith
275 Cornus macrophylla
276 Leycesteria formosa
277 Strobilanthes sp.
278 Fritillaria cirrhosa
279 Rhododendron lepidotum
280 Rhododendron cinnabarinum
281 Rhododendron anthopogon
282 Rosa sericea
283 Rhododendron campanulatum
284 Meconopsis napaulensis
285 Arisaema sp.
286 Rhododendron setosum
287 Rhododendron wightii
288 Senecio cappa
289 Inula cappa
290 Polygonum capitatum
291 Berberis sp.
292 Spiraea micrantha
293 Arisaema sp.
294 Rhododendron campanulatum
295 Piptanthus nepalensis
296 Boehmeria polystachya
297 Pinus wallichiana
298 Rhododendron virgatum
299 Vaccinium dunalianum
300 Rhododendron dalhousiae
301 Debregeasia longifolia
302 Vaccinium gaultheriifolium
303 Embelia floribunda
304 Clematis buchananiana
305 Rhododendron dalhousiae
306 Eunonymus echinatus
307 Acer sterculiaceum
308 Magnolia campbellii
309 Dianella ensifolia
310 Inula hookeri
311 Lonicera hispida
312 Rubus nepalensis
313 Rubus sp.
314 Rhododendron ciliatum
315 Rhododendron glaucophyllum
316 Rubus treutleri
317 Arisaema sp.
318 Cornus macrophylla
319 Vaccinium glaucoalbum
320 Gaultheria semi-infera
321 Coriaria terminalis var. xanthocarpa
322 Viburnum grandiflorum

323 Rhododendron hodgsonii
324 Rhododendron ciliatum
325 Rhododendron barbatum
326 Arisaema sp.
327 Rhododendron campanulatum
328 Gaultheria nummularioides
329 Rhododendron glaucophyllum
330 Rhododendron fulgens
331 Lonicera hispida
332 Rhododendron anthopogon
333 Juniperus squamata
334 Pedicularis sp.
335 Toricellia tiliifolia
336 Rhododendron vaccinioides
337 Pleione praecox
338 Rosa longicuspis
339 Corylus ferox
340 Gynura cusimbua
341 Daphniphyllum himalense
342 Rubus sp.
343 Polygonum sp.
344 Rhododendron campanulatum
345 Symplocos sp.
346 Daiswa polyphylla
347 Dichroa febrifuga
348 Hypericum uralum
349 Euonymus vagans
350 Lonicera glabrata
351 Quercus sp.
352 Gesneriaceae
353 Agapetes serpens
354 Mahonia napaulensis
355 Unnamed
356 Primula sp.
357 Primula sp.
358 Primula sp.
359 Corydalis sp.
360 Clematis montana
361 Corydalis sp.
362 Meconopsis discigera
363 Primula sp.
364 Gentiana recurvata
365 Gentiana sp.
366 Dicentra scandens
367 Corydalis sp.
368 Androsace globifera
369 Tetrastigma rumicispermum
370 Corydalis sp.

371 Lyonia villosa
372 Myricaria rosea
373 Leontopodium jacotianum
374 Salix calyculata
375 Potentilla microphylla
376 Rubus sp.
377 Cruciferae
378 Primula hookeri
379 Primula calderiana
380 Meconopsis villosa
381 Primula calderiana ssp. strumosa
382 Unnamed
383 Polygonum molle
384 Leguminosae
385 Fragaria daltoniana
386 Fragaria nubicola
387 Cardiocrinum giganteum
388 Potentilla microphylla var. achilleifolia
389 Fragaria nubicola
390 Unnamed
391 Hypericum monanthemum
392 Limnophylla sp.
393 Leguminosae
394 Mimosa pudica
395 Saxifraga brunonis
396 Pyrus pashia
397 Iris sp.
398 Abies spectabilis
399 Iris sp.
400 Leguminosae
401 Juniperus recurva
402 Juniperus squamata
403 Juniperus squamata
404 Juniperus squamata
405 Juniperus squamata
406 Juniperus recurva
407 Juniperus recurva
408 Juniperus squamata
409 Juniperus indica
410 Juniperus indica
411 Juniperus sp.
412 Juniperus sp.
413 Pinus wallichiana·
414 Juniperus sp.
415 Abies spectabilis
416 Abies spectabilis
417 Abies spectabilis

SELECT BIBLIOGRAPHY

The titles listed below are just a few of the many which I have consulted in the writing of the present account. Two of the most helpful to the traveller and student are Polunin and Stainton's *Flowers of the Himalaya* plus Supplement, whilst Edward Cronin's account, *The Arun,* though it may now be hard to obtain, gives the best description of the area through which the 1971 expedition travelled.

Allaby, M. (ed.) *The Concise Oxford Dictionary of Botany* (1992)

Alpine Garden Society, *Encyclopaedia of Alpines* (ed. Beckett, K.) 2 vols., 1993, 1994

Bean, W.J. *Trees and Shrubs Hardy in the British Isles,* 8th edn, revised vols. 1-4, (1970-80) and Supplement by D.L. Clarke (1988)

Brummitt, R.K. and Powell, E.C. (ed.) *Authors of Plant Names* (1992)

Brummitt, R.K. *Vascular Plant Families and Genera* (1992)

Chamberlain, D.F. *A Revision of Rhododendron* vol. 2 (1982)

Cobb, James L.S. *Meconopsis* (1989)

Cowan, A.M. and J.M. *The Trees of North Bengal* (1929)

Cox, E.H.M. *Plant Hunting in China* (1945)

Cronin, Edward W. Jr. *The Arun – A Natural History of the World's Deepest Valley* (1979)

Cullen, J. *A Revision of Rhododendron* vol. 1 (1980)

Davidson, H.H. *The Rhododendron Species* vols. 1-3 (1982-92)

Desmond, Ray *The European Discovery of the Indian Flora* (1992)

Desmond, Ray *Dictionary of British and Irish Botanists and Horticulturists* 2nd ed. (1994)

Dobremez, J.F., Vigny, F. and Williams, L.H.J. *Bibliographie du Nepal* vol. 3, *Science Naturelles* Tome 2 Botanique (1972)

Everist, Richard and Wheeler, Tony *Nepal a Travel Survival Kit* (1990)

Farrer, Reginald *The English Rock Garden* vols. 1 & 2 (1919)

Gabrielian, E. *The Genus Sorbus in Eastern Asia and the Himalayas* (1978)

Gamble, J.S. 'The Bambuseae of British India', *Ann. Roy. Bot. Gard. Calcutta,* 7:1-133 t.1-119 (1896)

Gelderen, D.M. van, de Jong, P.C. and Oterdoom, H.J., *Maples of the World* (1994)

Grey-Wilson, C. *Poppies* (1993)

Grierson, A.J.C. & Long, D.G. *Flora of Bhutan (including a Record of Plants from Sikkim)* vol. 1 pts.1-3 and vol. 2. pt. 1 (1983-1991)

Hagen, Toni *Nepal* (1972)

Halda, Joseph T. *The Genus Primula in Cultivation and the Wild* (1992)

Hara, H., Stearn, W.T. and Williams, L.H.J. *An Enumeration of the Flowering Plants of Nepal* vol. 1 (1978)

Hara, H. and Williams, L.H.J. *An Enumeration of the Flowering Plants of Nepal* vol. 2 (1979)

Hara, H. and Williams, L.H.J. *An Enumeration of the Flowering Plants of Nepal* vol. 3 (1981)

Heywood, V.H. (ed.) *Flowering Plants of the World* (1979)

Hooker, J.D. *Himalayan Journals* (1854)

Hooker, J.D. *Flora of British India* 7 vols. (1872-9)

Kohlein, Fritz *Gentians* (1991)

Lancaster, Roy 'An Account of the Species of *Rhododendron* collected by the University College Bangor Nepal Expedition 1971' *Rhododendrons* 24-32 (Royal Horticultural Society, 1972)

Lancaster, Roy 'Maples of the Himalaya', *The Garden* vol. 101, pt. 12, 589-93 (1976)

Lancaster, Roy *Travels in China – A Plantsman's Paradise* (1989)

Mabberley, D.J. *The Plant Book* (1987)

Mierow, D. and Shrestha, T.B. *Himalayan Flowers and Trees* (1978)

Nicholson, Nigel and Time Life *The Himalayas* (1975)

Noltie, H.G. *Flora of Bhutan including Sikkim and Darjeeling* vol. 3, pt. 1 (1994)

Philip, Chris and Lord, Tony *The Plant Finder* (1994/95)

Polunin, Oleg and Stainton, Adam *Flowers of the Himalaya* (1984)

Rajbhandary, K.B. *Natural Environment and Crop Distribution in Nepal* (1968)

Richards, J. *Primula* (1993)

Rushforth, K. *Conifers* (1987)

Stainton, Adam *Flowers of the Himalaya, a Supplement* (1988)

Stainton, J.D.A. *Forests of Nepal* (1972)

Stearn, W.T. *Botanical Latin* 4th ed. (1992)

Stearn's Dictionary of Plant Names for Gardeners (1992)

Stewart, R.R. *An Annotated Catalogue of the Vascular Plants of West Pakistan and Kashmir* (1972)

Swift, Hugh *Trekking in Nepal, West Tibet and Bhutan* (1989)

Taylor, George *An Account of the Genus Meconopsis* (1934)

Willis, J.C. *A Dictionary of the Flowering Plants and Ferns*, 8th ed., revised (1973)

Wilson, E.H. *A Naturalist in Western China* vol. 1 (1913)

GLOSSARY

Technical and botanical terms have been used in this book only when necessary for precision and brevity. The following are the most frequently used examples.

Acicular	Needle shaped
Acuminate	Tapering at the end, long pointed
Acute	Sharply pointed
Adpressed	Lying close and flat against
Anther	The pollen-bearing part of the stamen
Awl-shaped	Tapering from the base to a slender and stiff point
Bloom(y)	A white or pale-blue powdery-like wax covering as on a fruit
Bract	A modified, usually reduced leaf at the base of a flower
Bullate	Blistered or puckered
Calyx	The outer part of the flower, the sepals
Campanulate	Bell-shaped
Capitate	Head-like, collected into a dense cluster
Capsule	A dry, several-celled pod
Ciliate	Fringed with hairs
Cordate	Shaped like a heart, as base of leaf
Coriaceous	Leathery
Corolla	The inner, normally conspicuous part of a flower, the petals
Corymb	A flat-topped or dome-shaped flowerhead with the outer flowers opening first
Corymbose	Having flowers in corymbs
Crenate	Toothed with shallow, rounded teeth
Cuneate	Wedge-shaped
Cuspidate	Abruptly sharp pointed
Cyme	A flat-topped or dome-shaped flowerhead with the inner flowers opening first
Cymose	Having flowers in cymes
Decurrent	Extending down the stem
Dentate	Toothed with teeth directed outward
Denticulate	Minutely dentate
Downy	Softly hairy
Elliptic	Widest at or about the middle, narrowing equally at both ends
Emarginate	With a shallow notch at the apex
Entire	Undivided and without teeth
Epiphyte	A plant that uses another plant (usually a tree) or a rock as a physical support but does not draw nourishment from it
Exfoliating	Peeling off in thin strips
Exserted	Projecting beyond (stamens from corolla)
Ferruginous	Rust-coloured
Florets	Small, individual flowers of a dense inflorescence
Glabrous	Hairless
Glandular	With secreting organs
Glaucous	Covered with a 'bloom', bluish-white or bluish-grey
Hispid	Beset with rigid hairs or bristles

Indumentum	Dense hairy covering
Inflorescence	The flowering part of the plant
Lanceolate	Lance-shaped, widening above the base and long tapering to the apex
Linear	Long and narrow with nearly parallel margins
Lobe	Any protruding part of an organ (as in leaf, corolla or calyx)
Midrib	The central vein or rib on a leaf
Monocarpic	Dying after flowering and seeding
Mucro	A short fine point
Mucronate	Terminated abruptly by a spiny tip
Oblanceolate	Inversely lanceolate
Oblique	Unequal-sided
Oblong	Longer than broad, with nearly parallel sides
Obovate	Inversely ovate
Obtuse	Blunt (as in apex of leaf or petal)
Orbicular	Almost circular in outline
Ovary	The basal 'box' part of the pistil, containing the ovules
Ovate	Broadest below the middle (like a hen's egg)
Palmate	Lobed or divided in hand-like fashion, usually five or seven-lobed
Panicle	A branching raceme
Paniculate	Having flowers in panicles
Pectinate	Comb-like (as teeth on leaf margin)
Pedicel	The stalk of an individual flower in an inflorescence
Peduncle	The stalk of a flower cluster or of a solitary flower
Petal	One of the separate segments of a corolla
Petiole	The leaf-stalk
Pilose	With long, soft, straight hairs
Pinnate	With leaflets, arranged on either side of a central stalk
Pinnatifid	Cleft or parted in a pinnate way
Plumose	Feathery, as the down of a thistle
Prostrate	Lying flat on the ground
Pruinose	Bloomy
Pubescent	Covered with short, soft hairs, downy
Raceme	A simple elongated inflorescence with stalked flowers
Racemose	Having flowers in racemes
Rachis	An axis bearing flowers or leaflets
Recurved	Curved downward or backward
Reflexed	Abruptly turned downward
Reticulate	Like a network (as in veins)
Revolute	Rolled backwards, margin rolled under (as in leaf)
Rib	A prominent vein in a leaf
Rufous	Reddish-brown
Scabrid	Rough to the touch
Scale	A minute leaf or bract, or a flat gland-like appendage on the surface of a leaf, flower or shoot
Scandent	With climbing stems
Scape	A leafless flowering stem rising from the ground
Sepal	One of the segments of a calyx

Serrate	Saw-toothed (teeth pointing forward)
Serrulate	Minutely serrate
Sessile	Not stalked
Setose	Clothed with bristles
Spathulate	Spoon-shaped
Spike	A simple, elongated inflorescence with sessile flowers
Stamen	The male organ of a flower comprising filament and anther
Stellate	Star-shaped
Stigma	The summit of the pistil which receives the pollen, often sticky or feathery
Stipule	Appendage (normally two) at base of some petioles
Stolon	A shoot at or below the surface of the ground which produces a new plant at its tip
Stomata	Breathing pores in leaf surface
Strigose	Clothed with flattened fine, bristle-like hairs
Style	The middle part of the pistil, often elongated between the ovary and stigma
Tepals	Petals and sepals of similar appearance
Tomentose	With dense, woolly pubescence
Tomentum	Dense covering of matted hairs
Trifoliolate	A leaf with three separate leaflets
Type	Strictly the original (type) specimen, but used in a general sense to indicate the typical form in cultivation
Umbel	A normally flat-topped inflorescence in which the pedicels or peduncles all arise from a common point
Umbellate	Flowers in umbels
Umbellifer	Plant of the family Umbelliferae
Undulate	With wavy margins
Venation	The arrangement of the veins
Verrucose	Having a wart-like or nodular surface
Villous	Bearing long and soft hairs
Whorl	Three or more flowers or leaves arranged in a ring

PLANT INDEX

This index comprises those plants wild and cultivated seen in Nepal by the author in 1973 and by members of the University of North Wales Bangor expedition to Nepal in 1971.

The names currently accepted as correct (prior names) for the purposes of this account are shown in Roman type whilst those not accepted (synonyms) are shown in italics and are cross referenced to the accepted names.

All plant names are followed by the names in italics of the authors responsible for first publishing them. Authors' names have been abbreviated in accordance with *Authors of Plant Names* (1992) edited by R.K. Brummit and C.E. Powell, e.g. Acer pectinatum *Wall.* abbreviation for Wallich.

Authors' names in parentheses indicate the authority responsible for originally publishing a name for this plant, while the name(s) following the parentheses is the authority responsible for the present combination (name), e.g. Cardiocrinum giganteum *(Wall.) Makino:* the Giant Himalayan Lily was originally described by Wallich as *Lilium giganteum* and later transferred to the genus *Cardiocrinum* by Makino.

Where the names of two authors are connected by the letters *ex*, e.g. Daphne bholua *Buch.-Ham. ex D. Don,* this indicates that the second author, in this case D. Don validly published a name first given or suggested for this plant, but was not validly published by the first author, i.e. Buchanan-Hamilton.

Page numbers in bold refer to colour illustrations; in italics to black and white illustrations.